T0210478

Lecture Notes in Computer Science 9080

Commenced Publication in 1973
Founding and Former Series Editors:
Gerhard Goos, Juris Hartmanis, and Jan van Leeuwen

Editorial Board

David Hutchison
Lancaster University, Lancaster, UK
Takeo Kanade
Carnegie Mellon University, Pittsburgh, PA, USA
Josef Kittler
University of Surrey, Guildford, UK
Jon M. Kleinberg
Cornell University, Ithaca, NY, USA
Friedemann Mattern
ETH Zürich, Zürich, Switzerland
John C. Mitchell
Stanford University, Stanford, CA, USA
Moni Naor
Weizmann Institute of Science, Rehovot, Israel
C. Pandu Rangan
Indian Institute of Technology, Madras, India
Bernhard Steffen
TU Dortmund University, Dortmund, Germany
Demetri Terzopoulos
University of California, Los Angeles, CA, USA
Doug Tygar
University of California, Berkeley, CA, USA
Gerhard Weikum
Max Planck Institute for Informatics, Saarbrücken, Germany

More information about this series at http://www.springer.com/series/7409

Jérôme Gensel · Martin Tomko (Eds.)

Web and Wireless Geographical Information Systems

14th International Symposium, W2GIS 2015
Grenoble, France, May 21–22, 2015
Proceedings

 Springer

Editors
Jérôme Gensel
Université Grenoble Alpes
Saint Martin d'Hères
France

Martin Tomko
University of Zurich - Irchel
Zurich
Switzerland

ISSN 0302-9743   ISSN 1611-3349   (electronic)
Lecture Notes in Computer Science
ISBN 978-3-319-18250-6   ISBN 978-3-319-18251-3   (eBook)
DOI 10.1007/978-3-319-18251-3

Library of Congress Control Number: 2015937011

Springer Cham Heidelberg New York Dordrecht London
ⓒ Springer International Publishing Switzerland 2015
This work is subject to copyright. All rights are reserved by the Publisher, whether the whole or part of the material is concerned, specifically the rights of translation, reprinting, reuse of illustrations, recitation, broadcasting, reproduction on microfilms or in any other physical way, and transmission or information storage and retrieval, electronic adaptation, computer software, or by similar or dissimilar methodology now known or hereafter developed.
The use of general descriptive names, registered names, trademarks, service marks, etc. in this publication does not imply, even in the absence of a specific statement, that such names are exempt from the relevant protective laws and regulations and therefore free for general use.
The publisher, the authors and the editors are safe to assume that the advice and information in this book are believed to be true and accurate at the date of publication. Neither the publisher nor the authors or the editors give a warranty, express or implied, with respect to the material contained herein or for any errors or omissions that may have been made.

Printed on acid-free paper

Springer International Publishing AG Switzerland is part of Springer Science+Business Media (www.springer.com)

Preface

These proceedings report on the state of the art in the research on Web and Wireless Geographic Information Systems, as presented at the 14th W2GIS Symposium in Grenoble, in May 2015. Recent developments in Web technologies and advances in wireless Internet access have generated an increasing interest in the capture, processing, analysis, and diffusion of online geo-referenced data in and about the Web environment. Until recently only possible on desktop workstations, devices wirelessly connected to the Internet now offer ways of accessing and analyzing online geo-spatial information. These developments were the primary subject of this symposium series. This series has been capturing the developments in W2GIS since its earliest days. Alternating between Asia, Europe, and North America, the symposia have brought together researchers focusing on the technological and computational aspects of W2GIS, as well as on the human–computer interaction and dynamics afforded by this new technology. Over time, W2GIS has evolved into a mature field of research and this symposium series has become one of its principal annual meetings.

The 14th conference of the W2GIS Symposium was held in Grenoble, France, and hosted by the Grenoble University. In total, 43 researchers contributed by their work to the W2GIS 2015 Symposium. In an elaborate peer-review process, 12 original papers were selected for their high quality for single-track oral presentations, out of a total of 19 submissions. Each paper was reviewed by at least two (most often three) anonymous reviewers. Selected papers cover hot topics related to W2GIS including spatiotemporal data collection, processing and visualization, mobile user gencrated content, semantic trajectories, location-based Web search, Cloud computing, and VGI approaches.

Many people have contributed to the success of the W2GIS 2015 Symposium. First of all, we thank the authors for their excellent contributions and the members of the Program Committee for carefully reviewing their submissions. Second, the Local Organizers from the Grenoble University significantly contributed to the smooth running of the symposium and a very amicable atmosphere. We thank Prof. Mark Graham from the Oxford Internet Institute and Prof. Johannes Schöning from the ICT research institute of Hasselt University for delivering engaging and stimulating keynote speeches. We have been stimulated to think critically about the broader impact of the wealth of data held by the Web, and by their use in ubiquitous information systems. These views added tremendously to a broader perspective on the current research in the field of Web and Wireless Geographic Information Systems.

We are looking forward to the exciting developments of the field, which we hope will be presented in the future editions of the W2GIS Symposium.

May 2015
Jérôme Gensel
Martin Tomko

Organization

Symposium Chairs

Jérôme Gensel — Université Grenoble Alpes, France
Martin Tomko — University Zurich-Irchel, Switzerland

Steering Committee

Michela Bertolotto — University College Dublin, Ireland
James D. Carswell — Dublin Institute of Technology, Ireland
Christophe Claramunt — Naval Academy Research Institute, France
Max J. Egenhofer — NCGIA, The University of Maine, USA
Ki-Joune Li — Pusan National University, Korea
Steve Liang — University of Calgary, Canada
Kazutoshi Sumiya — University of Hyogo, Japan
Taro Tezuka — University of Tsukuba, Japan
Christelle Vangenot — University of Geneva, Switzerland

Local Organization Chair

Marlène Villanova-Oliver — Université Grenoble Alpes, France

Local Organization Committee

Mahfoud Boudis — Université Grenoble Alpes, France
Sylvain Bouveret — Université Grenoble Alpes, France
Paule-Annick Davoine — Université Grenoble Alpes, France
Philippe Genoud — Université Grenoble Alpes, France
Anthony Hombiat — Université Grenoble Alpes, France
David Noël — Université Grenoble Alpes, France
André Sales Fonteles — Université Grenoble Alpes, France
Danielle Ziébelin — Université Grenoble Alpes, France

Program Committee

M. Arikawa — University of Tokyo, Japan
S. Bell — University of Saskatchewan, Canada
A. Bouju — University of La Rochelle, France

T. Brinkhoff	IAPG, Germany
E. Camossi	JRC ISPRA, Italy
P. Corcoran	University College Dublin, Ireland
R.A. de By	ITC, The Netherlands
S. Dragicevic	Simon Fraser University, British Columbia, Canada
M. Gahegan	University of Auckland, New Zealand
R. Güting	FernUniversität Hagen, Germany
Y. Ishikawa	Nagoya University, Japan
B. Jiang	University of Gävle, Sweden
H.A. Karimi	University of Pittsburgh, USA
B. Kobben	ITC, The Netherlands
R. Larson	University of California, Berkeley, USA
D. Lee	Hong Kong University of Science and Technology, Hong Kong
H. Lu	Aalborg University, Denmark
S. Li	Ryerson University, Canada
M.R. Luaces	University da Coruna, Spain
G. McArdle	University College Dublin, Ireland
H. Martin	Université Grenoble Alpes, France
P. Muro-Medrano	Zaragoza University, Spain
K. Patroumpas	National University of Athens, Greece
C. Ray	Naval Academy Research Institute, France
B. Resch	Heidelberg University, Germany
P. Roose	University of Pau and Pays de lÁdour, France
A. Ruas	IFSTTAR, France
M. Schneider	University of Florida, USA
S. Shekhar	University of Minnesota, USA
M. Tsou	San Diego State University, USA
T. Ushiama	Kyushu University, Japan
W. Viana	Federal University of Ceara, Brazil
M. Villanova-Oliver	Université Grenoble Alpes, France
A. Voisard	FU Berlin and Fraunhofer FOKUS, Germany
X. Wang	University of Calgary, Canada
S. Winter	University of Melbourne, Australia
A. Zipf	Heidelberg University, Germany

Additional Reviewers

Z. Jiang
F. Hu

Contents

Computational Approaches, Algorithms and Architectures

User Generated Content – Data Collection, Processing and Interpretation

A Mobile Application for a User-Generated Collection of Landmarks

Marius Wolfensberger and Kai-Florian Richter(✉)

Department of Geography, University of Zurich - Irchel,
Winterthurerstrasse 190, 8057 Zurich, Switzerland
{marius.wolfensberger,kai-florian.richter}@geo.uzh.ch

Abstract. Landmarks are crucial elements in how people understand
and communicate about space. In wayfinding they provide references that
are preferred and easier to follow than distances or street names alone.
Thus, the inclusion of landmarks into navigation services is a long-held
goal, but its implementation has largely failed so far. To a large part this
is due to significant difficulties in obtaining a sufficient data set of landmark candidates. In this paper, we introduce a mobile application, which
enables a user-generated collection of landmarks. Employing a photo-
based interface, the application calculates and ranks potential landmark
candidates based on the current visible area and presents them to the
user, who then may choose the intended one. We use OpenStreetMap
as data source; the app allows tagging OSM objects as potential landmarks. Integrating users into the landmark selection process keeps data
requirements low, while a simple interface lowers the burden on the users.

Keywords: Landmarks · Volunteered geographic information · User-
generated content · OpenStreetMap · Location-based services

1 Introduction

Geographic landmarks are defined as "any element, which may serve as reference points" [10]. They are easily distinguishable environmental features that
are unique in or in contrast with their neighborhood [15,20]. Landmarks are
fundamental in how humans understand and represent their environment and
how they communicate about it [19].

Current navigation services construct their guidances exclusively based on
metrics (time or distance), orientation and street names [16]. However, the use
of metrics is not an effective way of indicating an upcoming decision point,
as the estimation of distances without any further tools constitutes a complex
task [2] and can easily be twisted by outside influences (traffic lights, crowded
pathways) [23]. To overcome these deficiencies, landmarks should be included
in routing instructions. Particularly at decision points, where a reorientation is
needed, they increase the performance and efficiency of users (e.g., [11]).

Currently, there are very few commercial systems that include landmarks in
their navigation instructions. The primary reason is the lack of available landmark data [5,17]. There are neither widespread possibilities to access and store

© Springer International Publishing Switzerland 2015
J. Gensel and M. Tomko (Eds.): W2GIS 2015, LNCS 9080, pp. 3–19, 2015.
DOI: 10.1007/978-3-319-18251-3_1

landmarks [23], nor standardized characteristics defining landmarks [5]. Previous research focused on automated methods to extract landmarks from existing data. A widespread use of these approaches was hampered by vast data requirements, uneven landmark distribution, or a focus on global landmarks [18].

We developed a mobile application that provides a tool for collecting and sharing of landmark data. This tool allows the in-situ labelling of objects as landmarks, i.e., while being in the environment and close to the landmark. Using their smartphone to take a photo of the desired landmark, users receive a list of potential landmark candidates, ranked by their probability of being the landmark the user intends to collect. In order to calculate the probability of the involved candidates, a ranking system is used, which estimates the visual and semantic suitability of the examined geographic objects. The suggested candidates need to be manually confirmed by the user in order to save them. Furthermore, the application enables the sharing of the gathered data on OpenStreetMap[1].

The next section will present relevant related work. In Section 3 we will discuss some of the challenges in enabling an in-situ landmark collection and illustrate our approach. The implemented Android app is presented in Section 4, while Section 5 shows results of a small case study we performed in order to evaluate the application. Section 6 discusses our approach in light of this case study, and Section 7 finally concludes the paper with an outlook on future work.

2   Previous Work

Several automated methods have been suggested in the past for the purpose of landmark extraction. The first method was developed by Raubal and Winter [16]. Their approach transforms the three main characteristics of landmarks proposed by Sorrows and Hirtle [21] into attributes that make these characteristics computable. Sorrows and Hirtle specified three main categories of landmarks: *Visual*, *semantic* and *structural* landmarks. *Visual* landmarks are considered landmarks due to their visual prominence. *Semantic* landmarks stick out because of their historical or functional importance. *Structural* landmarks are characterized by the importance of their location or their role in space (e.g., at intersections).

In Raubal and Winter's approach extracted attributes are compared to those of surrounding objects to decide whether something is a potential landmark. Since landmarks should be unique in their neighborhood, 'landmarkness' is a relative characteristic [13,19]. Accordingly, the identification process needs to account for nearby objects. Objects may be considered a landmark if their attributes differ significantly from those of the surrounding objects. However, this approach requires a vast amount of detailed data, which hinders its broad application [17].

Other approaches use data mining approaches for the identification of landmarks using various geographic and non-geographic data sources (e.g., [4,14, 22,23]. However, such approaches often only manage to detect the most famous,

---

[1] www.openstreetmap.org

'touristic' landmarks, but fail to pick up local landmarks, such as the small corner store in a residential neighborhood.

Duckham et al. [5] compared the category information of so-called points of interest (POI) with their surroundings in order to obtain their "landmarkness". Individual POIs were ranked by the general landmark suitability of their category (e.g., a church being generally more suited than a lawyer's office), and the uniqueness in their area. Category information is significantly more available than detailed data about an individual object's shape, color, or size. Thus, the amount of required data is greatly reduced. Nevertheless, this method still suffers from an unequal distribution of geographic (POI) information [17]. An additional limitation is that the employed heuristics may simply go wrong. Certain objects may be highly unsuitable landmarks despite their category being generally well suited. For example, while typical churches are highly suitable landmarks, as they are large, recognizable and semantically as well as architecturally distinct from their surroundings, some churches, for instance a small church-room inside an airport, cannot be considered salient [5].

To face the aforementioned difficulties arising from automated landmark identification, Richter and Winter [17,18] suggest applying principles and methods of "Volunteered Geographic Information" (VGI) in the collection process of landmark information. VGI is a form of user-generated content, specifically targeted at the acquisition of geographic information [7]. The goal is to provide a method allowing a straightforward way to collect and share landmark information. In such an approach, users perform the identification of what 'sticks out from the background', i.e., implicitly or explicitly filter objects with respect to their 'landmarkness'. Consequently, the lack of sufficient existing geographic data disappears. However, it is replaced by a need for a simple mechanism for collecting landmarks because otherwise it will be impossible to attract a sufficient number of users. Some previous work by Richter and Winter started off in this direction [6,18], but did not (yet) run on mobile devices and fell short in terms of usability. We believe that the mobile application presented in this paper solves these issues to a large extent.

3   In-Situ Collection of Landmark Candidates

Our aim is to provide a tool for the manual selection of landmarks while being in the environment close to a landmark. Since one of our requirements is a simple, easy-to-use interface, we opt for a photo-based collection procedure. This way, we create a kind of 'point&click' interface. Users take a photo of the geographic object they intend to mark as landmark. In that moment the application registers the user's position (via GPS) and heading (via the inbuilt compass sensor). With this sensor information the application calculates the geographic area visible to the user and retrieves the associated geographic data. This data is ranked according to the likelihood of being the intended object selected. In a final step, users have to confirm (or reject) any of the suggested landmark candidates.

It is important to note that we refrain from any content-based image retrieval approaches in our application. The resulting photo is saved to the phone, but not scanned or analyzed in any other form for possible landmark candidates. Our extraction method is based on location sensor data, and not on image content. Taking a photo is only used as a trigger to collect this sensor data, and because it offers an easy interface that for the user closely links the real-world geographic object with the selection process on the smartphone. Also, for the time being we restrict landmark selection to geographic objects in built environments.

Involving users in the process of landmark identification further has the advantage of creating a dataset directly based on human cognition. The application's main task is to automatically compute useful suggestions, so that the user can confirm the intended landmark. An important factor is to ensure a high performance, i.e., low latency between taking a photograph and confirming the selected object. This process provides several challenges; in this paper we focus on the following implementation aspects: Dealing with sensor inaccuracies in determining the visible area; extracting possible landmark candidates out of the objects in that area; quantification of the candidates' 'landmarkness' attributes; ranking of the remaining candidates by their suitability as landmarks.

3.1   Determining the Visible Area from Location Sensors

The first step is to determine the geographic objects visible to the user. As stated above, we obtain a user's position from the in-built GPS sensor and the heading (viewing direction) from the compass. Combining this sensor information allows for computing a field of view which includes all visible objects. Figure 1 shows an example of such a field of view, indicated by the triangle. Estimating the visible area is severely affected by a mobile device's sensor inaccuracies.

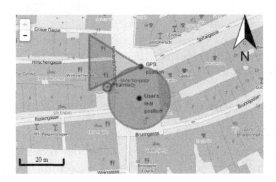

Fig. 1. Miscalculated field of view (triangle) due to GPS inaccuracies leads to missing the pharmacy. The circle indicates an inaccuracy radius of 15 meters (map source (c) OpenStreetMap users; CC BY-SA).

Smartphones use low-cost hardware parts. Consequently, their sensors have rather large inaccuracies [1]. GPS has an accuracy of 5 to 10 meters depending on satellite visibility, which is also achieved by smartphones. However, there is large variation in this accuracy. Even in wide streets inaccuracy can reach up to 15 meters, and much more in narrow lanes with tall surrounding buildings [12].

The compass of handheld devices typically has a mean error of 10 to 30 degrees (in either direction) while the device is moving [3], which differs from device to device. Also, the user is not meant to move while capturing a landmark. Therefore, we performed our own compass test in order to calibrate our application. The test used a mirror compass with a magnetic needle as ground truth (Recta DP-2) and two different cell phones (HTC One and Samsung Galaxy S II). Data was collected while keeping the phones stationary. The smartphone compass showed a mean error of approximately 16 degrees to the mirror compass.

These inaccuracies need to be accounted for when calculating the field of view and, accordingly, the visible objects. In Figure 1, the pharmacy is not detected due to a GPS inaccuracy of 15 meters. Although the compass returns an accurate result, instead the nearby restaurant will be shown as a landmark candidate. Similar errors can occur if the compass returns inaccurate results. Errors, such as this, cannot be fully avoided, but we implemented several strategies to decrease the influence of GPS and compass inaccuracies (discussed in Section 4.3).

3.2 Extracting Possible Landmark Candidates

The geographic data in the computed visible area needs to be scanned for possible landmark candidates. As the number of candidates can become very large if the viewing distance is not restricted, we focus on objects near to the users. We limit these candidates to either point entities or polygons of building size or smaller, since the capturing of paths or other linear features and of large areas is rather difficult to achieve with a mobile phone camera. The minimum demands of an entity to be a potential landmark candidate are to have a location, at least one tag and the possibility to derive a name out of the object's metadata. The name must either be directly available or other attributes, for example, category information or the address, must allow an appropriate naming. This ensures that the landmark can be referred to and users are able to recognize the suggested landmarks.

Furthermore, we restrict the categories of point data considered as landmark candidates. Categories, which frequently occur in clusters, such as pedestrian crossings or traffic signals, are excluded since it is difficult to reliably assign suggested candidates to the correct real world object. Some point objects are discarded as they only appear as part of larger units, such as building entrances. Vegetation is also excluded, based on the fact that trees and other plants are often subject to rapid change and, thus, are rather unreliable landmarks [24]. All objects in the visible area that do not meet these requirements are discarded. The remaining objects represent the set of potential landmark candidates.

3.3 Quantification of Landmarkness Attributes

In order to calculate the most probable candidate, a quantification of the given metadata and sensor information needs to be performed. For this reason, measurable attributes are allocated to the landmark characteristics of Sorrows and Hirtle (see Section 2). These attributes need to be available for a large part of objects in order to include and compare as many candidates as possible. Figure 2 shows characteristics determining a landmark's saliency. Characteristics that can be determined for most geographic entities are highlighted. These can be quantified and, thus, compared between different entities.

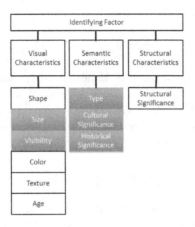

Fig. 2. The identifying characteristics defining landmark salience. Colored boxes show the characteristics which can be derived for most of the available data (after [18]).

In contrast to other approaches, which use similar characteristics to quantify their landmark candidates (e.g., [16]), our method incorporates also sensor data of a mobile device. The visual characteristics 'visibility' is calculated from sensor values. Characteristics not accounted for in our approach are either only rarely available (e.g., *color*) or not available at all (*3D shape*). In selecting the involved characteristics we keep the computational effort for quantification low to ensure a high level of performance. Consequently, 'structural significance' is not taken into account. A direct measurement would be rather challenging, as this would require involving factors such as the structural use, the accessibility and the role of the object within the transportation network. However, since the presented method relies on direct user input, we assume that users (implicitly or explicitly) account for structural significance in their selection of landmark candidates.

The selected characteristics are calculated using the following data. Apart from area and visible range, which are only available for polygons, the selected underlying data can be derived for all geographic entities that include at least category information.

- Size: Area (only available for polygons);
- Visibility: Distance and azimuth deviation to the user, visible range (the angle range in which an object is visible to the user - only for polygons);
- Type: Tags describing the function / category of an object (e.g., *amenity, leisure, shop*);
- Cultural / historical significance: Number of tags, background information (object's own website / Wikipedia article[2]), frequency of the category in surrounding area.

3.4   Ranking of Landmark Candidates

Geographical objects have differing suitability to act as landmarks. Therefore, a ranking system is introduced employing an entity's metadata and visibility to find the most appropriate landmark candidate. Based on the categorization of Sorrows and Hirtle [21], Raubal and Winter [16] developed a measure for determining the salience of a specific object:

$$s_{vis} \cdot w_{vis} + s_{sem} \cdot w_{sem} + s_{str} \cdot w_{str} \tag{1}$$

s stands for the salience measure and w is a weighting factor. The indices *vis*, *sem* and *str* describe visual, semantic and structural salience, respectively. As just discussed, structural characteristics are not taken into consideration in this approach. Thus, s_{str} is dropped from Equation 1. The remaining parameters s_{vis} and s_{sem} are calculated using the attributes listed in Section 3.3.

Calculating the Ranking Factor for Visual Characteristics
In order to derive the factor s_{vis} describing the visual salience, the size of an object (X_{size}), the visible range (X_{vis_range}), the azimuth (X_{az}), and distance to the user ($X_{distance}$) are accounted for. i refers to the current object and *min* and *max* to the respective minimum or maximum value for all objects. A normalization into the range [0,1] is performed for each parameter. Divisions by zero are handled in all cases with the return of the value 0.

Size (only polygons)

$$X_{size} = \frac{X_{size}^{i} - X_{size}^{min}}{X_{size}^{max} - X_{size}^{min}} \tag{2}$$

Visible range (only polygons)

$$X_{vis\_range} = \frac{X_{vis\_range}^{i} - X_{vis\_range}^{min}}{X_{vis\_range}^{max} - X_{vis\_range}^{min}} \tag{3}$$

The formulas for X_{az} and $X_{distance}$ are squared in order to prioritize nearness and compliance with the azimuth:

---

[2] www.wikipedia.com

Azimuth

$$X_{az} = \left(\frac{\pi - ((2\pi + X_{az}^{sensor} - X_{az}^{i}) \mod 2\pi)}{\pi} \right)^2 \tag{4}$$

X_{az}^{sensor} stands for the sensor's azimuth value. If the azimuth of the object is 180 degrees in the opposite direction, the candidate receives the value 0. If the azimuth value is equal to the sensor's azimuth it obtains the value 1. In the case of a polygon, the most outside edges of the entity are used as reference points to calculate the azimuth deviation.

Distance

$$X_{distance} = \left(\frac{X_{user\_max} - X_{dist}^{i}}{X_{user\_max}} \right)^2 \tag{5}$$

The maximum viewing distance X_{user_max} is set in the application as a parameter. This gives the following equations for the calculation of the factor s_{vis}. For polygons:

$$\begin{aligned} s_{vis} = {} & X_{size} \cdot w_{size} + X_{az} \cdot w_{az_{poly}} \\ & + X_{distance} \cdot w_{distance_{poly}} \\ & + X_{vis_{range}} \cdot w_{vis_{range}} \end{aligned} \tag{6}$$

And for points:

$$s_{vis} = X_{az} \cdot w_{az_{point}} + X_{distance} \cdot w_{distance_{point}} \tag{7}$$

Calculating the Ranking Factor for Semantic Characteristics
The factor s_{sem} defining the semantic characteristics is calculated in a similar way to s_{vis}. The involved parameters X_{type} (type) and X_{signif} (significance) are also normalized to the range [0,1].

Type
In order to calculate the value X_{type}, a weighting factor for each category is defined describing the "landmarkness" of a typical representative of that category. This is following Duckham et al.'s [5] approach to using categories in determining landmark candidates (see Section 2). We assigned each of the most frequent categories in our data a suitability factor in the range of [1,10]. Any entity of a category that is not assigned a value to will receive a factor of 1.

$$X_{type} = \frac{X_{type}^{i} - X_{type}^{min}}{X_{type}^{max} - X_{type}^{min}} \tag{8}$$

X_{type}^{min} is the lowest and X_{type}^{max} the highest category value in the visible area.

Significance

Cultural and historical significance are combined in a factor X_{signif}, since no clear distinction can be made between these two factors without checking other sources than the metadata. As stated in Section 3.3, this parameter captures the number of tags X_{tag}, the frequency of the category X_{freq} and potential background information, such as a website $\phi_{website}$ or a Wikipedia article ϕ_{wiki}.

$$X_{signif} = \left(1 - \frac{X_{freq}^i - X_{freq}^{min}}{X_{freq}^{max} - X_{freq}^{min}}\right) \cdot w_{freq}$$
$$+ \frac{X_{tag}^i - X_{tag}^{min}}{X_{tag}^{max} - X_{tag}^{min}} \cdot w_{tag}$$
$$+ \phi_{wiki} + \phi_{website} \tag{9}$$

Accordingly, s_{sem} is calculated as:

$$s_{sem} = X_{type} \cdot w_{type} + X_{signif} \cdot w_{signif} \tag{10}$$

4   Implementation

For our application, Android was chosen as the development platform due to its high market share (around 80% in 2014; [9]) and the openness of its system. As with most Android applications ours is implemented in Java.

4.1   Geographic Data

OpenStreetMap (OSM) is used as underlying geographic data. OSM allows for a world-wide unrestricted access to geographic data [8]. The associated geographic data in the calculated visible area is downloaded using the Overpass API[3].

The conceptual data model of OSM consists of three basic geometric components: *Nodes*, *ways* and *relations*.[4] Nodes represent specific coordinate points as standalone entities or as part of a more complex geometry. Ways consist of at least two nodes and represent polylines. If the first node is equal to the last one (closed ways), they represent polygons describing the geometry of areas, for example, of buildings. Relations are used to define logical or geographic relationships between elements, for example, a building with an inner and an outer geometry. All these elements can be described in more detail by using tags. A tag is a key/value pair, describing one feature of a specific element (e.g., stating that a particular polygonal entity represents a hotel). As there is no established OSM landmark tag, we use the tag "uzh_landmark" to label the collected landmarks.

---

[3] www.overpass-api.de

[4] http://wiki.openstreetmap.org/wiki/Elements; retrieved 04.06.2014

4.2   Collecting a New Landmark

On start-up the application ensures that there is a GPS signal and the device has Internet connection. Once the user takes a photograph and acknowledges that this is indeed the photo they wanted to take, the visible area is calculated and OSM data is downloaded. The data is filtered for potential landmark candidates, which are then ranked according to their suitability using the formulas presented in Section 3.4. Figure 3 shows a screenshot of how this ranking is presented to the users. In the top right corner is the photo previously taken by the user. Next to it is the top-ranked object (name, category and distance to the user) listed as the primary suggestion of a landmark candidate. Beneath are four additional suggestions (the next four objects in the ranking). The application also shows a map of the user's location and viewing direction.

Fig. 3. The interface for the list of suggested landmarks (map source (c) Open-StreetMap users; CC BY-SA)

4.3   Dealing with Sensor Inaccuracies

As discussed in Section 3.1, the application needs to deal with sensor inaccuracies, which may lead to suggesting unintended landmark candidates. Several strategies are used to prevent such errors. The GPS position and its accuracy as well as the calculated visible area are shown to the users (see Figure 3), so they are able to check the sensor performance. The size of the visible area is adapted to the current GPS accuracy to avoid missing any objects that may otherwise fall outside this area. GPS inaccuracy may not exceed 15 meters; otherwise the application refuses to take a photo. Tests during development showed that inaccuracies greater than 15 meters often resulted in unreliable performance.

The viewing angle is fixed at 120 degrees. This value provides good results in circumventing sensor inaccuracies without losing possible objects. The average compass inaccuracy showed a mean error of around 16 degrees (Section 3.1). Therefore, any azimuth deviation of an object to the provided compass value smaller than 16 degrees in either direction is still considered as in front of the user. Finally, five potential landmark candidates are suggested to the users. This increases the chance that the intended landmark is included in the results.

4.4 Weighting Parameters

Our current implementation uses the parameter values listed in Table 1. These values were determined empirically; they show good performance in the environments we ran our tests in. Accordingly, these values are not necessarily of general validity, and changing some of them slightly will likely not have any major impact. However, especially the weights w_{vis} and w_{sem} can significantly change the outcomes as our evaluation has shown (see Section 5). Overemphasizing the visual characteristics leads to unlikely results as distance to and size of objects become overriding factors. Overemphasizing semantic characteristics basically ignores sensor feedback and, thus, may miss out on landmark candidates.

Table 1. The weighting factor values used in the application

Weighting factor	Parameter	Weight
General Factors:		
Visual weight	w_{vis}	3
Semantic weight	w_{sem}	2
Individual visual Characteristics:		
Parameters for polygons:		
Size	w_{size}	2
Visible range	w_{vis_range}	2
Azimuth deviation	$w_{az_{poly}}$	10
Distance to user	$w_{distance_{poly}}$	10
Parameters for nodes:		
Azimuth deviation	$w_{az_{point}}$	12
Distance to user	$w_{distance_{point}}$	12

Weighting factor	Parameter	Weight
Individual semantic Characteristics:		
General semantic Factors:		
Type weight	w_{type}	8
Significance weight	w_{signif}	6
Individual parameters for significance:		
Frequency	w_{freq}	1
Tag Number	w_{tag_n}	1
Bonus for website	$\psi_{website}$	0.3
Bonus for Wikipedia article	ψ_{wiki}	0.6

5 Case Study

We performed a small case study as a proof of concept and to get a feel for the performance of our landmark collection application. This study has two parts. First, we marked different geographic objects as landmarks, seeing how often the intended objects show up in the list of suggestions. This test was run in an urban and a more rural (small town) environment. Second, we had a naive user collect (the same) landmarks to get some first impressions of usability.

5.1 Experimental Setup

We tested our application in an area in the inner city of Zurich, Switzerland, and the small town Zumikon. The geographic data of the chosen areas shows great variety in density and, thus, in the number of possible landmark candidates. By investigating these areas, conclusions can be drawn about the influence of data density on collecting landmarks. During this test, 30 landmarks were collected with the application; 20 in Zurich and 10 in Zumikon.

We did not predefine objects to mark, but selected them in-situ to cover a range of different landmarks. Candidates included prominent and less prominent geographic objects, located in regions with and without surrounding buildings, low and high density of candidates, and identical categories next to each other. In the first part of the test each object was captured either by considering only visual characteristics, only semantic characteristics, or both combined. Additionally every landmark was captured from a near (5-15m) and a far distance (15-35m). In every setting, each object was captured twice to reduce randomness of the results. The maximum viewing distance was set to 50 meters throughout the entire test. The test was performed with a HTC One smartphone.

In the second part of the study, a naive user, who did not know the application beforehand and has no background in geographic information or computer science, was asked to capture the same landmarks in the Zurich area as selected by us. In this test, we chose the optimal settings for the application, namely both rankings activated and capturing landmarks from a near distance, and used the same smartphone as before. This test with the naive user was performed in order to see whether people unfamiliar with the application achieve similar results, and whether there are any obvious usability issues that we had previously missed.

5.2 Results

For the inner city area in Zurich 838 landmark candidates were counted on an area of $0.351km^2$. Zumikon has 24 of such candidates in an area of $0.224km^2$.[5]

Table 2 lists the results of the study. It shows the number of missed and found landmarks, and the according success rate in finding the desired landmark. This rate is significantly higher in Zurich with a ratio of 87% (20 found, 3 missed) against 45 % (10 found, 12 missed) in Zumikon. Missed landmarks either have no representation in OSM, cannot be found by the application, or offer no possibility to derive a name from the metadata. A subsequent check showed that the missed landmarks were caused exclusively by non-existing OSM data for the desired geographic object. Therefore, missed landmarks are not included in the ranking results, as they would not explain the performance of the ranking system.

The second part of the table shows the 'hit rate' of the application, i.e., how often (in %) landmarks ended up on a particular ranking position. The average positions in Table 2 suggest that the best detection is achieved when both rankings are activated and landmarks are captured from a near distance

---

[5] Based on OSM data from 03.08.2014.

Table 2. Overall results of the study

Statistic	Zurich			Zumikon		
Found Landmarks	20			10		
Missed Landmarks	3			12		
Sucess Rate (%)	87			45		
Position Near (5-15m)	Both R.	Semantic R.	Visual R.	Both R.	Semantic R.	Visual R.
1. Place (%)	62.5	35.0	37.5	90.0	70.0	75.0
2. Place (%)	17.5	12.5	27.5	10.0	10.0	25.0
3. Place (%)	17.5	22.5	15.0	0.0	20.0	0.0
4. Place (%)	2.5	0.0	10.0	0.0	0.0	0.0
5. Place (%)	0.0	7.5	5.0	0.0	0.0	0.0
≥6. Place (%)	0.0	22.5	5.0	0.0	0.0	0.0
Average Position	1.6	3.625	2.525	1.1	1.5	1.25
Average Measurement Deviation	0.6	0.25	1.15	0.2	0	0.1
Position Far (15-35m)	Both R.	Semantic R.	Visual R.	Both R.	Semantic R.	Visual R.
1. Place (%)	47.5	40.0	25.0	80.0	55.0	60.0
2. Place (%)	12.5	7.5	30.0	15.0	25.0	15.0
3. Place (%)	17.5	12.5	7.5	5.0	10.0	0.0
4. Place (%)	7.5	12.5	15.0	0.0	10.0	5.0
5. Place (%)	7.5	2.5	0.0	0.0	0.0	20.0
≥6. Place (%)	7.5	25.0	22.5	0.0	0.0	0.0
Average Position	2.5	3.65	3.7	1.25	1.75	2.1
Average Measurement Deviation	0.6	0.2	1.1	0.1	0.1	0.4

with a mean ranking position of 1.6 (Zurich) and 1.1 (Zumikon), respectively. By increasing the distance to the landmark to 15 to 35 meters, this value deteriorates to 2.5 (1.25). The semantic ranking provides an average position of 3.625 (1.5) in near distance and 3.65 (1.75) from the far distance. The decline caused by the increased distance is considerably smaller when only using this ranking. The visual ranking has the highest decline in position between near and far distance with an average of 2.525 (1.25) for close distance and 3.7 (2.1) from far distance

In Zurich, nearly two-thirds (62.5%) of all near distance attempts using both rankings were placed on the first position, for the far distance this decreased to nearly half the attempts (47.5%). The separate rankings both had about one third "direct hits" (35% and 37.5%, respectively). In Zumikon, this difference is much smaller (90% against 70% and 75%).

With both rankings activated, only very few landmark capture attempts result in rankings below 5th place. With only semantic ranking, from both distances around a quarter of attempts ended below 5th place; for visual ranking this happened in 5% of the cases for the near distance (22.5% for the far distance). In Zumikon no intended object was ever ranked below 5th place since the number of landmark candidates in any visible area was small to begin with.

The average measurement deviation states the average difference in ranking between the two captures for each object. It gives an indication of the robustness of the results. In Zurich, the semantic ranking has the highest stability through lesser dependence on exact sensor data, whereas the visual ranking has the highest instability in the position (which is still only about 1). Accordingly, the combined ranking is in-between these two. Zumikon shows a similar pattern, although the difference between the different deviations is much smaller.

Results for the second part of the study–the naive user test–are very similar to those achieved in the first part with both rankings activated and capturing from a near distance. On average, the intended object has a ranking position of 1.675. In 65% of the cases, the object ended up on the first place of the ranking; only in one case it was ranked below fifth place.

6   Discussion

Overall, our research shows that collecting landmark candidates using principles and methods of user-generated content is a feasible approach. The smartphone application works reliably, achieves a very good hit rate, and presents results within a few seconds. The naive user test showed no significant problems with the interface. Thus, a widespread use of the application seems possible in principle.

For the purpose of identifying the intended object, we introduced a ranking system similar to the one introduced by Raubal and Winter [16]. The ranking is composed of visual and semantic characteristics. The purpose of the ranking is to distinguish between salient and non-salient (or less salient) objects in the field of view and to determine the object most probably intended by the user. The results of the strictly visual approach show that it is not possible to achieve stable results by relying only on sensor data. Hence, semantic characteristics need to be integrated to measure the 'landmarkness' of geographic objects.

Previous automated methods were hampered, among others, by the required amount of data to determine landmarks [17]. A main advantage of a user-generated approach is that the main part of the selection process is done by users through the manual confirmation of results. The application only suggests likely landmark candidates and does not prescribe them. This allows for a substantial reduction of data requirements.

The results of the case study demonstrate good performance in finding the intended landmarks. The accuracy of the integrated smartphone sensors seems to satisfy the demands. Restricting GPS accuracy to at least 15 meters and the need for a user to wait for a stable position ensured a viable sensor performance in most cases. This may not always be feasible in every situation, though. Other strategies, such as setting the viewing angle to 120 degrees, also contribute to improving the results. Without these strategies the success rate would drastically deteriorate, especially in situations with reduced satellite visibility.

Using OSM as data source turns out to be a limiting factor. This is especially apparent in the rural area, where the amount of available landmark candidates decreased drastically from 838 to 24 in a comparably sized area. This leads to an increased amount of missed landmarks, and asks for additional strategies that would, for instance, allow for adding missing objects on the fly.

Finally, objects may be considered to be landmarks due to many reasons, for example, their color or their age. And what makes an object salient often does not include the whole object, but instead an eye-catching feature of the object. In the current application, we only store that a specific object is a landmark, without specifying why or which parts make it a landmark. The submission of more detailed characteristics would allow the computation of more complex references to objects, such as "the blue building on the corner with the striking shop window". However, saving all associated information (landmark tag, justification, characteristics) on OSM would significantly increase the amount of stored data and, thus, the number of needed tags. Data volume would even further increase if photo-related information is stored as well, for example, the time of the recording, the azimuth angle to the landmark, and the location where the picture was taken. This might clutter the OSM data and be irritating to OSM users not interested in landmarks. As an alternative solution it would be possible to upload all gathered results on a dedicated publicly available server to offer a platform for the sharing of all landmark related information.

7 Conclusions

Compiling a set of landmark candidates that is of high enough quality to be uniformly useful has largely failed so far due to a mix of high demands on detailed geographic data and a lack of suitable base data. We believe that methods of user-generated content would alleviate these issues to a large extent. This paper presented first steps in that direction, namely a mobile application that allows for the in-situ collection of landmark candidates. Our work has shown the feasibility of such an approach and offered important insights into requirements and challenges that need to be dealt with to ensure a reliable data collection. However, more large-scale studies are needed to properly evaluate the usability and the scalability of the application.

Compared to automated methods to identify landmarks, the presented approach provides several advantages: First of all, it substantially reduces the amount of required data as a large part of the data filtering is done through direct input of the users. Second, in principle the application allows the landmark tagging of arbitrary geographic objects, large or small, world famous or only salient at a particular street corner. The level of detail is only limited by the completeness of the underlying OpenStreetMap data. However, this is also a major challenge for our approach. The results strongly depend on the quality of OSM data in a given area. OSM has known deficiencies of coverage in rural areas [8]. The low data density in these regions negatively affects the rate of identified landmarks and, thus, the usability of the application in such areas. This may be tackled by introducing further user-generated data collection methods.

The greatest challenge of any user-generated approach, however, is to find locals willing to contribute to such a project. To find enough users, people must be informed about and believe in the added value of landmarks and their possible uses. In addition, some mechanisms for quality checks need to be implemented, as user-generated content does not guarantee that the data is actually useful. Data correction and feedback mechanisms may be introduced towards this end.

Acknowledgments. We would like to thank Stephan Winter and Masha Ghasemi for their conceptual input in earlier stages of this project, as well as Kjartan Bjorset for his implementation of a first (map-based) prototype.

References

1. Bauer, C.: On the (in-) accuracy of GPS measures of smartphones: A study of running tracking applications. Studies **3**, 9 (2013)
2. Beeharee, A.K., Steed, A.: A natural wayfinding exploiting photos in pedestrian navigation systems. In: Proceedings of the 8th Conference on Human-Computer Interaction with Mobile Devices and Services, MobileHCI 2006, pp. 81–88. ACM, New York (2006)
3. Blum, J.R., Greencorn, D.G., Cooperstock, J.R.: Smartphone sensor reliability for augmented reality applications. In: Zheng, K., Li, M., Jiang, H. (eds.) MobiQuitous 2012. LNICST, vol. 120, pp. 127–138. Springer, Heidelberg (2013)
4. Crandall, D.J., Backstrom, L., Huttenlocher, D., Kleinberg, J.: Mapping the world's photos. In: Proceedings of the 18th International Conference on World Wide Web, pp. 761–770. ACM, New York (2009)
5. Duckham, M., Winter, S., Robinson, M.: Including landmarks in routing instructions. Journal of Location Based Services **4**(1), 28–52 (2010)
6. Ghasemi, M., Richter, K.F., Winter, S.: Landmarks in OSM, State of the Map 2011 (2011)
7. Goodchild, M.F.: Citizens as sensors: The world of volunteered geography. GeoJournal **69**(4), 211–221 (2007)
8. Haklay, M.: How good is volunteered geographical information? A comparative study of OpenStreetMap and Ordnance Survey datasets. Environment and Planning B **37**(4), 682 (2010)
9. Lomas, N.: Android still growing market share by winning first time smartphone users. http://techcrunch.com/2014/05/06/android-still-growing-market-share-by-winning-first-time-smartphoneusers/ (retrieved on: July 23, 2014)
10. Lynch, K.: The Image of the City. The MIT Press, Cambridge (1960)
11. May, A.J., Ross, T., Bayer, S.H., Tarkiainen, M.J.: Pedestrian navigation aids: Information requirements and design implications. Personal and Ubiquitous Computing **7**(6), 331–338 (2003)
12. Modsching, M., Kramer, R., ten Hagen, K.: Field trial on GPS accuracy in a medium size city: the influence of built-up. In: 3rd Workshop on Positioning, Navigation and Communication, pp. 209–218. Hannover, Germany (2006)
13. Nothegger, C., Winter, S., Raubal, M.: Selection of salient features for route directions. Spatial Cognition & Computation **4**(2), 113–136 (2004)
14. Papadopoulos, S., Zigkolis, C., Kompatsiaris, Y., Vakali, A.: Cluster-based landmark and event detection on tagged photo collections. IEEE Multimedia **18**(1), 52–63 (2010)
15. Presson, C.C., Montello, D.R.: Points of reference in spatial cognition: Stalking the elusive landmark. British Journal of Developmental Psychology **6**, 378–381 (1988)
16. Raubal, M., Winter, S.: Enriching wayfinding instructions with local landmarks. In: Egenhofer, M., Mark, D.M. (eds.) GIScience 2002. LNCS, vol. 2478, pp. 243–259. Springer, Heidelberg (2002)
17. Richter, K.F.: Prospects and challenges of landmarks in navigation services. In: Raubal, M., Mark, D.M., Frank, A.U. (eds.) Cognitive and Linguistic Aspects of Geographic Space - New Perspectives on Geographic Information Research. Lecture Notes in Geoinformation and Cartography, pp. 83–97. Springer, Heidelberg (2013)
18. Richter, K.F., Winter, S.: Harvesting user-generated content for semantic spatial information: the case of landmarks in OpenStreetMap. In: Proceedings of the Spatial Sciences & Surveying Biennial Conference, Wellington, NZ (2011)

19. Richter, K.F., Winter, S.: Landmarks – GIScience for Intelligent Services. Springer, Cham (2014)
20. Siegel, A.W., White, S.H.: The development of spatial representations of large-scale environments. In: Reese, H. (ed.) Advances in Child Development and Behaviour, pp. 9–55. Academic Press, New York (1975)
21. Sorrows, M.E., Hirtle, S.C.: The nature of landmarks for real and electronic spaces. In: Freksa, C., Mark, D.M. (eds.) COSIT 1999. LNCS, vol. 1661, pp. 37–50. Springer, Heidelberg (1999)
22. Tezuka, T., Tanaka, K.: Landmark extraction: a web mining approach. In: Cohn, A.G., Mark, D.M. (eds.) COSIT 2005. LNCS, vol. 3693, pp. 379–396. Springer, Heidelberg (2005)
23. Tomko, M.: Case study – assessing spatial distribution of web resources for navigation services. In: Proceedings of the 4th International Workshop on Web and Wireless Geographical Information Systems, pp. 90–104 (2004)
24. Vinson, N.G.: Design guidelines for landmarks to support navigation in virtual environments. In: Proceedings of the SIGCHI Conference on Human Factors in Computing Systems, pp. 278–285. ACM, New York (1999)

Leveraging VGI for Gazetteer Enrichment:
A Case Study for Geoparsing Twitter Messages

Maxwell Guimarães de Oliveira[1,2]([⊠]), Cláudio E.C. Campelo[1],
Cláudio de Souza Baptista[1], and Michela Bertolotto[2]

[1] Information Systems Laboratory, Department of Computer Science,
Federal University of Campina Grande, Campina Grande, Brazil
`maxwell@ufcg.edu.br`, {`campelo,baptista`}`@dsc.ufcg.edu.br`
[2] School of Computer Science and Informatics,
University College Dublin, Dublin, Ireland
`michela.bertolotto@ucd.ie`

Abstract. With the advent of Volunteered Geographical Information
(VGI), the amount of user-contributed spatial data grows around the
world each day. Such spatial data may contain valuable information
which may help other research fields, such as the Digital Gazetteers used
in Geographic Information Retrieval (GIR), for instance. The Digital
Gazetteers have a powerful role in the geoparsing process. They need to
keep themselves up-to-date and as complete as possible to enable geopar-
sers to perform lookup and then resolve toponym recognition precisely
over digital texts. In this context, this paper proposes a method of gazetteer enrichment leveraging VGI data sources. Indeed VGI environments
are not originally developed to work as gazetteers, however, they often
contain more detailed and up-to-date information than gazetteers. Our
method is applied in a geoparser environment by adapting its heuristics set besides enriching the corresponding gazetteer. A case study was
performed by geoparsing Twitter messages focused solely on the microtexts in order to evaluate the performance of the enriched system. The
results obtained were compared with previous results of a case study that
used the same dataset and both the gazetteer and the geoparser without
improvements.

Keywords: Gazetteer · Geoparsing · OpenStreetMap · Twitter · VGI

1 Introduction

Digital Gazetteers are known as huge geographical knowledge databases and
have been fundamental for Geographic Information Retrieval (GIR) tasks in
order to resolve place names to geographical features or footprints [11]. The
wide variety of such gazetteers are enriched by geography experts endowed with
skilled knowledge in order to provide geographical data of acceptable quality.
Although it is desirable, this way of spatial data production is costly, requires

© Springer International Publishing Switzerland 2015
J. Gensel and M. Tomko (Eds.): W2GIS 2015, LNCS 9080, pp. 20–36, 2015.
DOI: 10.1007/978-3-319-18251-3_2

time and leads to a lack of free services availability as well. GeoNames[1] is one of the most known open gazetteers and its database covers all countries and contains over ten million[2] place names.

The problem with current open gazetteers is that they do not cover geographical features at a high level of detail e.g. Points-Of-Interest (POIs), Streets and Districts. Considering that gazetteers are mainly used by geoparser systems, which work aiming to identify geographical locations in digital texts (i.e. geoparsing), those systems are only able to resolve toponyms relying on the level of detail provided by the gazetteers. Thereby, it is necessary to enrich gazetteers in order to perform geoparsing with high level of detail regarding geographical features.

Our research is motivated by the Location-Based Social Networks (LBSN) related to city issues as the Crowd4City system [5]. In LBSN environments, we might have users in the role of residents interested in gathering information about specific urban events and small areas of their cities of residence. Such small areas can be simply specific POIs, for example, instead of information about an entire city. Despite initiatives like Crowd4City, one of the main challenges in the use of human sensors has been keeping them willing to contribute and consequently maintain the LBSNs in continuous operation. Typically, only a few users are in charge of providing a significant volume of information. This phenomenon is visible in terms of geographic location, where many areas around the world are mapped by only few users [9]. One of the factors regarding users' motivation can be associated with the existence of costs for these volunteers. These costs can be inherent to the learning curve for correct operationalization of a LBSN, or related to the contribution routines. These costs can also be associated with the volunteers' available time and demands persistence from them. Therefore, it becomes necessary to find alternatives that will allow keeping the LBSNs up-to-date even when the volume of contributions of the volunteers is below the expected. One alternative we are considering is the integration of GIR techniques and VGI for LBSN improvement.

In our previous work [15], we proposed an approach for the automated production of Volunteered Geographic Information (VGI) [8] based on geoparsing of microtexts published on social media. In this way, we call VGI all discovered information that could be produced by microtexts which might refer to specific geographical locations. Thus, writers from social media can become nonintentional volunteers in the production of the VGI in an automated way and such produced VGI could be explored by the users of LBSN systems for city issues. The proposed approach encompassed the geoparser of the GeoSEn system [3, 4] and its own gazetteer. Although we achieved good results, the adopted gazetteer only resolves toponyms in a city-scale level like other gazetteers. Social media users may refer to cities in their messages, however they often refer to specific buildings and vernacular toponyms instead, particularly on a lower-scale

---

[1] http://www.geonames.org/
[2] Information updated in February 2015.

level. Thus, we need a gazetteer which enables to resolve toponyms at a higher level of detail.

The amount of VGI continues to grow around the world each day. OpenStreetMap (OSM) [9] is one of the most representative VGI environments and has approximately 2.8 billion spatial features or 500 GB of XML data[3] available to be freely downloaded and used. OpenStreetMap has approximately 1.8 million registered users, nevertheless only 25% are considered active contributors[4]. We believe using VGI derived from OSM data for gazetteer enrichment can enable gazetteers to resolve toponyms at a higher level of detail. Another advantage of using VGI in gazetteer enrichment is to continuously present an up-to-date database, as the number of active volunteers around the world is increasing and the VGI quality is improving. In 2013, for instance, over 5 million spatial features have changed in the OSM database[6].

In this paper, we present a method for gazetteer enrichment leveraging VGI. We developed a method with the aim to classify retrieved VGI features based on its metadata and also on the previous knowledge already stored into the gazetteer. These two classifiers are considered due to known VGI quality issues, as Keßler et al. [11] highlighted. This forced us to not rely solely on VGI metadata for the gazetteer enrichment. We also present an extension of the GeoSEn system [3,4] in order to enable the toponym resolution at a higher level of detail according to the enriched gazetteer. While the GeoSEn system only works for the Portuguese language, in this paper we use examples in English.

We evaluate our enriched gazetteer with a case study applied to manually checked Twitter messages harvested from social media. Then we compare our results with results achieved in our previous study [15], when we used the previous gazetteer of the GeoSEn system.

The remainder of this paper is structured as follows. Section 2 discusses related work. Section 3 describes briefly the GeoSEn system geoparser. Section 4 presents our developed method in details. Section 5 addresses a case study carried out to evaluate the enriched gazetteer. Finally, section 6 concludes the paper and highlights further work to be undertaken.

2   Related Work

The next generation of gazetteers was prophesied by Keßler et al. [11] few years after the OpenStreetMap become popular. They linked the geographical information contribution and retrieval with the aim of using VGI in order to enrich gazetteers, and discussed challenges to make it real. In their opinion, the next generation gazetteer needs to cope with harvesting and integration of information, assessing fitness for purpose, and enabling retrieval, querying and navigation. The key topic is the time-dynamic behavior of spatial features facing a world where things change quickly and that goes against the idea of static

---

[3] http://wiki.openstreetmap.org/wiki/Planet.osm
[4] http://wiki.openstreetmap.org/wiki/Stats

gazetteers. Our proposed work fits with some ideas discussed by Keβler et al. [11] as we explore harvesting VGI in order to enrich a gazetteer.

The current literature comprises some proposals concerning digital gazetteers and leveraging VGI sources for making gazetteers up to date. Lamprianidis et al. [13] proposed a method for extraction and integration of Points-Of-Interest (POIs) from several crowdsourced media, e.g. DBPedia, OpenStreetMap, Wikimapia and Foursquare. The main idea is to classify such POIs by a common taxonomy in order to gather POIs from different sources into a unique database.

Gelernter et al. [7] addressed gazetteer enrichment motivated by the fact that GeoNames is not rich in local toponyms. They proposed a fuzzy SVM-based algorithm that checks both OpenStreetMap and Wikimapia for approximate spelling and approximate geocoding in order to find duplicates as confirmation of reliability in a way of noise reduction for the purpose of integration into a gazetteer. They suggest that OSM and Wikimapia would make suitable sources for gazetteer enrichment although the OSM coordinates have proved to be more geographically accurate. While Gelernter et al. [7] focus on comparing different VGI sources, our proposal is related to the usage of just one VGI source in order to harvest geographical features at a city-scale level for gazetteer enrichment based on spatial characteristics and a hierarchical classifier.

Moura and Davis Jr. [14] proposed a gazetteer enriched with semantic relationships and connections with non-geo entities through combining GeoNames and DBPedia. Such work is motivated by the fact that currently there is no single gazetteer which has detailed coverage of places as intra-urban places. Their experiments show DBPedia has more urban details than GeoNames. However, neither has much information at such level of coverage. Similarly, our aim is to provide a gazetteer with detailed coverage of places like POIs and streets. While their approach is based on Linked Data, our approach relies on VGI and its power of providing much information about urban places in a simple way.

Beard [1] proposed an ontology-based gazetteer model for organizing VGI and outlined some characteristics of VGI regarding its usage for a gazetteer approach. Peng et al. [16] also relied on ontologies and proposed an architecture which mixes folksonomy and ontology into a digital gazetteer. Furche et al. [6] performed gazetteer enrichment by automatically extracting web pages. They proposed a system which performs page segmentation, attribute alignment among different pages and then extending existing gazetteers.

The usage of VGI for gazetteer enrichment has been applied in several researches and in different ways, as we could notice. Our proposal fits in this field and aims to provide an improvement in geographical coverage of gazetteer through VGI, which provides more geographically precise data than a city-scale level empowered by crowds. Our main difference from related work is that we relied on two classifiers for VGI, where one explores the VGI metadata and the other explores the knowledge from previously stored data into the gazetteer. In addition, we are also considering the usage of the enriched gazetteer in geoparsing messages from social media (e.g. Twitter).

3 The GeoSEn Parser

Campelo and Baptista [3, 4] proposed a model for extraction of geographic knowledge from web documents. They developed GeoSEn, a search engine with geographic focus, which enables the geographic indexing of documents extracted from the web.

The architecture of the GeoSEn system was developed as an extension of the Apache Nutch Framework[5], by adding the ability to manipulate and retrieve geographic information. Since Nutch is based on a plugin-oriented architecture, some plugins were implemented and they are the essence of the GeoSEn system. The focus of this paper is on the GeoSEn Parser, which is one of these plugins.

The GeoSEn Parser is responsible for the detection of geographic terms from texts written in Portuguese. It enables to infer toponyms eventually cited in a text following the Brazilian political-division hierarchy, which goes from the least precise levels (countries) to the most precise ones (cities). The GeoTree [3] is a tree-based data structure which establishes the hierarchical relationship between toponyms stored into the GeoSEn gazetteer. There are six levels of toponyms in the GeoTree: Country, Region, State, Mesoregion, Microregion and City. An example of a GeoTree instance is illustrated in Fig. 1.

The process of detecting geographic references is based on a set of heuristics. For example, the geoparser considers information such as the position of a term in the text and its length (i.e. the number of words that form a term). Such information about position of the terms can be useful to correlate spatial terms

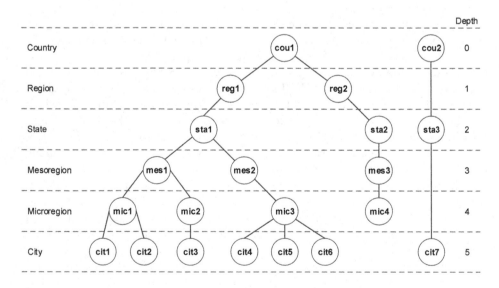

Fig. 1. An example of a GeoTree instance

---

[5] http://lucene.apache.org/nutch

which are close in the messages. All the details about how the GeoSEn Parser works are described in the previous work [3,4].

The GeoSEn system includes a gazetteer which is composed of all the toponyms from Brazil, according to the GeoTree structure. Each toponym is stored by `loc:id`, the unique identification; `loc:type`, the type of the toponym, which means the respective level in the GeoTree; `loc:name`, the full name; `loc:ancestor`, the identification of the toponym which is a direct ancestor; and `loc:geometry`, the embedded geometry. The GeoSEn gazetteer is the object of our study and will be enriched by geographical data derived from VGI in order to enable storing more specific toponyms in a city context.

4 The Gazetteer Enrichment Leveraging VGI

Our aim in enriching the GeoSEn gazetteer is to enable it to geoparse texts which may contain more specific locations like Points-Of-Interest, for example. For such, we believe the power of VGI can provide a huge volume of up-to-date geographical locations instead of data provided by agencies. In addition, there is a lack of official data about specific locations in several parts of the world. When such data exists, they are not often freely available.

We developed an extension of the GeoSEn system which comprises the gazetteer enrichment and the heuristics adjustments in order to enable the GeoSEn parser to perform toponym resolution for more geographically specific locations. In the following, we show such extension in details.

4.1 The Gazetteer Enrichment Method

As discussed in section 3, the GeoSEn gazetteer is composed of toponyms related to the Brazilian's political subdivision and its most geographically precise level for stored toponym of the city-scale level (See Fig. 1). This may imply an inaccurate toponym resolution while geoparsing messages (e.g. Twitter messages, etc.) related to a big city which may contain more precise information like districts or known buildings. This can cause too many toponym resolutions into the same location (typically the centroid of that big city). The citizens interested in specific regions within their cities would need to manually filter all the information related to such cities, for instance.

We have extended both the GeoSEn gazetteer and the GeoTree in order to store and enable toponyms related to more specific locations within a city. We focused on three types of toponyms: points of interest (POI's), such as well-known buildings, shops or touristic targets; street names and districts. Thus, we organized and included these types into the previously established GeoTree. An example of the new GeoTree instance is shown in Fig. 2.

The original structure of the GeoTree has been used in this work since our current focus is on geoparsing documents written in Portuguese that relates to Brazilian toponyms. Indeed, further work should investigate how such structure could be generalized to allow us to classify worldwide toponyms.

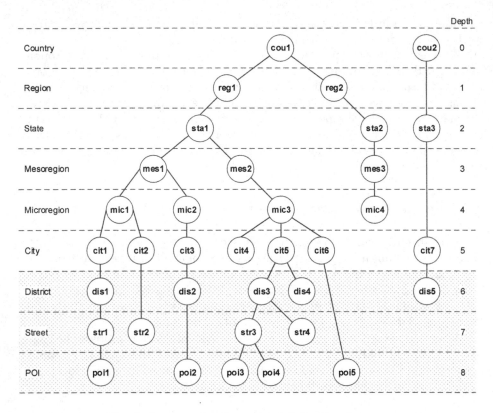

Fig. 2. An example of an extended GeoTree instance

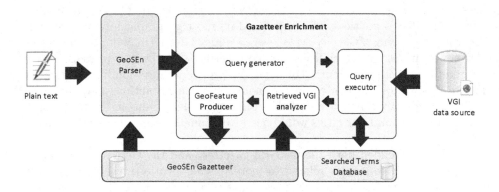

Fig. 3. The gazetteer enrichment architecture

In the preliminary version of our gazetteer enrichment method implementation, the requests are delivered on-demand as soon as a text is delivered to the GeoSEn parser. Fig. 3 presents the architecture of our proposal.

The gazetteer enrichment method can be subdivided into four stages: query generation, query execution, retrieved VGI analysis and geoFeature production. In the following, we explain each stage considering Twitter messages as our text data.

Query generation: performs the preprocessing over the text, which includes the removal of hashtags, URLs, "RT"s (a token commonly used in retweets, when a tweet is shared by other users), usernames preceded by "@", and the generation of queries to be delivered to the query execution stage.

Query execution: establishes the communication between the gazetteer enrichment method implementation and a VGI source using an API.

Retrieved VGI analysis: performs the classification of the retrieved features and also seeks for duplicates into the GeoSEn gazetteer.

GeoFeature Production: produces the record of new geographical features which will enrich the gazetteer and also produces adjustments into the previously stored features.

In order to store a high number of different toponyms into the GeoSEn gazetteer, we can produce several different search terms from a single microtext during the query generation stage. The basic idea of the algorithm is to combine between one and four neighbor words to form a search term using white spaces between them. This strategy enables to get toponyms from a VGI source formed by just one and up to four words properly. Stop words, special characters and punctuation are discarded. Fig. 4 illustrates some iterations of such algorithm in a sample text.

In the five iterations shown in Fig. 4, we can notice only three produced search terms delivered to VGI source. It is important to notice that although the query "grove road" should retrieve the same results as "grove road D6", this is not guaranteed by the VGI source. Duplicate results eventually retrieved by a

---

Tweet:	**@user:** heavy traffic jam in grove road D6 today	

Iteration	...	Status
i	**@user:** heavy traffic jam in grove road D6 today	*ignored*
i+1	**@user:** heavy traffic jam in grove road D6 today	*searched term*
i+2	**@user:** heavy traffic jam in grove road D6 today	*searched term*
i+3	**@user:** heavy traffic jam in grove road D6 today	*searched term*
i+4	**@user:** heavy traffic jam in grove road D6 today	*ignored*

Fig. 4. Some iterations of the search-term-generator algorithm in a sample text

most specific search are discarded in the retrieved VGI analysis stage. The two iterations which have not produced and delivered a search term contain special words that would not help in the search.

The number four was empirically chosen for the maximum word count in a term which may refer to a location name after observing typical toponym patterns around the world. Toponyms with more than four words tend to be rare.

One auxiliary database for keeping previously searched terms and avoiding duplicated requests was developed. Such database is quite useful during the query execution stage. The historical database stores the searched terms and also the timestamp and information about retrieved features from VGI source for each searched term. As the VGI changes all the time, we believe an expiration time for each searched term should be established. Thus, new searches could be performed periodically in order to store updated toponyms into the gazetteer, keeping a permanent enrichment process. We are currently not taking this into consideration but it forms part of our plan for further work.

The OSM Nominatim[6] service - which indexes the entire OpenStreetMap spatial database and provides toponym lookup - was used as a VGI data source for the GeoSEn gazetteer enrichment. We implemented an API using Java programming language for automatically performing searches on such service and receiving the JSON (JavaScript Object Notation) responses with the geographical location features.

Geographical data retrieved during the query execution stage is analyzed before being finally stored into the GeoSEn gazetteer. This analysis is performed during the retrieved VGI analysis stage and consists of discovering the level of the toponym in the new GeoTree and its direct ancestor into the GeoSEn gazetteer. Fig. 5 shows the process flow of the retrieved VGI analysis in details.

The analysis of a retrieved VGI feature consists of four steps: 1) the checking for duplicates; 2) the classification; 3) the definition of a direct ancestor; and 4) the search of candidates for children. The first step consists of looking for similar features into the GeoSEn gazetteer comparing its geometries and/or names with the retrieved feature. Duplicated features are discarded and not stored into the gazetteer.

The classification of a retrieved VGI feature involves the extended version of GeoTree structure since such feature needs to fit with one of the levels in the tree. For example, a retrieved feature can be classified as a Point-Of-Interest or as a City. The classification step is based on both the VGI metadata classifier and the spatial-search-driven classifier.

The OSM metadata structure, for instance, provides some fields which can help to identify where a retrieved feature can fit in the GeoTree. An OSM feature which satisfies the condition "`class:place` && `type:hamlet`" in its metadata fields, for example, can be mapped onto the District level in the new GeoTree. Another feature which has the field "`class:highway`", for example, can be mapped onto the Street level.

---

[6] http://nominatim.openstreetmap.org/

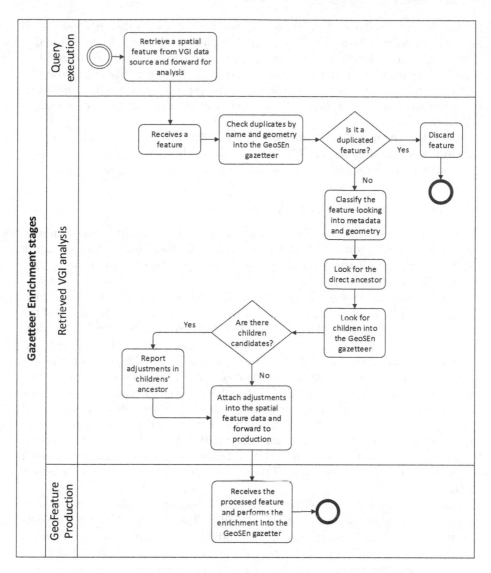

Fig. 5. The process flow of retrieved VGI analysis stage

As OpenStreetMap allows users to simply not fill up the metadata fields or even to put wrong information, we chose to develop a classifier based on performing spatial searches within the GeoSEn gazetteer. The main idea of this second classifier is to find out spatial relationships between retrieved features and the previous stored toponyms by using known spatial operations e.g. contains, intersects, touches and overlaps.

The step for definition of a direct ancestor consists of searching for a previously stored spatial feature suitable to be the direct ancestor of the retrieved feature in the GeoTree. It takes use of the spatial-search-driven classifier to find the immediate feature which spatially contains the new feature. Finally, the search of candidates for children is applied to find previously stored features of which the new feature is an ancestor. This step is also based on the spatial-search-driven classifier. Obviously, this step does not apply to new features classified as Point-Of-Interest since they could not assume the ancestor's role in the GeoTree.

Once the retrieved VGI analysis finishes, the last stage of the gazetteer enrichment method is responsible for generating the new toponym entry into the GeoSEn gazetteer and performing the updates on its children as well.

4.2   The GeoSEn Heuristics Adjustments

Once we have enriched the GeoSEn gazetteer in order to store more precise toponyms in a city-context, it was necessary to perform some changes in the GeoSEn heuristics for toponym recognition and toponym resolution considering the new GeoTree structure (see Fig. 2).

The internal GeoTree production method, which is responsible for structuring the hierarchical tree of each toponym resolved, was remodeled. We included the three new toponym levels (POI, Street and District) so that the GeoTree production could recognize them correctly. The spatial distance calculation was included into the GeoSEn parser's module that is responsible for checking cross-references between every toponym-resolved candidate. Cross-references are geographic references found in a document which has topological spatial relationships in relation to other reference [4]. The previous version of such module only considered the textual distance (word-by-word) and the hierarchical relationship between such candidates into a message. Thus, the spatial distance is used in addition to the textual distance only when two compared toponym candidates have a common ancestor and at least one of these candidates is classified as POI, Street or District.

For example, let us consider two tuples in the format ("name", "type") representing a toponym-resolved candidate: ("Eiffel Tower", "POI") and ("Rue la Fayette", "Street"). In such case, both candidates have at least one common ancestor in the GeoTree: Paris (of the city level). Thus, as the spatial distance decreases, the cross-reference coefficient for both candidates increases.

The GeoSEn system uses a metric called Confidence Rate (CR). The CR is a measure which represents the probability of a toponym-resolved candidate to be a valid place. The CR value varies between 0 and 1, inclusive. In the GeoSEn system, each toponym level in the GeoTree has a specific CR calculation. A specific CR for each toponym type is necessary as there are several different ways that influence people mentioning a toponym depending on such type. Therefore, we needed to define the CR calculation for each toponym-resolved candidate from one of the new included toponym levels in the GeoTree.

The CR values are calculated based on Confidence Factors (CFs). A CF is a measure associated with an analyzed feature of a toponym during the parsing process. The GeoSEn system uses four different CFs:

- CF_{ST}, which is related to the occurrence of a special term[7] before or after the term that results in a toponym-resolved candidate;
- CF_{FMT}, which is related to the spelling correctness of a toponym-resolved candidate when it is compared to terms from the source text;
- CF_{CROSS}, which is related to other toponym-resolved candidates;
- CF_{TS}, which is related to textual searches performed by the GeoSEn search engine.

As our focus is on the GeoSEn parser and not on its search engine, the CF_{TS} was not considered in our study. Each CF has a weight in the CR computation for a toponym type. We needed to define the weights for CFs in the CR computation for the additional toponym types. As CR value may vary between 0 and 1, we defined the weight set below:

$$CR_{(POI)} = 0.40\ CF_{ST} + 0.15\ CF_{FMT} + 0.45\ CF_{CROSS}$$

$$CR_{(Street)} = 0.25\ CF_{ST} + 0.15\ CF_{FMT} + 0.60\ CF_{CROSS}$$

$$CR_{(District)} = 0.30\ CF_{ST} + 0.15\ CF_{FMT} + 0.55\ CF_{CROSS}$$

We considered the weights of the previous toponym types found in the GeoSEn system in defining such weight set. We also considered the addition of the spatial distance for CF_{CROSS} calculation involving the additional toponym types as well as the empirical nature of occurrence of these types in text messages. One idea for future work is to automate the definition of such weights based on a historical analysis of occurrences for each toponym type. Although we have obtained satisfactory results so far, we are aware that the empirical definition may cause misinterpretation in the toponym resolution task.

Another change performed was implementing a cut function in order to discard less-geographically-precise toponym-resolved candidates while geoparsing microtexts. Although such redundancy has been relevant for the search engine of the GeoSEn system, it is unsuitable for our proposal of LBSN integration, which requires high geographical precision for toponym resolution. The main idea here is to keep only the most precise toponym-resolved candidates. For example, suppose we have a microtext "very beautiful view from Eiffel Tower in Paris". In this case, we will have two toponym-resolved candidates ("The Eiffel Tower, Paris, France", "POI") and ("Paris, France", "City"), and both candidates will be resolved at the end of the geoparsing process. Once the GeoTree knows that the Eiffel Tower is in Paris (France), it is not necessary to resolve for the less precise toponym even they are both present in the source text.

We also performed other minor changes in the GeoSEn parser, such as: the definition of new special terms in Portuguese like "rua" (street), "avenida" (avenue), "travessia" (crossing), "vila" (village/hamlet/town), among others which

---

[7] Special terms are words (or terms) that frequently appear before or after a toponym (e.g. "in", "at", "near") and can be used in order to help the toponym recognition task in the geoparsing process.

are usually used when Brazilian people describe streets or districts in Portuguese language; and the definition of some stop words in English like "at", "I'm", once we have experienced messages written in Portuguese with fragments in English.

This set of changes provides a new strategy for toponym resolution in the GeoSEn parser. Obviously, such strategy should be improved as new experimental results and new ideas arise. The next section describes a case study we carried out to evaluate the extended version of the GeoSEn parser.

5   Case Study: Automated Geoparsing of Twitter Microtexts

The extended version of GeoSEn was tested on a case study so that we could evaluate the changes performed and make comparisons with the previous one. In the following, we discuss the results.

5.1   Methodology

We carried out a study in order to compare the GeoSEn parser before and after the modifications described in section 4, aiming to measure the performance when geoparsing with more precise toponym types available in the improved gazetteer.

In our previous work [15], we carried out a study with a dataset formed by over 300,000 microtexts written in Portuguese, published on Twitter during the FIFA's Confederations Cup, which took place in Brazil in 2013. Such dataset was processed by the GeoSEn parser in order to identify toponyms based solely on the Twitter microtexts. The main idea was to establish a linkage between twitter messages and locations mentioned in its body instead of the location where users were at the time such messages were delivered. A random sample of these processed microtexts was validated by human volunteers. Besides accuracy of the geoparsing, the volunteers were able to report the microtexts that could have toponyms resolved to places within a city, even if they knew that the version of the GeoSEn parser they used was not able to identify locations at a more detailed level such the city level.

In our most recent evaluation, discussed in this paper, we took the microtexts classified as "could be more precise" from the previous study and applied the extended version of the GeoSEn parser presented in the previous section. The microtexts classified as "could be more precise" are those tweets which have resolved toponyms until the city level (according to the previous GeoTree) even with the messages referring to more precise level toponyms than a city, such as a district or part of a street.

5.2   Results

The results obtained from our experiments show that some tweets have more than one toponym resolved by the extended version of the GeoSEn parser. The processed microtexts and its toponyms resolved were manually validated in order to compute occurrences of true/false positives and negatives.

The GeoSEn gazetteer was enriched with 9,858 additional toponyms from OpenStreetMap database, our adopted VGI data source. Such places were searched on demand during the tweets processing and were classified as Districts (11%), Streets (59%) and points of interest (30%). By the processed tweets, in comparison with results obtained in our previous study, we could report:

– 80% have at least one toponym resolved, an increase of only 3% over the same set of tweets processed in the previous study. This reinforces the good rate of true negatives reported in our previous case study;
– 20% presented the same result observed in the previous study. This may be related to messages which reported more than one toponym resolved and where both the previous and the additional toponym types were mentioned;
– 32% have more than one toponym resolved. This corresponds to microtexts which refer to different locations;
– 91% of the toponyms-resolved set are from one of the recently added toponym types. This confirms the human-volunteer validation trust but is not sufficient to conclude the extended version of the GeoSEn parser is accurate.

By the manual validation over the processed microtexts, we could report:

– 39% of True Positives - i.e., accurate toponym resolution;
– 15% of True Negatives - i.e., no toponym resolution when there were no toponyms to resolve;
– 41% of False Positives - i.e., wrong toponym resolution;
– 5% of False Negatives - i.e., no toponym resolution when there were toponyms to resolve.

Table 1 presents four calculated statistical metrics in order to measure the overall performance of the extended GeoSEn parser and its enriched gazetteer.

Table 1. Statistical results of the extended version of the GeoSEn parser

Accuracy	Precision	Recall	F-Measure
53.68 %	48.37 %	88.11 %	0.624561

Analyzing the achieved results we can conclude the extended version of the GeoSEn system presented a good overall performance. A decrease in accuracy and precision rates, in a comparison with the statistical results of the previous study considering the previous version of the GeoSEn system, were expected. The addition of three toponym levels into the GeoTree and the gazetteer enrichment with places from VGI data source added substantial complexity for the geoparsing process due to uncertainty and unguaranteed data quality. However, these changes have enabled to resolve toponyms in a higher level of detail.

The additional features presented in this paper improved considerably our geoparser, in the sense that it can now perform toponym-resolution at a higher level of detail. However, given this significant change in the level of geographic detail the system can deal with, comparing the geoparser with its previous version in terms of precision and recall would not be meaningful.

It is clear that both accuracy and precision need to be improved in order to have more accurate geoparsing. It will be necessary to analyze in detail occurrences of false positives to discover whether these can be related to our classifiers used in the gazetteer enrichment, to problems concerning VGI quality or to the GeoSEn heuristics. In this latter case more adjustments to the heuristics set of the GeoSEn system and also perhaps to the confidence rate calculation for the added toponym types should be required.

6   Conclusion and Further Work

In this paper, we proposed a gazetteer enrichment using VGI in order to provide an up-to-date and a more accurate toponym lookup. We presented a gazetteer enrichment implementation based on the GeoSEn gazetteer which incorporates a term-query generator, a query executor, a VGI analyzer and a geo-feature producer.

We also extended the GeoTree in order to include three toponym levels within a city: Districts, Streets and Points-Of-Interest; and performed several relevant changes within the GeoSEn heuristics set as well, in order to enable the recognition of the added toponym levels. Although we have presented a gazetteer enrichment method based on a specific gazetteer, we would like to highlight that our proposal could be applied in other gazetteers like GeoNames, for instance. We do not discard novel studies applying our techniques in other gazetteer systems.

A case study was carried out with the aim of evaluating the extended version of the GeoSEn system. The overall results are promising since we have a good accuracy and precision regarding the known VGI quality issues. These achieved results shows that the accuracy of the GeoSEn parser can be over 50%, even using the deeper GeoTree, that increases the complexity of the geoparsing process. Such results can be considered good for this kind of task, though they can potentially be further improved. It is also important to highlight that any specific heuristics aimed to geoparsing microtexts were applied since this is out of the scope of the presented work. The enabling of more precise levels of toponyms into the geoparsing process provides more precise geoparsing over Twitter microtexts.

Even though our results are not conclusive, the lessons learned from this work can provide an interesting basis for discussion. VGI quality, for instance, is an open research field which has received several contributions [2,10,12]. Since our proposal requires good quality VGI, in the future we could apply trust techniques to ensure that the data we use meets this requirement.

The next research steps will consider techniques to increase the precision rate, that is, to decrease false positives occurrence. The case study enabled the identification of some issues related to the quality of OSM data and how it can negatively affect the classification of toponyms added to the GeoSEn gazetteer. One way to address this issue is to combine different VGI data sources.

Further developments will enable the GeoSEn system to deal with other languages, such as English. In parallel with this, an investigative study on the generalization of the GeoTree will be carried out so that it can be applied to classify worldwide toponyms.

Acknowledgments. The authors are grateful to the CNPq, "Conselho Nacional de Desenvolvimento Científico e Tecnológico" - Brazil, for funding this research project by the Science Without Borders Programme.

References

1. Beard, K.: A semantic web based gazetteer model for VGI. In: Proceedings of the 1st ACM SIGSPATIAL International Workshop on Crowdsourced and Volunteered Geographic Information, GEOCROWD 2012, pp. 54–61. ACM, New York (2012). http://doi.acm.org/10.1145/2442952.2442962
2. Bishr, M., Kuhn, W.: Geospatial information bottom-up: a matter of trust and semantics. In: Fabrikant, S., Wachowicz, M. (eds.) Lecture Notes in Geoinformation and Cartography, pp. 365–387. The European Information Society (2007)
3. Campelo, C.E.C., Baptista, C.d.S.: Geographic scope modeling for web documents. In: Proceedings of the 2nd International Workshop on Geographic Information Retrieval, pp. 11–18. GIR 2008, ACM, New York, NY, USA (2008). http://doi.acm.org/10.1145/1460007.1460010
4. Campelo, C.E.C., de Souza Baptista, C.: A model for geographic knowledge extraction on web documents. In: Heuser, C.A., Pernul, G. (eds.) ER 2009. LNCS, vol. 5833, pp. 317–326. Springer, Heidelberg (2009)
5. Falcão, A.G.R., Baptista, C.d.S., Menezes, L.C.d.: Crowd4City: utilizando sensores humanos como fonte de dados em cidades inteligentes (in portuguese). In: Proceedings of the 8th Brazilian Symposium on Information Systems, pp. 144–149. São Paulo, Brazil (2012)
6. Furche, T., Grasso, G., Orsi, G., Schallhart, C., Wang, C.: Automatically learning gazetteers from the deep web. In: Proceedings of the 21st International Conference Companion on World Wide Web, pp. 341–344. WWW 2012 Companion, ACM, New York, NY, USA (2012). http://doi.acm.org/10.1145/2187980.2188044
7. Gelernter, J., Ganesh, G., Krishnakumar, H., Zhang, W.: Automatic gazetteer enrichment with user-geocoded data. In: Proceedings of the Second ACM SIGSPATIAL International Workshop on Crowdsourced and Volunteered Geographic Information, pp. 87–94. GEOCROWD 2013, ACM, New York, NY, USA (2013). http://doi.acm.org/10.1145/2534732.2534736
8. Goodchild, M.F.: Citizens as voluntary sensors: spatial data infrastructure in the world of Web 2.0. International Journal of Spatial Data Infrastructures Research **2**, 24–32 (2007)
9. Haklay, M., Weber, P.: OpenStreetMap: User-Generated Street Maps. IEEE Pervasive Computing **7**(4), 12–18 (2008)

10. Jilani, M., Corcoran, P., Bertolotto, M.: Automated highway tag assessment of open-streetmap road networks. In: Proceedings of the 22nd ACM SIGSPATIAL International Conference on Advances in Geographic Information Systems, pp. 4–7. Dallas, Texas, USA (2014)
11. Keßler, C., Janowicz, K., Bishr, M.: An agenda for the next generation gazetteer: geographic information contribution and retrieval. In: Proceedings of the 17th ACM SIGSPATIAL International Conference on Advances in Geographic Information Systems, pp. 91–100. GIS 2009, ACM, New York, NY, USA (2009). http://doi.acm.org/10.1145/1653771.1653787
12. Koukoletsos, T., Haklay, M., Ellul, C.: Assessing Data Completeness of VGI through an Automated Matching Procedure for Linear Data: Assessing Data Completeness of VGI. Transactions in GIS **16**(4), 477–498 (2012). http://discovery.ucl.ac.uk/1354847/
13. Lamprianidis, G., Skoutas, D., Papatheodorou, G., Pfoser, D.: Extraction, integration and analysis of crowdsourced points of interest from multiple web sources. In: Proceedings of the 3rd ACM SIGSPATIAL International Workshop on Crowdsourced and Volunteered Geographic Information, pp. 16–23. GeoCrowd 2014, ACM, New York, NY, USA (2014). http://doi.acm.org/10.1145/2676440.2676445
14. Moura, T.H.V.M., Davis Jr., C.A.: Integration of linked data sources for gazetteer expansion. In: Proceedings of 8th ACM SIGSPATIAL Workshop on Geographic Information Retrieval (GIR 2014) (2014)
15. Oliveira, M.G.d., Baptista, C.d.S., Campelo, C.E.C., Acioli Filho, J.A.M., Falcão, A.G.R.: Automated production of volunteered geographic information from social media. In: Proceedings of XV Brazilian Symposium on GeoInformatics, pp. 118–129 (2014)
16. Peng, X., Chen, R., Cheng, C., Yan, X.: A folksonomy-ontology-based digital gazetteer service. In: 2010 18th International Conference on Geoinformatics, pp. 1–6 (2010)

Measuring Crowd Mood in City Space Through Twitter

Shoko Wakamiya[1](✉), Lamia Belouaer[2], David Brosset[2], Ryong Lee[3],
Yukiko Kawai[1], Kazutoshi Sumiya[4], and Christophe Claramunt[2]

[1] Kyoto Sangyo University, Kyoto, Japan
{shokow,kawai}@cc.kyoto-su.ac.jp
[2] Naval Academy Research Institute, Brest, France
{lamia.belouaer,david.brosset,christophe.claramunt}@ecole.navale.fr
[3] Korea Institute of Science and Technology Information (KISTI), Daejeon, Korea
lee.ryong@gmail.com
[4] University of Hyogo, Kobe, Japan
sumiya@shse.u-hyogo.ac.jp

Abstract. In this paper, we measure crowd mood and investigate its spatio-temporal distributions in a large-scale urban area through Twitter. In order to exploit tweets as a source to survey crowd mind, we propose two measurements which extract and categorize semantic terms from texts of tweets based on a dictionary of emotional terms. In particular, we focus on how to aggregate crowd mood quantitatively and qualitatively. n the experiment, the proposed methods are applied to a large tweets dataset collected for an urban area in Japan. From the daily tweets, we were able to observe interesting temporal changes in crowd's positive and negative moods and also identified major downtown areas where crowd's emotional tweets are intensively found. In this preliminary work, we confirm the diversity of urban areas in terms of crowd moods which are observed from the crowd-sourced lifelogs on Twitter.

Keywords: Emotion-based urban semantics · Spatial and temporal distribution · Microblogs · Location-based social networks · Twitter

1 Introduction

Social networks have been a useful and important source, with which we are able to study a variety of urban dynamics and characteristics [10]. In particular, Twitter provides valuable opportunities to observe crowd mind and behavior by analyzing the written texts and metadata such as location and user's social relationship [12].

In this paper, we study the possibility of surveying crowd mind with massive crowd-sourced lifelogs on Twitter [21]. In fact, estimating crowd mind in city space is worth being explored for many socio-economical, transportation and urban studies. In our daily lives, sentiments and moods play a critical role, fundamentally directing our attention and responses to environment, framing our attitudes and impacting our social relationships. Consumer research, health

© Springer International Publishing Switzerland 2015
J. Gensel and M. Tomko (Eds.): W2GIS 2015, LNCS 9080, pp. 37–49, 2015.
DOI: 10.1007/978-3-319-18251-3_3

care, urban development, etc. are just a few of the domains that would benefit from social network/media automated systems for tracking population behaviors and minds. Several recent researches have interestingly studied the capability of Twitter to aggregate crowd's sentiment [1, 8, 14] and behavior [9, 11]. In order to advance techniques to take advantages of social networks for a variety of real-life businesses and social surveys, in this paper, we will examine crowd mood in city space with the popular social network, Twitter.

The research presented in this paper explores the geographical and temporal distribution of crowd mood observed through geo-tagged tweets over Twitter. The approach is grounded on a semantic extraction of the terms identified in tweets messages, those being classified and valued by a sentiment dictionary introduced in related work [19]. In order to measure and categorize crowd mood, we present two types of functions with which tweets are classified: 1) a 5-level categorization of the positive/negative terms and 2) score-based categorization of the positive and negative terms.

In the experiment, we explore spatio-temporal distributions of crowd mood by applying the proposed two methods to massive geo-tagged tweets in a local area around Osaka in Japan. We first measure and categorize the tweets on a daily basis over a period of one week by the count-based method and score-based method. Then, we compare the ratios of tweets categorized into 5 sentimental classes; Very Positive (VP), Positive (P), Neutral $(Neut)$, Negative (N), and Very Negative (VN). In addition, we observe geographic distribution patterns of crowd mood on a weekday and weekend by focusing on specific areas in a downtown and a bedroom town.

The remainder of this paper is as follows. Section 2 describes related work. Section 3 explains two measurements to extract and categorize the sentiments from crowd's located tweets. Section 4 illustrates the experiment to evaluate the proposed methods with a large tweets dataset of a local area in Japan, and discusses some of the main findings. Finally, Section 5 concludes the paper and briefly describes future work.

2   Related Work

An increasing amount of work in the social network and media domains has been recently oriented to the analysis and understanding of examining and exploiting sentiments and emotions in human behavior [16, 22]. In Ferrara et al.'s work [4], the origins and pathways of tweets in the US have been studied, and how those reflect local consumption behaviors and clusters, and reveal that those coincide with major air traffic hubs. The spatial variability and structure of population's response to various stimuli such as large scale sportive, political or cultural events have been also studied [6, 17].

In particular, several recent studies have been oriented to the detection and classification of positive and negative sentiments reflected by tweets in order to better understand human opinions on various topics and contexts. Golder et al. [5] studied how individual mood varies in time (hourly and daily), and across seasons and cultures by measuring positive and negative sentiments and moods in Twitter posts. In Choudhury et al.'s work [3], more than 200 moods have been extracted from tweets, based on psychology research, and in order to derive a representation of human mood landscape. The principle behind this approach is to classify the terms and moods identified according to an sentiment-based dictionary. Several recent dictionary-based approaches have been oriented to the analysis, clustering and prediction of sentiments expressed by tweets [2,7,20].

In [15], Mislove et al. spatio-temporally explore the pulse of mood throughout a day using Twitter. Although the aim of this study is quite similar to the work, we attempt to analyze the semantics which are contained in the tweets, particularly positive and negative sentiments. This will allow us to qualitatively explore and evaluate reasonable crowd-sourced cognition, as well as the relationships between these tweets and the place and time where and when those tweets were broadcasted.

3   Measuring Crowd Mood from Geo-Tagged Tweets

This section introduces measurements to extract and categorize sentiments from crowd's located tweets. This idea behind this approach is to explore the spatio-temporal distributions of crowd mood when compared to the underlying properties of the geographical space.

In general, a tweet T_1 can be modeled as follows:

$$T_1 = < u_1, t_1, l_1, m_1 >$$

This means that a tweet T_1 is triggered from one location l_1 by a given user u_1 at a given time t_1. Let us show an example of a tweet whose ID is 34558124.

$$T_{34558124} = < 1324246478, \text{"}Fri\ Jun\ 14\ 16:39:25\ +0000\ 2013\text{"},$$
$$[139.55224609, 35.64853287], \text{"}I'm\ very\ happy\text{"} >$$

Furthermore, in order to estimate crowd mood in a geographic region for a period time, we define a generalized function as follows.

$$Crowd\_Mood(G, P_1, P_2) = \sum_{l_i \subseteq G, P_1 \leq t_i \leq P_2} (f(m_i)),$$

where G is the area of a targeting geographic region and $< P_1, P_2 >$ is a time period of interest, and $f(m_i)$ is a measurement function of sentiment for a tweet T_i.

3.1   Dictionary-Based Sentiment Extraction

In order to estimate emotions from tweets, a sentiment dictionary introduced in related work [19] is used as a non-sensitive reference and dictionary[1]. The

---

[1] The Japanese dictionary used is at: http://www.lr.pi.titech.ac.jp/~takamura/pubs/pn_ja.dic and the English dictionary used is at: http://www.lr.pi.titech.ac.jp/~takamura/pubs/pn_en.dic

Table 1. An example of Japanese sentiment dictionary

Positive terms				Negative terms			
Term	Reading	Part of speech	Value	Term	Reading	Part of speech	Value
優れる (superior)	すぐれる	動詞 (Verb)	1	悪い (bad)	わるい	形容詞 (Adjective)	-1
良い (good)	よい	形容詞 (Adjective)	0.999995	死ぬ (die)	しぬ	動詞 (Verb)	-0.999999
喜ぶ (delight)	よろこぶ	動詞(Verb)	0.999979	病気 (disease)	びょうき	名詞 (noun)	-0.999998
褒める (praise)	ほめる	動詞(Verb)	0.999979	酷い (terrible)	ひどい	形容詞 (Adjective)	-0.999997
めでたい (auspicious)	めでたい	形容詞 (Adjective)	0.999645	ない (no)	ない	形容詞 (Adjective)	-0.999997

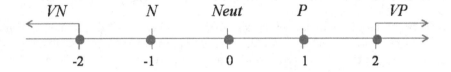

Fig. 1. Criteria of count-based categorization

Japanese dictionary is composed of a term, its reading, its main part of speech, its qualitative evaluation of the sentiments ranged from -1.0 to $+1.0$ as shown in Table 1. The sign of the values in the table represents the polarity of sentiments; positive $(+)$ and negative $(-)$ moods.

When a tweet is given, our method first splits the message into terms using a morphological analyzer [13]. Then we determine whether each term is in the dictionary and look up the value of its semantic value when available. Next, we classify the terms based on their semantic values into positive and negative categories.

In the following subsections, tweets are measured by two types of sentiment measurement functions: 1) a 5-level categorization of the positive/negative terms and 2) score-based aggregation of the positive and negative terms in each tweet. The first one counts the most prominent sentimental term in a tweet, while the second one aggregates the scores of all significant terms and then provides a more precise view.

3.2   Count-Based Measurement and Categorization

The method classifies tweets based on the number of positive/negative terms with respect to the sentimental classes: Very Positive (VP), Positive (P), Neutral

($Neut$), Negative (N), and Very Negative (VN).

$$f_1(m_i) = |PosTerms_{m_i}| - |NegTerms_{m_i}| \tag{1}$$

$$\begin{cases} VP, \text{ if} & f_1(m_i) >= 2 \\ P, \text{ if} & f_1(m_i) = 1 \\ Neut, \text{ if} & f_1(m_i) = 0 \\ N, \text{ if} & f_1(m_i) = -1 \\ VN, \text{ if} & f_1(m_i) <= -2 \end{cases}$$

where, a function $f_1(:)$ evaluates the superior sentimental direction of a given tweet's message m_i by computing the difference between the number of positive terms $|PosTerms_m|$ and the number of negative terms $|NegTerms_m|$. Overall, each tweet is categorized according to the derived value of sentiment count. For instance, a message "I'm very happy" has two sentimental words; "very" and "happy" and the values of the words are -0.169067 and 0.995837, respectively, according to the sentimental dictionary. Then, on the basis of their semantic values, the message has one negative word and one positive word, and both $|PosTerms_m|$ and $|NegTerms_m|$ are 1. As a result, the message is classified into the category $Neut$, because $f_1(m)$ becomes 0. Fig. 1 also depicts the criteria of the count-based categorization of crowd mood.

3.3   Score-Based Measurement and Categorization

Next, in order to consider the scores given in each term, we propose the other categorization method by summing up all the scores of the sentimental terms appeared in each tweet as follows.

$$f_2(m_i) = \begin{cases} \frac{\sum ScorePosTerms(m_i)}{|PosTerms_{m_i}|} + \frac{\sum ScoreNegTerms(m_i)}{|NegTerms_{m_i}|}, \\ \quad \text{if } |PosTerms_{m_i}| > 0 \ \wedge \ |NegTerms_{m_i}| > 0 \\ \frac{\sum ScorePosTerms(m_i)}{|PosTerms_{m_i}|}, \\ \quad \text{if } |PosTerms_{m_i}| > 0 \ \wedge \ |NegTerms_{m_i}| = 0 \\ \frac{\sum ScoreNegTerms(m_i)}{|NegTerms_{m_i}|}, \\ \quad \text{if } |PosTerms_{m_i}| = 0 \ \wedge \ |NegTerms_{m_i}| > 0 \\ 0, \\ \quad \text{if } |PosTerms_{m_i}| = 0 \ \wedge \ |NegTerms_{m_i}| = 0 \end{cases} \tag{2}$$

$$\begin{cases} VP, \text{ if} & f_2(m_i) > 0.5 \wedge f_2(m_i) <= 1.0 \\ P, \text{ if} & f_2(m_i) > 0 \wedge f_2(m_i) <= 0.5 \\ Neut, \text{ if} & f_2(m_i) = 0 \\ N, \text{ if} & f_2(m_i) >= -0.5 \wedge f_2(m_i) < 0 \\ VN, \text{ if} & f_2(m_i) >= -1.0 \wedge f_2(m_i) < -0.5 \end{cases}$$

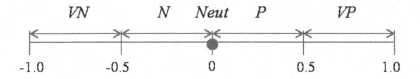

Fig. 2. Criteria values of the score-based categorization

where, a function $f_2(:)$ computes the sum of the average values of scores of positive terms and negative terms. For instance, the message "I'm very happy" has two sentimental words; "very" and "happy" and their values are -0.169067 and 0.995837, respectively, according to the sentimental dictionary. In this case, $f_2(m)$ is 0.82677 by the sum of the values, so the message is classified into the category P. Fig. 2 shows the criteria distribution applied to the score-based categorization.

The main characteristics of this score-based approach is that it allows to take into account the weight of all sentiments that are found in a given tweet. The sentiment values derived are refined and give a more balanced sentiment value, in contrast to the count-based measurement.

4   Experimental Study

4.1   Experimental Setting

The functions for measuring and categorizing crowd mood introduced in the previous section will be applied to a real large database of Japanese tweets. At first, we collected about 0.2 millions geo-tagged tweets from Twitter on a daily basis as shown in Fig. 3. In this figure, dotted points represent locations of the collected geo-tagged tweets. It clearly appears that high density locations are found in urban areas such as Tokyo, Nagoya, Osaka, Kyoto, and Kobe.

The objective of this experiment is to observe the spatio-temporal distribution of crowd mood in a local area around Osaka (longitude range = [134.358, 136.244] and latitude range = [34.2044, 35.185]). Therefore, geo-tagged tweets around Osaka had been extracted from the database about one week. In detail, we used geo-tagged tweets emitted in the region around Osaka between Tuesday, June 18, 2013 and Monday, June 24, 2013. We could on average extract $51,840$ geo-tagged tweets on a weekday and $99,255$ geo-tagged tweets on a weekend, respectively. Then, the two methods developed in Section 3 are applied to study crowd mood. The terms of each tweet were analyzed by a Japanese morphological analyzer, Mecab [13]. The semantic orientations of each term was measured by matching them to the index words of the Japanese sentimental dictionary developed in [19].

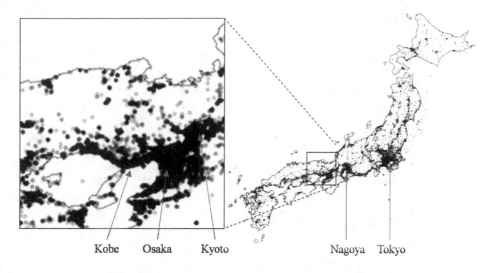

Kobe   Osaka   Kyoto   Nagoya   Tokyo

Fig. 3. Geographic distribution of geo-tagged tweets

4.2   Experimental Results

When applying the first function that gives a count-based crowd mood measurement, sentiments for each tweet are aggregated based on the number of positive and negative terms (Equation (1) in Section 3). Specifically, the semantic orientation of each tweet is given by the difference of positive and negative sentiment values. Next, when applying the score-based crowd mood measurement and categorization, sentiments are categorized for each tweet based on the respective score of positive/negative terms (Equation (2) in Section 3).

Fig. 4(a) and (b) present the temporal changes of the occurrence ratio of respective sentiments measured and categorized by the two methods, respectively. Crowd mood measured and categorized by the count-based function were extremely biased in negative sentiments. As shown in Fig. 4(a), very little positive sentiments (VP and P) were measured. This was caused by extracting sentiments based on the number of terms regardless of the intensity of their sentiments. On the other hand, in Fig. 4(b), these show that the score-based method could measure and categorize crowd mood in a more balanced way compared to the count-based method, though it was still biased in negative sentiments. Overall, we could observe a pattern which negative sentiments were higher than on average on the middle of weekdays, Wednesday and Thursday, and where these decreased from the end of weekends to the weekend.

Therefore, Fig. 5(a) and (b) present the geographic distributions of the crowd mood based on the count-based method and score-based method, respectively. In Fig. 5(a), we show geographic distributions of crowd mood measured by the count-based method on Friday, June 21 and Saturday, June 22. These distributions showed a clear predominance of negative sentiments over positive sentiments. Furthermore, we could observe positive sentiments are more predominant

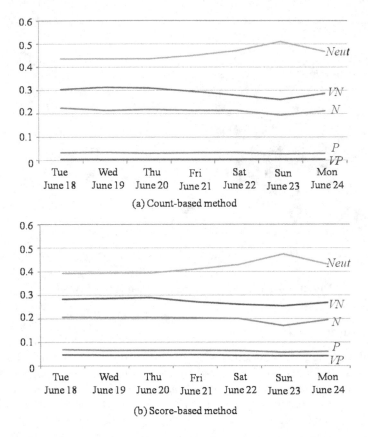

Fig. 4. Temporal changes of crowd mood in the local area around Osaka measured and categorized by (a) count-based method and (b) score-based method

in urban centers such as Osaka and Kyoto, especially over the weekend as shown in Fig. 5(b), where we present geographic distributions of crowd mood measured by the score-based method on the days, respectively. This approach favors a more balanced valuation of the different terms and then of the overall sentiment value from each tweet.

In order to study crowd mood on weekdays and weekends, we examined geographic distributions by focusing on two sentimental classes; Very Positive (VP) and Very Negative (VN) on Friday, June 21 an example of weekdays and Saturday, June 22 as an example of weekends as illustrated in Figs. 6 and 7. In these figures, locations of VP are in crowded areas around Osaka station, Nanba station, and on the north of Kyoto station on both the weekday and the weekend. This is probably reflecting the fact that these areas are multifunctional areas including downtowns and lots of famous sightseeing places for not only tourists but also working people and local residents. Although we cannot identify types of crowds who emitted the tweets in these areas whether tourists, working people,

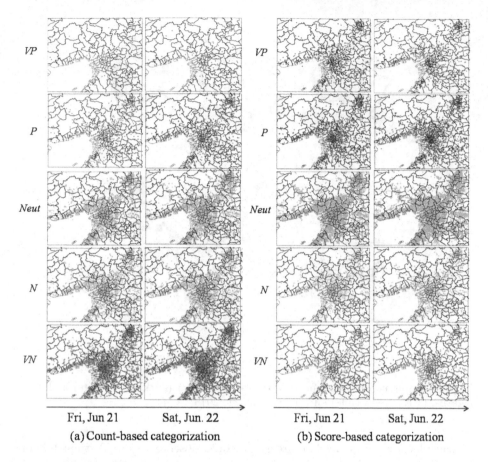

Fri, Jun 21   Sat, Jun. 22   Fri, Jun 21   Sat, Jun. 22

(a) Count-based categorization   (b) Score-based categorization

Fig. 5. Geographic distributions of crowd mood on Friday, June 21, 2013 and Saturday, June 22, 2013. (a) crowd mood base on the number of semantic terms and (b) crowd mood based on the scores of semantic terms.

or local residents, these results show that these areas are potentially places where humans are more likely to express positive sentiments.

On the other hand, we could find a different pattern which appears in an area around Kobe station; there were lots of locations of VN on the weekday (in Fig. 6) and crowd mood VP became superior to VN on the weekend (in Fig. 7). We might conclude as a first approximation that this can be caused by the fact that many people work in this area on weekdays because there are lots of office buildings and weekends are their off-days. In addition, we could observe another pattern which would be caused by different functions of locations such as urban centers and bedroom towns. Specifically, in bedroom towns in Kobe and Osaka such as Ashiya city, Nishinomiya city, Toyonaka city, Suita city, and Sakai city, there were some locations of VP on the weekday, but crowd mood at these locations changed to VN on the weekend as shown in Fig. 7.

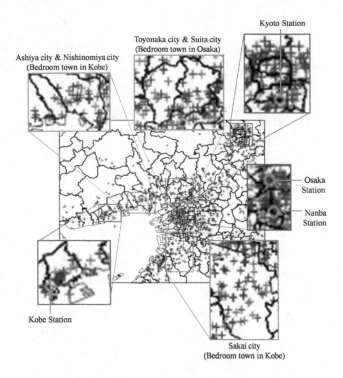

Fig. 6. Geographic distributions of Very Positive (VP) (dark blue points) and Very Negative (VN) (red points) on Friday, June 21, 2013

At other locations in suburban areas, we could observe more VN than VP on the weekend. One might conclude that those places with relative negative sentiments encompass several causes to crowd activities and minds: positive aspects generated from popular attractions while predominant negative aspects might be generated by heavy traffic.

4.3 Discussion

We discuss the results of this experimental study which applied our proposed methods for measuring and categorizing crowd mood to massive tweets dataset and explored spatio-temporal patterns of crowd mood in the local area of Japan. A first noteworthy result of the count-based method is that there is a clear predominance of negative sentiments over positive sentiments. From the point of view of geographic distributions of crowd mood, we could observe positive sentiments are more predominant in urban centers, especially over the weekend. Against the results of the count-based method which were inclined towards negative sentiments, we could obtain the favorable results from the score-based method which successfully measured crowd mood which were highly biased by the count-based method, though there were still negative sentiments over positive

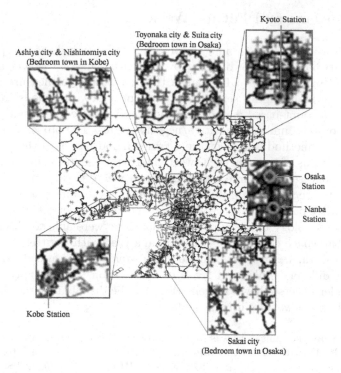

Fig. 7. Geographic distributions of Very Positive (VP) (dark blue points) and Very Negative (VN) (red points) Saturday, June 22, 2013

ones. From this result, we could confirm one common trend: the tweets generally follow several spatio-temporal patterns based on the difference of functions of places, we can easily imagine that people emit VP sentiment when they are out on both weekdays and weekends, and they emit VN sentiment when they are at home, especially on weekends.

The proposed approaches are still preliminary but allow to observe several valuable trends. First one significant pattern is that the geography from this large tweet database matches very much the main urban areas and suburbs as reflected by the experimental study. This is not a completely surprising result as humans are more likely to write more tweets, and as the higher the population the higher the probability to have tweets. However, the approach offers some promising avenues of research to study temporal and spatial differences, as well as the impact of specific events in the distribution of tweets (typically in the case of a disaster or emergency to study how people react in such situations). One specific trend that appears in the study is the importance of negative sentiments when the most significant terms are retained. Of course this preliminary result should be confirmed by a more precise analysis of the semantics behind the tweets by confronting our results with a close examination of a sample of tweets, as this is confirmed by the more balanced results of the score-based approach. This is one of direction that we have to explore when extending our experimental study.

5 Conclusions and Future Work

This paper introduced a preliminary approach for the analysis of the spatial and temporal distribution of crowd mood by exploiting massive tweets in a large geographical area in Japan. The goal in this paper was to measure and categorize tweet terms using an sentimental dictionary. Two methods were developed. Firstly, a count-based method in which sentiments were measured in each tweet based on the number of positive/negative terms. The objective of the second score-based method was to measure crowd mood based on the score of the semantic directions of terms in each tweet. The experimental study were applied to a massive dataset in a large region in Japan where tweets were categorized according to the sentiments' patterns and then allows for an exploration of positive and negative patterns in space and time. While more work is still required to refine the methodology to measure crowd mood, we were able to observe crowd mood in urban space can be extracted and analyzed with Twitter.

In future work, we plan to examine much sophisticated and detailed urban dynamics at different scales and levels of aggregation. Additionally, we would like to consider tweets followers as emotions can be distributed from humans to humans in terms of various urban events.

Acknowledgments. This work was supported by the Strategic Information and Communications R&D Promotion Programme (SCOPE) of the Ministry of Internal Affairs and Communications of Japan, and JSPS KAKENHI Grant Number 26280042.

References

1. Barbosa, L., Feng, J.: Robust sentiment detection on twitter from biased and noisy data. In: Proc. of the 23rd International Conference on Computational Linguistics: Posters (COLING 2010), pp. 36–44 (2010)
2. Bollen, J., Mao, H., Pepe, A.: Modeling public mood and emotion: twitter sentiment and socio-economic phenomena. In: Proc. of the Fifth International AAAI Conference on Weblogs and Social Media (ICWSM), pp. 450–453 (2011)
3. Choudhury, M.D., Counts, S., Gamon, M.: Not all moods are created equal! exploring human emotional states in social media. In: Proc. of the Sixth International AAAI Conference on Weblogs and Social Media (2012)
4. Ferrara, E., Varol, O., Menczer, F., Flammini, A.: Traveling trends: social butterflies or frequent fliers? In: Proc. of the first ACM Conference on Online Social Networks, pp. 213–222 (2013)
5. Golder, S.A., Macy, M.W.: Diurnal and Seasonal Mood Vary with Work, Sleep, and Daylength Across Diverse Cultures. Science **333**(6051), 1878–1881 (2011)
6. Kim, H.-G., Lee, S., Kyeong, S.: Discovering hot topics using twitter streaming data: social topic detection and geographic clustering. In: Proc. of the 2013 IEEE/ACM International Conference on Advances in Social Networks Analysis and Mining, pp. 1215–1220 (2013)
7. Kivran-Swaine, F., Naaman, M.: Network properties and social sharing of emotions in social awareness streams. In: Proc. of the ACM 2011 Conference on Computer Supported Cooperative Work (CSCW 2011), pp. 379–382 (2011)

8. Kontopoulos, E., Berberidis, C., Dergiades, T., Bassiliades, N.: Ontology-based Sentiment Analysis of Twitter Posts. Expert System Application **40**(10), 4065–4074 (2013)

9. Lee, R., Wakamiya, S., Sumiya, K.: Discovery of Unusual Regional Social Activities using Geo-tagged Microblogs. World Wide Web **15**(4), 321–349 (2011)

10. Lee, R., Wakamiya, S., Sumiya, K.: Urban Area Characterization based on Crowd Behavioral Lifelogs over Twitter. Personal and Ubiquitous Computing **17**(4), 605–620 (2013)

11. Lee, R., Wakamiya, S., Sumiya, K.: Exploring Geospatial Cognition based on Location-based Social Network Sites. World Wide Web 1–26 (2014)

12. Lee, R., Wakamiya, S., Sumiya, K.: Geo-social media analytics: exploring and exploiting geo-social experience from crowd-sourced lifelogs. SIGWEB Newsletter Spring, article 4 (2014)

13. Mecab: http://mecab.googlecode.com/svn/trunk/mecab/doc/index.html   (in Japanese)

14. Mahalia, M., Conal, S., Daniel, W., Jure, L., Christopher, P.: Sentiment flow through hyperlink networks. In: Proc. of the Fifth International AAAI Conference on Weblogs and Social Media (ICWSM), pp. 550–553 (2011)

15. Mislove, A., Lehmann, S., Ahn, Y.-Y., Onnela, J.-P., Rosenquist, J. N.: Pulse of the nation: US mood throughout the day inferred from twitter. http://www.ccs.neu.edu/home/amislove/twittermood/ (accessed February 8, 2014)

16. Palmer, A., Nicole, K.-L.: The effects of pre-enrolment emotions and peer group interaction on students satisfaction. Journal of Marketing Management **27**(11–12), 1208–1231 (2011)

17. Pozdnoukhov, A., Kaiser, C.: Space-time dynamics of topics in streaming text. In: Proc. of the 3rd ACM SIGSPATIAL International Workshop on Location-Based Social Networks (LBSN 2011), pp. 1–8 (2011)

18. Silva, T.H., Vaz de Melo, P.OS., Almeida, J.M., Salles, J., Loureiro, A. AF.: A comparison of Foursquare and Instagram to the study of city dynamics and urban social behavior. In: Proc. of the 2nd ACM SIGKDD International Workshop on Urban Computing (2013)

19. Takamura, H., Inui, T., Okumura, M.: Extracting semantic orientations of words using spin model. In: Proc. of the 43rd Annual Meeting on Association for Computational Linguistics (ACL 2005), pp. 133–140 (2005)

20. Tsagkalidou, K., Koutsonikola, V., Vakali, A., Kafetsios, K.: Emotional aware clustering on micro-blogging sources. In: Proc. of the 4th International Conference on Affective Computing and Intelligent Interaction - Volume Part I (ACII 2011), pp. 387–396 (2011)

21. Twitter: https://twitter.com

22. Yang, L., Yang, H.: Research on characteristics and reasons of current internet group events. In: Proc. of International Academic Workshop on Social Science (IAW-SC-13), pp. 980–983 (2013)

Representation and Interaction: Generalization, Visualization, and Mobility

On-Demand Generalization of Guide Maps with Road Networks and Category-Based Web Search Results

Masaki Murase, Daisuke Yamamoto, and Naohisa Takahashi$^{(\boxtimes)}$

Department of Computer Science and Engineering
Graduate School of Engineering, Nagoya Institute of Technology
Gokiso-cho, Showa-ku, Nagoya-shi, Aichi, Japan
{murase,daisuke,naohisa}@moss.elcom.nitech.ac.jp

Abstract. The production of strokes according to the perceptual grouping of arcs in a road network provides a good basis for the generalization of road networks, but a large amount of time is required for their creation and selection, and they lack associations with the map objects along them. In this study, we propose a system for generalizing a guide map with road networks and category-ry-based web search results on demand in response to a user request, or a triplet of an area, a size, and a category. The main features of the proposed system are as follows. (1) It constructs a database of strokes and refines the strokes by considering the actual movements of people. It also introduces a data structure called a "fat-stroke," which combines web search results with the strokes. Pre-construction of the fat-stroke database facilitates the generalization of a guide map on demand to satisfy a user request. (2) It ranks the strokes in order of significance in a guide map according to the web search results combined with the strokes, as well as their length. (3) It determines the number of strokes that need to be drawn on a map based on the map scale and the proportion of road area relative to the whole area in the map. We developed a prototype of the proposed system and a preliminary evaluation demonstrated that pre-construction of the fat-stroke database reduced the response time for guide map generalization to less than 1 s, and thus it can be applied to web map services.

Keywords: Guide map · Road generalization · Spatial database · Web map

1 Introduction

Web maps such as Google Maps [1] and Yahoo! Maps [2] can be used in various environments such as PCs, smartphones, and tablet PCs. Many web maps are precise and they display map images where objects such as roads and landmarks at specific locations are determined according to their scale.

They are useful for checking the location of a map object and for planning a route to a destination. When a user specifies a category of facilities such as restaurants, shops, or schools, the objects included in this category are presented on the map. After the user finds the target object on the map, they can plan a route to the destination by tracing a road on the map.

© Springer International Publishing Switzerland 2015
J. Gensel and M. Tomko (Eds.): W2GIS 2015, LNCS 9080, pp. 53–70, 2015.
DOI: 10.1007/978-3-319-18251-3_4

However, if a user requests a map showing the locations of specific facilities, the web maps might simply overlay the locations of the facilities on an existing map image. In many cases, a user wants to investigate the location and the roads related to the location, i.e., the roads required to reach the location. Displaying an excessive number of roads in an area that includes few facilities will reduce the visibility of the objects in the map, possibly making it difficult to plan a route to the facilities.

Therefore, some roads need to be eliminated according to the map scale and the locations of the objects. Road generalization methods based on "strokes" have been proposed to solve this problem [3-4].

The fundamental idea of these methods is to group the network data such as rivers and roads as a stroke if continuity is observed based on cognitive psychology features [3]. Thomson et al. defined a stroke as a: "curvilinear segment that can be drawn in one smooth movement and without a dramatic change in style" [3]. Extracting only long strokes will remove small branches while still showing the main trunks of the rivers and roads, which increases the visibility of maps.

Our research goal is to develop a system for generalizing a guide map with road networks and category-based web search results on demand in response to a user request, or a triplet of an area, a size, and a category. A road network comprises nodes and links. Thus, a node represents the location of an intersection and a link is a line between two adjacent nodes, as shown in Fig. 1(a). We apply the idea of the perceptual grouping, strokes mentioned above, to actual road networks. A stroke is a group of chained links that does not branch, although they may cross, as shown in Fig. 1(b). It is represented as a sequence of links. For example, stroke S3 in Fig. 1(b) is a sequence of links, i.e., L5, L10, and L17 in Fig. 1(a), which is represented as S3 = (L5, L10, L17).

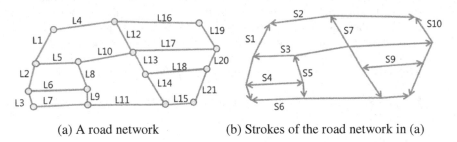

(a) A road network   (b) Strokes of the road network in (a)

Fig. 1. Example of a road network and strokes

The following problems occur when we apply the stroke-based generalization method to a guide map showing search results or the locations of facilities, such as restaurants and schools, via a web service.

— **Problem 1** This method identifies all of the strokes in a road network and selects the most significant strokes among them, which requires a large amount of time, and thus the web service may have difficulty responding to a user request in real time.

- **Problem 2** The method produces strokes by analyzing a road network independently of the locations of the facilities. Thus, it is necessary to analyze the relationships between the strokes and the locations of facilities when the web service draws the strokes along which many facilities are located, before drawing the facilities along a stroke. This analysis requires a large amount of time, which could make the web service impractical.
- **Problem 3** The method selects long strokes and removes short strokes, and thus it could remove the routes to the destination point and the locations of the facilities.
- **Problem 4** There may also be problems when drawing a generalized guide map because methods are not provided to determine how many strokes should be drawn on the map. If the number of strokes is inadequate, the guide map may have low visibility or it could be less informative.

In this study, we propose a system for the on-demand generalization of guide maps with road networks and category-based web search results. The main technical contributions of this study are as follows.

- We propose a data structure called a "fat-stroke," which associates strokes with the facilities obtained in a category-based search. This can be calculated in advance before a user specifies a map area, a map size, and a search category during a map-drawing request. Constructing a fat-stroke database (DB) in advance facilitates the creation of the guide map for the user request in real time.
- We propose a method that ranks strokes in order of their significance in a guide map, which is determined by considering the stroke length, facility search results, and access points.
- We propose a method that determines the number of strokes that need to be drawn on a map based on the map scale and the relative proportion of the stroke area in the map.

The remainder of this paper is organized as follows. Section 2 describes related research in this area. Sections 3 and 4 provide an overview and descriptions of the implementation of the proposed system, respectively. Section 5 presents a prototype of the novel proposed system. Section 6 discusses preliminary experiments conducted using the prototype. Section 7 gives our conclusions.

2   Related Work

Several previous research studies have focused on the creation of guide maps [5-6]. In particular, Maruyama et al. modeled guide map creation according to the following steps [7].

1. Select the features from the map according to the user request.
2. Deform the road shape to improve the visualization of the selected features.
3. Reallocate features other than roads via morphing and road deformation.
4. Allocate the textual labels to the features.

The proposed system corresponds to step 1, which selects the roads required for the guide map.   Selection of important reads from a road network is one of the essential operators in generalization of road networks, which has been studied by many researchers.

Thomson and Richardson introduced the concept of stroke into road generalization using road geometry [3].Strokes are network elements that combine both functional importance and perceptual significance in map generalization and are derived by introducing the 'good continuation' principle of perceptual grouping into networks. Strokes are constructed and ordered according to predefined rules and the selection of roads is then simplified as selection of strokes with higher order. Their stroke-based generalization orders strokes based on stroke length and road class.

Zhang presented a method to select salient roads based on connection analysis [4]. It counts the number of connections at each junction, which acts as a parameter indicating the association between salient roads. Several strategies were proposed to combine connection criterion with road length and road attributes, so as to order roads corresponding to their relative importance in road network generalization.

An algorithm for the elimination of arcs in road maps was presented based on information theory [8]. The perceptual properties of the map reader and the resolution of the display unit are brought into the algorithm by a similarity function. It is computed based on the length between any two points called information points. Based on the information points and the similarity function, the entropy and the equivocation of the road map can be computed. The conditional probabilities are derived from a similarity function, and mutual information is derived from the relation between similarity and conditional probability. By using information theory, the elimination algorithm computes how many roads that can be presented in a map by maximizing the amount of useful information.

Yungang et al. propose selective omission for streets based on a ratio of an area and length of the road that surrounds the area, called a mesh density [9]. The place that mesh density is higher narrow interval of road. Omitting these roads enables to create small scale road network.

Jinang and Claramunt proposed a generalization model for selecting characteristic streets in an urban street network [10]. The proposed model retains the central structure of a street network, it relies on a structural representation of a street network called connectivity graph. Local and global measures are introduced to qualify the status of each vertex within the graph.

We adopt the stroke-based approach and construct a data structure called a fat-stroke, which associates strokes with the facilities obtained in a category-based search. We also design a method of constructing a fat-stroke database by pre-computation, and design a selection method of fat-strokes so as to realize on-demand generalization of a guide map in a Web service.

3   Proposed System

3.1   Features of the Proposed System

The proposed system has the following features.

— **Feature 1: Preparing a stroke table and associating strokes with facilities.**
Our system constructs a table of strokes and it refines the strokes by considering the actual movements of people. It also associates a stroke with the facility search results as a fat-stroke. Fat-strokes can be computed in advance before a user specifies a request. Therefore, the construction of a fat-stroke DB facilitates the creation of a guide map on demand when a request is received. This approach addresses Problems 1 and 2.
— **Feature 2: Ranking strokes in order of their significance in a guide map.**
Our method selects the strokes that need to be drawn in a guide map by considering the locations of facilities and significant points such as access points, as well as the lengths of the strokes. We use the stroke length as a criterion for stroke selection in a similar manner to conventional methods [3] because longer strokes often become major roads such as motorways and trunk roads. Furthermore, if there are many facilities along a stroke and significant points, such as railway stations, the stroke can be regarded as significant because it will tend to have heavy traffic and people flows, and thus it may be part of a route to the destination. Ordering strokes as described above solves Problem 3.
— **Feature 3: Determination of the number of strokes in a guide map.**
We propose a method for determining the number of strokes when drawing a map based on the map scale and the proportion of the road area relative to the whole area in the map. Even if the size and the scale of a map are small, the method maintains the visibility of the map to solve Problem 4.

3.2   System Structure

As shown in Fig. 2, the proposed system includes the three functions: Stroke Generator, Fat-Stroke Generator, and Map Drawing. It also includes four data: Road, Loop Road, Stroke, and Facility. The Road table contains vector data for the road networks and traffic signals. Stroke table and Loop Road table store intermediate data created from the Road table. Facility data are classified into groups according to categories such as restaurants, schools, and hospitals, where their locations are displayed in a map, as shown in Fig. 3(a). The Loop Road table contains all of the loop roads that can be created from the Road. A loop road is represented as a sequence of links. For example, the loop road that surrounds Point P, i.e., loop road LR1 shown in Fig. 3(b), is represented as LR1 = (L1, L4, L12, L10, L5).

The Stroke Generator generates strokes from the road data. The Fat-Stroke Generator generates a fat-stroke by associating a stroke with facility data. Because the above data are independent of a user input, or a triplet of the area and the size of the map, as well as the category of facility, the Fat-Stroke DB can be constructed in advance. This approach facilitates rapid road generalization. The Map Drawing function selects appropriate strokes and draws a guide map on demand when users input their requests.

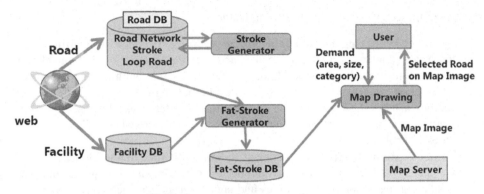

Fig. 2. Structure of the proposed system

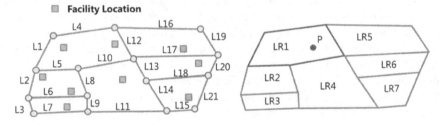

(a) A map with a road network and facilities   (b) Loop roads included in the map (a)

Fig. 3. Examples of a map and loop roads

4   Implementation of the Proposed System

This section describes the data and methods used to implement the three functions described in the previous section, as shown in Fig. 2, using spatial data types (Point, LineString, MultiLineString, Polygon) and spatial operations (st_crosses(), st_buffer(), st_contains(), st_split()) in PostGIS [11-12].

4.1   Construction of Fundamental Data

First, the Road table is constructed using road network data and traffic signal data. A road network comprises a set of nodes and links. A node represents an intersection and a link connects adjacent nodes. The road network data are stored in a link table, as shown in Table 1, which contain four columns related to links, i.e., link ID, a line or a sequence of edge nodes of links, link length, and link class. A link class represents a road type such as a motorway and trunk road. The traffic signal data comprise IDs and locations, as shown in Table 2.

To create the Loop Road table, the loop road extraction method [13] is applied to all of the links in the Road table. The data structure used in the loop road table is shown in Table 3. The facility data are gathered from the web servers and stored in a facility table, as shown in Table 4, which comprises four columns: ID, location, category, and the name of the facility.

Table 1. Link table

column	type	description
link_id	int	ID of the link
link_line	LineString	line connecting the end node
link_length	double	length
link_class	int	road class

Table 2. Traffic signal table

column	type	description
traffic_signal_id	int	ID of the traffic signal
traffic_signal_point	Point	location

Table 3. Loop road table

column	type	description
looproad_id	int	ID of loop road
looproad_poly	Polygon	shape of loop road

Table 4. Facility table

column	type	description
facility_id	int	ID of the facility
facility_location	Point	location
facility_category	int	facility category
name	string	name

4.2   Creation of Strokes

The Stroke table is constructed by using all of the links in the road table. The proposed system is created based on the concept of "good continuation" in the perceptual grouping principle [3]. Moreover, it splits the strokes at the locations where the movement is prevented by considering the actual movements of people. Table 5 shows the data structure of the Stroke table.

Before describing the rules to form consecutive links into a stroke, we define some notations and system parameters.

First, we define the following symbols and functions for some link L in the road table is connected with k (>=1) links at the edge of L as shown in Fig. 4.

- $LS = \{L_1, L_2, \ldots, L_i, \ldots, L_k\}$: the set of links connected with L.
- $LS_i = \{L_{i1}, L_{i2}, \ldots, L_{ij}, \ldots, L_{ik_i}\}$: the set of links connected with L_i.
- L_i_length: the length of the link L_i
- $angle(A, B)$: returns the angle between the two links A and B,
- $minAngle(A, S)$: returns the minimal among the angle(A,B) for all B in the set S.

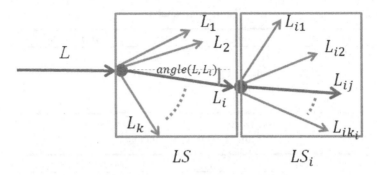

Fig. 4. Consecutive links from the link L

Next, we define the following two system parameters to introduce the good continuation principle of perceptual grouping into actual road networks.

- Δ : the length of tolerances , e.g., 5m,
- δ : the upper limit of the θ_i in consideration of   good continuation , e.g. 45°

Occasionally quite short links exist in an actual road network data, which a map reader cannot recognize even when the map scale is relatively large. We will neglect these short links and avoid their influence on the judgment of good continuation. This is a similar idea called tolerance in pgRouting[14], which provides the route between the specified two nodes even when the road network data lack some small segments between the two nodes.

Now, we define the rules to form consecutive links into a stroke. The consecutive links L, L_i and L_{ij} shown in Fig.4 are determined whether they are grouped as a stroke according to the following there rules (a) to (c) as shown in Fig. 5

- (a) $LS = \{L_1\}$
  →L and L_1 belong to the same stroke
- (b) $LS = \{L_1, \ldots L_k\}(k \geq 2)$
  and $angle(L, L_i) < \delta$
  and $minAngle(L, LS) = L_i$
  →L and L_i belong to the same stroke
- (c) $LS = \{L_1, \ldots L_k\}(k \geq 2)$
  and $L_i\_length \leq \Delta$
  and $angle(L, L_{ij}) < \delta$
  and $minAngle(L, LS_i) = L_{ij}$
  → L and L_{ij} belong to the same stroke

Table 5. Stroke table

Column	Type	Description
stroke_id	Int	ID of stroke
stroke_line	MultiLineString	series of link
stroke_length	double	Length

Fig. 5. Conditions for grouping links as a stroke

Stroke Generator contains a function of stroke split. This function is to split one stroke into two strokes. Suppose that two strokes cross a stroke that is a heavy traffic road and a traffic signal is located on one of the two intersections, or the right intersection as shown in Fig. 6. In this case, the stroke without a traffic signal is split at the intersection, as shown in Fig. 6. The stroke splitting algorithm is as follows.

1. Find a set of all strokes, S, the road class of which indicates that it is higher than a criterion length defined as a system parameter.
2. For each element S_i in S ($i=1, \ldots, N_s$, where N_s is the number of strokes in Stroke table), apply the following procedure.
   (a) Find a set of strokes (IS_i) that intersects with stroke (S_i).
   (Execute the following SQL query:
   Select IS_i from stroke_table where st_crosses(S_i, stroke_line);)
   (b) For each element $IS_{i,j}$, in IS_i, apply the following procedure.
   (i) Find an intersection point (IP) where S_i intersects with $IS_{i,j}$.
   (ii) Calculate the domain(D_{buf}) of buffer (ε) for IP, and search for a traffic signal inside D_{buf} from Road table. (Execute the following SQL query:
   Select traffic_signal_point from traffic_signal_table
   where st_contains(st_buffer(IP,ε), traffic_signal_point);)
   (iii) If the above search fails, apply the following procedure.
   (1) Split $IS_{i,j}$ into two strokes ($IS_{i,j,1}, IS_{i,j,2}$).
   (Execute the following SQL query:
   Select st_split($IS_{i,j}$, IP);)
   (2) Remove $IS_{i,j}$ from Stroke table.
   (3) Insert $IS_{i,j,1}$ and $IS_{i,j,2}$ into Stroke table.
3. Finish

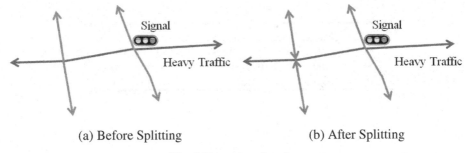

(a) Before Splitting   (b) After Splitting

Fig. 6. Examples of strokes

4.3   Creation of Fat-Strokes

Fat-strokes are created from the Stroke, Loop Road, and Facility according to the procedure shown in Fig. 7.

- **(i)** For each loop road LR_i in the Loop Road table ($i = 1, ..., N_{LR}$, where N_{LR} is the number of loop roads in Loop Road table), obtain all of the facility data inside the LR_i and place them into the loop road and facility table, as shown in Table 6 (Fig. 7. (i)). (Execute the following SQL query:
  select looproad_id, facility_id from looproad_table, facility_table
  where st_contains(LR_i, facility_location);)
- **(ii)** For each stroke S_j in the Stroke table ($j = 1, ..., N_{ss}$, where N_{ss} is the number of strokes in Stroke table after split operations), obtain all of the loop roads for which the components or links are the same as those in S_i and place them into the stroke and loop road table, as shown in Table 7 (Fig. 7(ii)). (Execute the following SQL query:
  select stroke_id, looproad_id from stroke_table, looproad_table
  where st_intersects(S_j, looproad_poly);)
- **(iii)** Create a stroke and facility table from the table created in (i) and (ii) above, as shown in Table 4 (Fig. 7(iii)).
- **(iv)** Create a fat-stroke from the stroke table and the table created in (iii) above (Fig. 7(iv)).

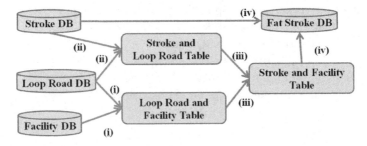

Fig. 7. Procedure for fat-stroke creation

Table 6. Loop road and facility table

column	type	description
looproad_id	int	ID of the loop road
shop_id	int	ID of the shop
facility_category	int	facility category

Table 7. Stroke and loop road table

column	type	description
stroke_id	int	ID of the stroke
looproad_id	int	ID of loop road

Table 8. Stroke and facility table

column	type	description
stroke_id	int	ID of the stroke
facility_id	int	ID of the facility
facility_category	int	facility category

Table 9. Fat-stroke data structure

column	type	description
stroke_id	int	ID of the stroke
stroke_length	double	length
facility_num	int	number of facilities
facility_category	int	facility category

In Fig. 1 and Fig. 3, stroke S3 has common links to five loop roads: LR1, LR2, LR4, LR5, and LR6, and there are eight facilities in these loop roads. Therefore, facility_num is seven for stroke S3.

4.4   Drawing a Guide Map

The function of guide map drawing is to select appropriate strokes and to draw them on a map image, or a raster map, thereby generating a guide map when the user inputs a request. This includes two important methods for ranking strokes and determining the number of strokes.

Method for Ranking Strokes
This method ranks strokes in order of their significance in a guide map based on the following observations of the significance of roads in a guide map.

— **Road on the route to the destination.**
   The route to the destination is an essential component of the guide map, and thus these roads should always be selected.

— **Many target facilities along the road.**
A road with many facilities related to the target facilities along the road is significant because the road is on the route to the target facilities.

— **Many pedestrians and vehicles tend to follow a long stroke.**
A long stroke is often a major road such as a motorway or trunk road. Major roads are crowded with heavy traffic; thus, these roads are significant because they might be part of the route to the target facilities.

First, we define the following symbols for strokes.

- N_f: number of facilities along the stroke.
- L_s: length of the stroke.
- $w_{facility}$, w_{stroke}: weights for N_f and L_s.
- NearestStroke(l): nearest stroke to a location l.
- MSL: a set of the most significant locations, such as the locations of target facilities particularly specified by the user and their access points.

We calculate the significance of stroke s or S_s using the following equation.

$$S_s = \begin{cases} \dfrac{N_f}{\sum N_f} w_{facility} + \dfrac{L_s}{\sum L_s} w_{stroke} & (if\ s == NearestStroke(l)\ where\ l \in MSL) \\ 1 & (otherwise) \end{cases}$$

The stroke significance can be used to adjust which value should be more important depending on the number of facilities or the length of the stroke by changing the ratio of $w_{facility}$ relative to w_{stroke}, where $w_{facility}$ and w_{stroke} are system parameters. A user specifies a set of significant locations (or MSL) on the map, the equation is applied and all of the strokes are ranked in order of their significance in the map.

Method for Determining the Number of Strokes Drawn in a Map
In order to determine the number of strokes drawn in a map, the ratio of the stroke area relative to the whole area in the map should be considered. If this ratio is high, the visibility of the map is reduced because the road interval is narrow. By contrast, if this ratio is low, it is difficult to understand the map because it contains less information. Setting an adequate number of strokes to be drawn in a map will improve the visibility of the map because the ratio of the stroke area relative to the other area in the map remains constant.

If we assume that all of the strokes are drawn with the same width on a map, we can calculate the ratio of the stroke area relative to the whole area in the map, or $\alpha(n)$, using the following equation, where the top n strokes in the ranking of the strokes are drawn. The stroke drawn is determined by finding n such that $\alpha(n) < \alpha_0$ might be the minimum. Thus, α_0 is a criterion that determines the number of strokes.

This method ensures that the relative ratio of the area occupied by the drawn roads in the map is constant:

$$\alpha(n) = \frac{\sum_{i=0}^{i=n}(s_i\_length \cdot s\_width)}{S_{map}} \leq \alpha_0,$$

where

- s_i: i th stroke in the ranking of the strokes in order of significance,
- s_i_length: length of the stroke s_i,
- s_width : width of the drawing stroke (system parameter),
- S_{map}: whole area of the map,
- α_0: criterion (system parameter).

5   Prototype System

5.1   Overview of the Prototype

We implemented all of the functions of the proposed system described in Section 4 using Java [15]. We obtained road and facility data from OpenStreetMap [16], and we used PostgseSQL [17] and PostGIS [11] to construct the proposed DB.

5.2   Examples of Generalized Guide Maps

When a user specifies a map area (e.g., longitude = (136.924–136.943), latitude = (35.146–35.162498)) and window size (700 × 700 pixels), the prototype system creates a generalized map, as shown in Fig. 8(a). When the user drags the corner of the map window to make the map small, the prototype updates the map as shown in Fig.8 (b). In the two maps, a red dot represents the location of a facility and a black bold line represents a stroke, or a road selected by the prototype system. The system parameters are as follows: $w_{shop} = w_{stroke} = 0.5, width(s) = 5, \alpha_0 = 0.15$. The size of the map in Fig. 8(a) is $S_{map} = 700 \times 700$ pixels, and the number of strokes selected is 67. The size of the map shown in Fig. 8(b) is $S_{map} = 350 \times 350$ pixels, and the number of strokes selected is 17. These maps both include the same district and the categories of facilities, but their sizes are different. When the map size is small, the prototype system reduces the number of strokes in the map. This approach prevents the visibility from being reduced.

Fig. 9 shows three generalized guide maps for three different values of α_0. The number of strokes drawn in the guide maps varies according to the value of α_0. Fig. 10 shows generalized guide maps for different categories. The prototype system produced a generalized guide map, as shown in Fig. 10(a), when a convenience store was specified for a search category. It generated the map shown in Fig. 10(b) when a parking area was specified as a search category. These figures show that the prototype system selects strokes by considering the locations of facilities that belong to the specified category.

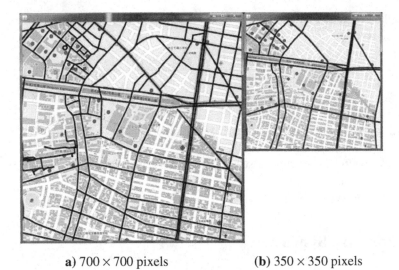

a) 700×700 pixels   **(b)** 350×350 pixels

Fig. 8. Generalized guide maps for two map sizes

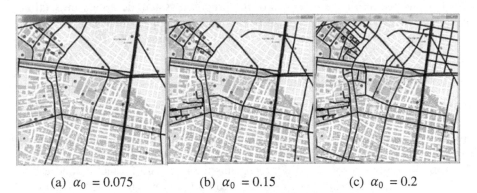

(a) $\alpha_0 = 0.075$ (b) $\alpha_0 = 0.15$ (c) $\alpha_0 = 0.2$

Fig. 9. Generalized guide maps for different values of α_0

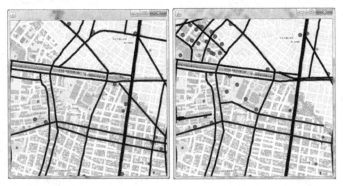

(a) Convenience store   (b) Parking Area

Fig. 10. Generalized guide maps for different categories

6   Preliminary Experiments

6.1   Objective of the Experiments

Web maps are important for responding to requests in real time. Because many web maps use raster images that are prepared in advance, the web clients only have to arrange tiled images obtained from the map server. However, during map generalization using vector data, such as the proposed system, large amounts of time may be required to make a map compared with the method described above. Therefore, we measured the time required to create guide maps in a preliminary experiment and we checked whether the proposed system satisfied the responsiveness requirements for the web map. We also conducted a preliminary experiment to measure the time required to obtain the data for map generalization. This experiment aimed to demonstrate the benefits of DB creation by calculating the fat-strokes in advance. Moreover, this experiment aimed to demonstrate the effectiveness of using the fat-stroke DB comparing with not using the DB.

6.2   Methods

We conducted the following two experiments using map scale = 25000:1, center co-ordinates of (longitude = 35.154, latitude = 136.933), and various map sizes. The numbers of facilities and links used in the experiments are shown in Table 10. Fig. 11 shows the execution times measured in the experiments.

Experiment 1
We measured the following two times when changing the map size, as shown in Table 10 because fat-stroke creation consists of two steps.

— (i) T_1: Time spent producing strokes from road data.
— (ii) T_2: Time spent preparing fat-strokes using strokes, facility data, and loop road data.

Experiment 2
We compared the following two execution times when changing the map size.

— (iii) T_3: Time spent producing a generalized map without strokes and the fat-stroke DB.
— (iv) T_4: Time spent producing a generalized map with the fat-stroke DB.

For (iii), we measured the time T_3 which is the sum of the time spent creating strokes and fat-strokes from facilities and roads data, which were within the range of the specified map area, and the time spent in generalization. For (iv), we created the fat-stroke DB in advance using a range that was appropriate for the experiment. We measured T_4 which is the sum of the time spent obtaining the range data within the specified map area from the stroke table, and the time spent in generalization.

Table 10. Number of facilities and links included in the map

Map size (number of pixels on a side)	Number of facilities	Number of links
300	59	201
500	141	566
700	279	1138
900	499	1907
1100	933	3054
1300	1368	4359

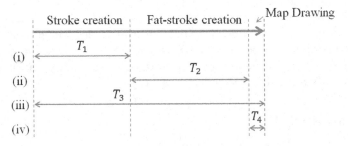

Fig. 11. Execution times measures in the two experiments

6.3   Results

(1) Results of Experiment 1

The time spent creating strokes, or T_1 increased exponentially, as shown in Fig. 12(a). Stroke creation includes many steps such as checking the relationships between the links. The proposed system could create fat-strokes from strokes almost in linear time, as shown in Fig. 12(b). Thus, the time spent associating strokes with facility data was short due to the use of the loop road table, and thus the fat-strokes could be created simply by referring to the stroke and facility data table (Table 8).

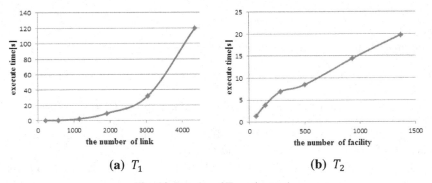

(a) T_1 (b) T_2

Fig. 12. Results of Experiment 1

(2) Results of Experiment 2

Fig. 13 compares the generalization time in two cases: without strokes and the fat-stroke DB (iii), and with the fat-stroke DB (iv). For (iii), the number of links and facilities increased when the map size was larger, and the time required to create fat-strokes increased exponentially. For (iv), it was possible to generalize rapidly at any map size because the fat-strokes could simply be obtained from the strokes in the fat-stroke DB. Note that the execution times were always less than 1 s which is tolerable response time in web map services. A large amount of time was required to construct the fat-stroke DB, but it could be prepared in advance independently of user requests. Therefore, the proposed system could be generalized rapidly after receiving a user request.

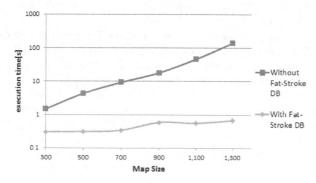

Fig. 13. Execution time for producing a generalized map

7   Conclusions

In this study, we proposed a system that generalizes a guide map with road networks and category-based web search results on demand, and we described the methods required for its implementation. We implemented strokes for the guide map and associated them with facility data in a new data structure called fat-strokes. Fat-strokes can be calculated in advance and the production of a Fat-Stroke DB facilitates the rapid drawing of a generalized map on demand to satisfy a user request. We also implemented a prototype of the proposed system and performed preliminary experimental evaluations. The experimental results obtained demonstrated that the used of a Fat-Stroke DB facilitates rapid road generalization. Furthermore, the response time was less than 1 s, which means that the proposed system can be used for road generalization to obtain guide maps at an acceptable speed for web services.

In the future, we plan to evaluate the visibility of the road network generalized by the proposed system. For conducting this experiment, we have to consider the conditions of the roads that most people need by examining how they use a guide map in more detail.

Acknowledgments. We would like to thank anonymous reviewers for their fruitful comments on the previous version of this manuscript.

This research was supported by JSPS KAKENHI 26330136 and 25700009.

References

1. Google Maps. https://maps.google.com/
2. Yahoo! Maps. http://map.yahoo.co.jp/
3. Thomson, R.C., Richardson, D.E.: 'Good continuation' principle of perceptual organization applied to the generalization of road networks. In: Proceedings of the 19th International Cartographic Conference (ICC), pp. 1215–1223 (1999)
4. Zhang, Q.: Road network generalization based on connection analysis. In: Development in Spatial Data Handling 2005, pp. 343-353 (2005)
5. Fujii, K., Sugiyama, K.: Route Guide Map Generation System for Mobile Communication. Information Processing Society of Japan (IPSJ) Journal **41**(9), 2394–2403 (2000)
6. Nagata, T., Maeda, Y.: Agent-based geographic information selection in the deformed map. In: Human Interface Symposium 2006, pp. 479-484 (2006)
7. Maruyama, K., Tanizaki, M., Shimada, S.: Mathematical transformation model of road network for deformed map generation and its system evaluation. The Institute of Electronics Information and Communication Engineers (IEICE) Technical Report, ITS2002-192, pp. 77–84 (2003)
8. Bjrke, J.T.: Generalization of road networks for mobile map services: an information theoretic approach. In: Proceedings of the 21st International Cartographic Conference (ICC), pp. 127–135 (2003)
9. Hu, Y., Chen, J., Li, Z., Zhao, R.: Selection of streets based on mesh density for digital map generalization. In: Proceedings of the International Conference on Image and Graphics 2007, pp. 903–908 (2007)
10. Jiang, B., Claramunt, C.: A Structual Approach to the Model Generalization of an Urban Street Network. GeoInformatica **8**(2), 157–171 (2004)
11. PostGIS. http://postgis.refractions.net/
12. OpenGIS Consortium, Simple Features for SQL. http://www.opengeospatial.org/standards/sfs
13. Yamamoto, D., Itoh, H., Takahashi, N.: One click focusing: an SQL-based fast loop road extraction method for mobile map service. In: Proceedings of the 4th International Conference on Advanced Geographic Information Systems, Applications, and Services (GEOProcessing 2012), pp. 7–16 (2012)
14. pgRouting. http://pgrouting.org/
15. Java https://www.java.net/
16. OpenStreetMap. http://www.openstreetmap.org/
17. PostgreSQL. http://www.postgresql.org/

Compass-Based Navigation in Street Networks

Stefan Funke[1], Robin Schirrmeister[2], Simon Skilevic[2], and Sabine Storandt[2](✉)

[1] FMI, University of Stuttgart, Stuttgart, Germany
funke@fmi.uni-stuttgart.de
[2] Department of Computer Science, University of Freiburg,
Freiburg im Breisgau, Germany
storandt@informatik.uni-freiburg.de

Abstract. We present a new method for navigating in a street network using solely data acquired by a (smartphone integrated electronic) compass for self-localization. To make compass-based navigation in street networks practical, it is crucial to deal with all kinds of imprecision and different driving behaviors. We therefore develop a trajectory representation based on so-called inflection points which turns out to be very robust against measurement variability. To enable real-time localization with compass data, we construct a custom-tailored data structure inspired by algorithms for efficient pattern search in large texts. Our experiments reveal that on average already very short sequences of inflection points are unique in a large street network, proving that this representation allows for accurate localization.

1   Introduction

Mobile devices are one of the primary tools for navigation nowadays. They more and more replace integrated navigation systems in cars, and can also be used when going by bicycle or foot. Typically, mobile devices rely on GPS, GSM or Wifi for localization. GPS allows for a rather precise determination of the actual position (up to few meters) if the GPS receiver gets signals from at least four satellites. Unfortunately, this might not always be possible due to signal blockage (e.g. by high buildings or foliage), furthermore signal reflections might induce imprecisions. To use GSM, one has to be connected to a cell phone network, with the signal strength of nearby base stations revealing the position (with a precision of $\approx$50m). Wifi localization works in a similar fashion. Here, companies like Google georeference wireless access point IDs, and as soon as signals are received, a certain geographic location can be estimated (with a precision of $\approx$20m). So for GSM and Wifi, interaction with a third party is required to self-localize. And even for GPS, to obtain a faster position lock, third party servers are contacted via GSM or 3G. This raises privacy issues, as the own position is revealed to these third parties. There are recent attempts, though, to crowd-source GSM and Wifi access points and make the data openly available[1]. But the coverage of mapped data is still poor. Moreover, GSM and Wifi is simply not

---

[1] https://location.services.mozilla.com/

© Springer International Publishing Switzerland 2015
J. Gensel and M. Tomko (Eds.): W2GIS 2015, LNCS 9080, pp. 71–88, 2015.
DOI: 10.1007/978-3-319-18251-3_5

available everywhere; especially in rural or sparsely inhabited areas one cannot expect precise localization based solely on those signals.

We propose a new way of navigating in street networks, by making use of the electronic compass present in most of the current smartphones and other mobile devices. We acquire sequences of absolute directions and use them to identify the trajectory the vehicle has taken in the network. So for a given road map and the measured absolute directions, we aim at identifying the path in the map that most likely is the one that led to those measurements. The problem of pinpointing measurements to a path in a map is commonly referred to as *map matching*. The advantage of our scheme is the ability to self-localize in a completely autonomous way. No interaction with third parties is required. Moreover we do not rely on any kind of distance measurements, which are typically imprecise if conducted with a mobile device.

We will describe in detail how to obtain, process and store compass data, and how to instrument this for precise and fast self-localization.

1.1   Related Work

In the classical *map matching* problem, we are given a sequence of possibly imprecise location measurements (obtained e.g. with GPS, GSM or WLAN). This setting is well-studied in different variations. The on-line version (measurements have to be processed the moment they are taken) is described e.g. in [1]. In the off-line case the best possible path in the map for a given measurement sequence is chosen as the optimal one according to some scoring function. The score might for example be the Frechet-Distance, see [2], or the objective function value of an integer program [3]. In [4], the authors have shown that even very imprecise GSM localization allows for a very accurate reconstruction of the route a mobile user has traveled along in a network if measurements for a long enough period can be gathered.

Alternative sources of information for localization (besides GPS, GSM or WLAN) have been investigated before. In [5] the authors introduce so called *path shapes* which describe the sequence of *relative* movements of a vehicle (e.g. '500m straight, 40 degree left turn, 200m straight, 90 degree right turn, $\cdots$'). Experiments show, that different paths quickly exhibit differing path shapes, which allows for high-precision self-localization. The relative movement data is acquired by reading information from the on-board computer of a car.

Smartphones do not have access to this data, as typically there is no open interface for communication with the on-board computer. Of course, most smartphones also have integrated gyro sensors and accelerometers, which allow to measure turning angles and (increase in) velocity. In theory, this yields the same kind of data as needed for the path shape localization scheme. In practice, though, due to the imprecision of this data, such methods only make sense to *complement*, not replace GPS localization. The latter is the goal of this work.

In [6] the concept of *elastic pathing* is introduced. The authors show that fine-grained speed information is also sufficient for self-localization. Every path in the street network exhibits a typical 'speed profile' to which actual measurements can be compared. In contrast to *path shapes*, this localization scheme requires knowledge about the starting location. We aim to be able to compute the actual position without the start position being known beforehand. Moreover we have the same problem here as with path shapes: While the car itself monitors the driving speed autonomously, speeds measured by a smartphone normally involve GPS usage. And even more severe, a huge amount of historical data is necessary to have good typical speed profiles at hand. This data is not easily available with sufficient coverage (especially for bicycles).

In [7], positions of pedestrians are determined using gyro sensors and a heuristic which mitigates direction errors by incorporating the underlying street network data. They do not use smartphones, though, but specially constructed devices attached to a shoe. Again, they require the user to provide the starting location. No large-scale study is conducted and no timings are given; hence, it is unclear whether this methods can be used for real-time localization.

In other navigation domains where vehicles do not have to follow streets but move around almost freely e.g. considering ships, planes, missiles or robots, navigation based on the movement alone is known as inertial navigation system (INS). Here, given the start point, the current position is calculated based on speed and direction of the moving object as well as the elapsed time since departure. Unfortunately, when using INS already small measurement errors translate into large positional errors accumulating over time, as the new position is always computed relative to the last one. Hence in regular intervals the actual position has to be corrected using e.g. GPS; therefore the autonomy of the system is compromised. An incarnation of INS for pedestrians was described in [8]. They use the built-in electronic compass of modern smartphones and employ an approach based on Bayesian networks, which combines GPS and compass information in a neat manner. As indicated before, they do not consider an underlying path or street network, but investigate free spaces and buildings where people can wander around. In contrast to this, a car or bicycle has to follow streets or paths. Therefore the effect of measurement errors is mitigated in our scenario. Even better, we gain information while driving around, hence the positioning becomes more and more accurate over time – quite the opposite of the INS paradigm.

1.2   Contribution

This paper presents a novel localization scheme purely based on absolute directions acquired by an electronic compass. We describe how to retrieve such data using a conventional smartphone, and how to deal with numerous sources of imprecision. We propose a new compass-based representation for trajectories, which is far more robust in particular against variations of driving speed than temporal subsampling of the absolute directions (e.g. by measuring every second). We show experimentally that already short paths in a network are characterizable by our compass representation, i.e. their representation is unique among all possible paths. As our framework does not rely on a known starting position, naively, we have to consider every node in the network as a potential starting point and then compute the one that most likely led to the observed measurements. An implementation of this naive approach scales very badly with the network size. To enable real-time self-localization, we therefore develop a custom-tailored data structure inspired by algorithms for efficient pattern search in large texts. This data structure allows for self-localization within fractions of a second even in large road networks. Finally, we provide an experimental study, including results on real-world data (collected by bicycle).

2   Wireless Acquisition of Compass Data

The first step in the pipeline is to acquire precise absolute direction information while driving around. In the following, we provide the details for collecting such data with the help of an electronic compass.

2.1   Electronic Compass

We implemented an Android app to gather electronic compass data. Five different methods based on different kinds of virtual and physical sensors provided by the android API[2] were employed:

Orientation Sensor. This used to be the standard way of acquiring compass data, but is officially deprecated now. The orientation sensor is a virtual sensor which directly returns the actual orientation. No parameters are required.

Magnetometer and Accelerometer to Rotation. This is one current standard way of getting absolute direction information. It returns the rotation matrix resulting from reading out the sensor values. No parameters are required.

Low Pass. This method is also based on the magnetometer and the accelerometer but additionally includes a low-pass filter to take care of short-term fluctuations. The higher the input parameter α, the less short-term fluctuations influence the resulting orientation.

Rotation Sensor. This sensor is similar to the orientation sensor but returns a rotation matrix and an estimation for the precision of the measured values.

Attitude Heading Reference System (AHRS)[3]. Apart from the accelerometer and the magnetometer, this method also uses the gyro sensor to estimate the orientation. There are several tuning parameters.

We stored direction values once per second for our real-world experiments. The data collected during an hour of measuring directions is below 300kB, so there is no problem with storing the measurements locally on the phone.

---

[2] http://developer.android.com/guide/topics/sensors/sensors_overview.html
[3] http://www.x-io.co.uk/open-source-imu-and-ahrs-algorithms/

2.2 Smoothing

Naturally, no sensor is flawless and the measured angles are perturbed by all kind of external factors. To take care of these fluctuations, we apply a smoothing technique. For that purpose we convert the measurements into a polyline. We do this by starting at $(0,0)$ in a two-dimensional coordinate system, and then elongate the line by a straight segment in the direction of the measured angle. We always use the same length for each straight segment, i.e. we assume constant travel speed. Then we apply the Douglas-Peucker algorithm [9] to this polyline. Douglas-Peucker reduces the number of points on a polyline but faithfully preserves the overall shape at the same time, therefore we regard this algorithm as very useful in our scenario.

3 Compass Paths

Once the compass data is acquired, the challenge is to match these measurements to a path in the underlying street network. This means paths in the network and gathered measurements have to be made comparable by a common representation. A natural way of encoding a trajectory is just the sequence of absolute directions measured e.g. every second while driving. It turns out that this approach is too error-prone to be practical, though. In the following, we first discuss in detail why this is not the envisioned representation. Then we introduce a new representation, based on so called inflection points which is much more suitable for matching a compass-based trajectory to a path in the network.

3.1 Representation as Sequence of Absolute Directions

The problem of using the sequence of measurements received from the electronic compass directly for map matching, is that the descriptions of turns in the network and in a real trajectory might differ considerably. In a given network representation, a turn happens typically at a single point. So a turn is a sequence of two absolute directions, the one in which the vehicle headed before, and the one in which the vehicle headed after. For example, $30°,60°$ describes a $30°$ turn. But measuring the direction every second or even more fine-grained, we have to expect that the description of the trajectory for the very same turn looks more like this: $30°,37°,51°,60°$. In fact, every angle between the entrance and the exit angle might appear in real measurements. And depending on the sampling rate, even driving the same turn in the exact same way might lead to a new representation each time. From the pure sequence of absolute direction measurements, it is very difficult to tell which angles are artefacts of turns. Therefore we consider this kind of representation unsuitable for map matching.

3.2 Inflection Point Representation

We aim for a compass-based path representation which is robust against different driving styles and the problem of modelling (sharp) turns as described above.

So let $\phi : [0,1] \rightarrow$ be the function mapping points along the path (parametrized over $[0,1]$) to an absolute direction. Driving the same path twice at different speeds, we get two different functions ϕ_1, ϕ_2 with different parametrizations of the path (here ϕ_2 could also be interpreted as the path in the underlying network). The question is in what respect could they be considered equal?

A typical path includes both curves or turns to the left as well as to the right. So a possible characterization is to consider the sequence of angles where there is a change from increasing angles to decreasing angles or vice versa. This means in particular, that the sequence of angles resulting from a right/left turn is completely ignored. In fact, this is nice, as there is no way to predict how the subsampling of a turn will look like – and the chances it is the same as in the underlying network is miniscule. On the contrary, points that indicate a change of turn direction tend to be in the middle of almost straight segments or at least at sections where the directional change is not as pronounced as in sharp curves, see Figure 1 for an illustration. Hence restricting the measurements to such points seems to be a more robust and clean way to compare ϕ_1, ϕ_2. In differential calculus these points of turn direction change are called *inflection points*. They are characterized by the second derivative changing sign. If we map directions to points in time, the inflection points turn out to be local maxima/minima. In our case, the function ϕ need not be differentiable, but we will still call the resulting representation the *inflection point representation (IPR)* or *compass path*. Obviously, the IPR of a path in the street network and of (smoothed) real-world measurements can be computed in linear time, by sweeping over the induced angles and extracting local extrema.

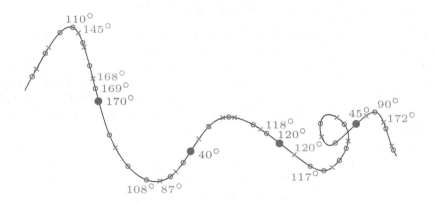

Fig. 1. Continuous trajectory with induced inflection points (blue). Two discrete measurement sequences conducted on this trajectory are indicated by the red circles and the green crosses, respectively. The labelled points near inflection points show that absolute directions are rather stable, while in curves even small sampling differences lead to drastic direction variations.

4   Map Matching

Having a common representation for paths in the network and compass paths, the next step is to find for a given compass path the network path that fits best, i.e. solving the map matching problem for our specific input. The notion of similarity for compass paths is yet to be defined. Ideally, we would like to declare two compass paths equal if and only if the sequence of inflection points is exactly the same. But obviously this will yield no match in the map most of the time. An electronic compass is hardly free from error; and even if it were, people do not drive exactly in the middle of the lane, heading in exactly the direction of the respective road segment. So we have to introduce some degree of fuzziness here.

4.1   Curve Matching

In computational geometry, the same problem arises when (polygonal) curves have to be matched. Transferred to our scenario, we are given a collection of polygonal curves (represented by the underlying graph) and want to select the one, that matches our reference curve (the given trajectory) best. One classical measure here is the Frechet-Distance which was already applied to planar maps in [2]. The Direction-Based Frechet-Distance [10] also allows for partial matchings which is beneficial in our envisioned scenario, as our trajectory naturally is only a small part of the whole graph. But these methods require integral calculus and have a runtime of $\Omega(ab)$ with a and b being the number of vertices on the two curves. With b denoting the number of all vertices in the network in our application, this is far from being practicable in a reasonable amount of time. Moreover curve similarity measures like the Frechet-Distance do not necessarily capture the similarity one aims for when considering trajectories. Especially if typical angle fluctuations are known for compass paths (due to experimental studies), there is no easy way to incorporate such knowledge in the measure.

4.2   Tolerance Ranges and Shape-Preserving Search

As argued before, the sequence of inflection points is never going to be *exactly* the sequence of inflection points on the respective path in the underlying map. So we have to allow inflection points to differ by at least some degrees. We realize that by introducing a tolerance value t. Hence, two compass paths $P = p_1, p_2, \cdots, p_a$ $P' = p'_1, p'_2, \cdots, p'_a$ are equal if $|p_i - p'_i| \leq t$ for $i = 1, \cdots, a$. The parameter t captures the imprecision of the electronic compass as well as differing absolute directions induced by individual driving behaviour.

Now the question is how to a extract matching compass paths from the network. Lets assume for the moment that the start location $s \in V$ is known. In [5], a shape-preserving Dijkstra algorithm (SPD) was introduced. Here, a Dijkstra run is started in s, but paths are only explored if their encoding is declared equal (according to our introduced comparison oracle) to the encoding of the reference path (aka the trajectory we want to match). So a node v is only looked at, if the respective path from s to v in the actual Dijkstra search tree yields a prefix of the reference encoding (including tolerance ranges). For an SPD to be as efficient as possible, a newly explored edge should be encodable in constant time. Therefore, in our scenario, we do not only store predecessor labels with every node, but also sign labels, that tell whether we are actually in a right bend, a left bend or in no bend at all. This information along with the difference of the absolute directions of the last two edges on the path is sufficient to decide whether a new inflection point arises.

With the help of this modified SPD, we can search for the longest match of the trajectory in the map that starts at s. As the number of paths that are compatible with the reference trajectory should be very small for reasonable values of t, a single SPD computation is typically very quick. But it is the starting point s itself that is unknown and that we want to discover. Hence, theoretically, we have to start an SPD in every single vertex of the network, as each of them might be the start location we are looking for. Obviously this scales very badly with the network size. Our experiments will reveal that in networks with millions of nodes and edges query times are in the order of minutes. This is absolutely impractical for navigation purposes. Therefore, in the next section we will describe a data structure which allows to speed up queries significantly.

5   A Data Structure for Fast Inflection Point Recognition

Checking for every node in the network if it is a valid starting point of the trajectory in question is far too time-consuming. Of course, once we have identified the correct start location, we can invoke SPD computations for updating the location of the vehicle if it moves on. But to get the initial correct match, we need an alternative approach.

To accomplish fast localization queries, we follow the idea presented in [5] to transfer the map matching problem to a pattern search problem in texts. So the encoding of the trajectory is regarded as a concatenated string. The text describing the network consists naively of all encodings of possible (shortest) paths in the map. Several preprocessing methods for large text corpora exist, which allow to find a pattern in time linear in the pattern length (so completely independent of the length of the text). One way to achieve this, is the creation of a generalized suffix tree (GST) on the text [11]. A GST requires only linear space in the length of the text, if the alphabet has bounded size. This is of course the case in our application, as our 'letters' correspond to absolute directions with a precision of one degree. Therefore our alphabet has 360 letters only.

In the following, we first describe the way a conventional GST is constructed and how queries are answered using this data structure. Then, we briefly review how the GST construction on *path shapes* works (as proposed in [5]). This GST construction scheme is based on some basic assumptions about the encoding that are not fulfilled with our inflection point representation of trajectories. Therefore we subsequently describe how to adapt the GST creation to be applicable to compass paths as well.

5.1   Conventional Generalized Suffix Trees

For a set of strings $S_1, \cdots S_k$ a GST represents all suffixes of those strings, fulfilling the following characteristics: (1) Each tree edge is labelled with a non-empty string. (2) There is no inner node with degree 1. (3) Any suffix of a string corresponds to a unique path in the tree (starting from the root) with the concatenated edge labels along that path starting with this suffix.

A suffix is grafted into the GST by first identifying its longest prefix that already exists in the tree by tree traversal. If the path of this prefix ends in a node, a new edge and a new leaf are created, representing the last part of the suffix (if there are remaining characters). Also, the path could end implicitly, that means the edge label contains additional characters that are not in the suffix. Hence this edge has to be split together with its label, creating a new inner node that represents the longest prefix. Then one can proceed as described before. By performing this for every suffix occurring in $S_1, \cdots, S_k$ a GST of this set of strings is obtained. Note, that there are even more efficient ways of constructing GSTs, see e.g. [11]. But for the specific construction of the GST for the map matching application these are not applicable, as we will discuss later.

After the GST is constructed, the question whether a given pattern is contained in $S_1, \ldots, S_k$ can be answered in time linear in the size of this pattern, if the alphabet size is bounded, since a bounded alphabet size allows to associate an array with every node, which for each letter of the alphabet stores the edge (if any) whose label starts with this letter. So a query starts in the root of the GST, looking for an outgoing edge with a label, that begins with the first letter of the pattern. If such an edge exists, we have to compare the edge label to the respective pattern prefix element by element. If they are equal, we can go to the end point of the edge and repeat the search with the remaining elements of the pattern. If we always find a match, the pattern is contained in the underlying set of strings, otherwise it is not.

5.2   GSTs for Path Shapes

To construct the GST conventionally, all strings, i.e. all path shapes of all (shortest) paths in the network have to be explicitly available. But for larger networks this is clearly impractical. In fact, there are $\mathcal{O}(n^2)$ shortest paths in a network on n vertices. Even if their encoding length is rather small, the space consumption is far too high to store them all explicitly. Furthermore it is waste of time and space, to store all possible (long) paths. In fact, it suffices to store the prefixes of all paths until they are *unique* in the network. Because at this point, if a trajectory matches this prefix, the starting point can already be identified correctly, and the current location of the vehicle can be deduced. To determine efficiently whether a path encoding is unique in the network is non-trivial. Therefore the GST scheme as presented in [5] interleaves this classification with the GST creation. So the strings that are contained in the final GST are not available a priori, but are constructed in an online manner.

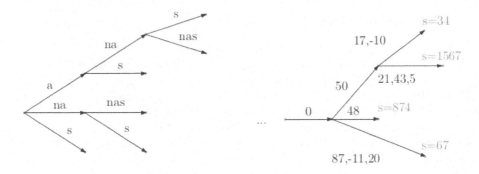

Fig. 2. Left: Conventional GST, here on the single string 'ananas'. Right: Small cutout of a GST on path shapes. The letters on the edges are now angles. Every leaf is labeled with the source vertex of the encoded path.

The detailed construction works as follows. A Dijkstra run is started in every vertex of the network, but with a given maximal distance. After each Dijkstra explored all nodes up to that distance (or the respective priority queue ran empty) it is frozen and all contained paths (implicitly given by the predecessor labels) are extracted and encoded. These encodings are grafted into the GST, with each node in the GST knowing the source and target vertex of the network, whose shortest path led to the creation of the node. Moreover every node has a boolean tag, that is initially set to true. If a path with different target vertex results the very same node in the GST, the tag is turned to false (this can be decided as a by-product of the grafting). Having done this for all vertices, the nodes in the GST with a true tag represent unique paths in the network. Hence the respective targets can be removed from the Dijkstra search tree of the respective source, pruning the search space. As long as not all priority queues of the Dijkstra have run empty, the process is repeated with an increased maximal distance. At the end, all necessary path prefixes are encoded in the GST. In Figure 2, examples of a conventional GST and our specialized GST-based data structure are provided.

When dealing with tolerance ranges, the construction has to be adapted slightly. In fact, it has to be checked whether a path prefix is unique with respect to that tolerance. If not, the respective search spaces cannot be pruned.

5.3   GSTs for Compass Paths in IPR

There are basically two requirements for the path shape GST construction scheme to work:

1. If an encoding of length l is unique among all other occurring encodings with length $\leq l$, a longer occurring encoding cannot destroy the uniqueness.
2. The length of a path encoding is equivalent to the path length.

The first condition is naturally fulfilled in our scenario, but using inflection points the code length does not have to be proportional to the path length at all.

So the second condition is violated. Therefore we have to modify the suffix tree construction. To ensure that every path with an encoding length of a given value l is known, we proceed as follows: For every vertex we run Dijkstra with an upper bound on the number of polls (i.e. extractions of elements from the priority queue). After this number of polls is processed (or the priority queue ran empty), we extract the set UL of unsettled leaves in the Dijkstra search tree. For each node in UL we compute the respective path via predecessor-labels and encode it using IPR. If all encodings have a length equal to or exceeding l we are done. Otherwise we increase the poll limit and continue the Dijkstra run. After we ensured that every leave in the search tree is either settled or leads to a long enough encoding, we backtrack all paths from leaves nodes (i.e. all longest paths) and encode them. If an encoding exceeds l, we just use its l-long prefix. All resulting encodings can then be grafted into the suffix tree.

Note, that using inflection point encoding some of the Dijkstra runs might explore a very large search space in order to achieve the required encoding length for every path, e.g. in the case of long straight highways the code length will remain zero. As this increases runtime and space consumption significantly, it should be prohibited as possible. If the path $p = s, u, v$ of a settled node v from the related source s consists of two edges with the same absolute direction, then every elongation of this path will have the same encoding as the suffix of the path starting at node u. Hence there is no need to explore these paths starting in s and therefore in such a case we remove v from the search tree. We can proceed analogously, if we have a path $p = s, u, v, w$ with w being a settled node and the directions of the three edges $(s, u), (u, v), (v, w)$ increase or decrease strictly monotonous. Here again all path elongations will have the same encoding as the path's suffix starting at u and therefore the search space can be pruned.

5.4 Answering Queries

The complete pipeline for answering a map matching query on compass-based data looks like this:

- gather absolute directions via an electronic compass, e.g. every second
- smooth the data to get rid of artefacts
- extract the inflection point representation
- search for the resulting encoding in the GST in order to determine the source vertex in the street network
- if such a source vertex was found, run a SPD (with the trajectory as reference) from this node to determine the end point of the trajectory and hence the current location of the vehicle

Note, that we could also construct the GST backwards, i.e. on reversed paths. Then searching for the reversed inflection point representation of the trajectory, the GST would provide us with the actual position of the vehicle right away – without the necessity to run a SPD. But on the one hand, a single SPD is very efficient, and on the other hand, it allows to display the whole trajectory driven so far on the map. Hence we stick to the forwards approach anyway.

6   Experimental Results

To show the practicability of our approach, we implemented the described algorithms and methods and tested them on several input networks. Our implementation is written in C++, timings were taken on a single core of an AMD Opteron
6172 with 2.1GHz and 96 GB RAM. Table 1 shows on overview of the sizes of
our networks (ST -Stuttgart, MA - Massachusetts, BW - Baden-Wuerttemberg,
SG - Southern Germany, all extracted from OSM[4]), along with several characteristics. We included Massachusetts as it contains many grid-like substructures
(especially in the area of Boston) which we consider challenging for our approach. We observe that the ratio of inflection points to all points on the average
shortest path is rather high in larger graphs, in fact about 50%.

Table 1. Characteristics of the used test graphs. Averaged values are calculated on the
basis of 1000 randomly chosen shortest paths (SPs). The number of inflection points
(IPs) on a path equals its encoding length according to our model.

	ST	MA	BW	SG
# nodes	122,334	294,345	999,591	5,588,146
# edges	243,593	731,874	2,131,490	11,711,088
avg. path length	15.9km	120.4km	78.2km	173.7km
avg. # IPs on SP	119	209	664	1373
avg. % IPs on SP	30.0	51.2	45.5	48.6

6.1   Characterizability of Street Networks

The first crucial step is to show that the inflection point representation really
suffices for accurate localization. For that purpose, we conducted the following
experiment: We randomly choose a vertex pair $s, t \in V$ and compute the shortest
path π between them. Then we use our SPD for every possible start vertex to find
the longest match of the inflection point encoding of π. Naturally, the longest
match will be π itself or even a superpath, as depicted in Figure 3. To find out,
if there is a path really different from π but sharing its encoding, we restricted
the result to matches with at least 80% of the edges being different from the
reference path. In Table 2 the average prefix lengths can be found, grouped by
the number of inflection points we demand the match to contain at least. If we
set this number to zero, the longest match simply is the longest shortest path
in the network with no encoding, completely independent of the reference path.
Increasing the number of inflection points that have to be equal, the prefix sizes
decrease dramatically. Already using 5 IPs, the IPR becomes unique quite early,
even when using an angle tolerance that allows the IPs to differ by 5 degrees
($t = 5$). The first 10 IPs are rarely matched by any other path in the map even
for Southern Germany. There, 10 IPs correspond to less than one percent of the
total number of IPs on an average path.

---
[4] openstreetmap.org

Fig. 3. Left image: Reference path (blue) and its longest match in the map. Without restrictions, the match (red+blue) is naturally a superset of the reference path (blue), as there are prefixes/suffixes with zero encoding length. The two images on the right show long pure right or left turns which do not exhibit encodings in IPR.

Table 2. Unique prefix length (in meters) in dependency of the number of inflection points (IPs) a match has to contain for exact queries (left table), and with an angle tolerance of $t = 5$ (right table). The respective query times (in seconds) denote the time that was necessary to finish a SPD computation for every vertex in the network. Values are averaged over 1000 random queries.

	ST	MA	BW	SG
exact	avg. prefix length (m)			
0 IP	4,822	28,430	4,289	91,941
1 IP	2,509	21,388	3,060	45,083
2 IP	582	9,085	1,269	31,757
5 IP	13	114	66	1,596
10 IP	0	2	1	4
time	7.86	17.18	36.73	245.63

	ST	MA	BW	SG
t= 5	avg. prefix length (m)			
0 IP	5,255	31,931	4,731	94,146
1 IP	4141	31,293	4,441	81,934
2 IP	3,047	23,445	3,778	62,309
5 IP	835	8,853	1,210	4,998
10 IP	5	175	14	3
time	8.03	19.01	42.81	287.12

Hence IPR encoding for shortest paths in street networks seems to be a feasible way to solve the map matching problem accurately. But the running time of the naive approach is a drawback, increasing significantly with the network size – resulting from a SPD run started in *every* vertex. It is almost unaffected by the required number of IPs, as the paths with zero encoding have to be explored anyway, leading to a total runtime of over 4 minutes for a single query in Southern Germany.

6.2 GST Construction

We computed GSTs for all our test graphs, for an exact as well as an imprecision-tolerant comparison model. Table 3 contains the characteristics of the created GSTs. The depth of the GST – reflected by the maximal code length we had to consider – is quite small for all test graphs. For every path in Southern Germany that contains at least 17 inflection points, we can be sure to find a proper source node with the help of the GST. Moreover for exact queries this means that at most 17 comparisons are necessary to retrieve this source node. Having a look at the number of explored nodes per Dijkstra run, the search spaces are very small on average. Nevertheless some of the Dijkstra search trees contain very long path sections with zero encoding, leading to very long maximal distances in that tree, e.g. over 37 km for Massachusetts and over 155 km for Southern Germany. But even with the majority of the Dijkstra runs being very fast, the run time of the preprocessing scales badly with the network size and the introduction of an angles tolerance t. While the depth of the GST only doubles for $t = 5$, the runtime increases significantly. This is due on the one hand to the larger search spaces for the Dijkstra computations and on the other hand to the increased time for checking whether a node in the temporary GST is unique. On a single core we needed about one hour to preprocess BW with exact comparison and about a day with $t = 5$. It took already two days to preprocess Southern Germany without considering tolerances. Future work will include the parallelization of the Dijkstra computations to speed up the preprocessing and permit to use even larger graphs and higher tolerances. But the preprocessing step only has to be performed once – for the queries the resulting GST suffices. For Southern Germany the respective data structure is less than 4 GB in size and hence could be stored on a SD-card of a mobile device.

Table 3. Experimental results of the online GST creation

	exact				t=5			
	ST	MA	BW	SG	ST	MA	BW	SG
max code size	12	15	13	17	30	37	31	33
avg. #expl. nodes	191	279	202	154	428	498	359	215
max dist (m)	8,697	37,650	9,923	155,481	12,746	37,824	17,111	162,582
time (min)	5.75	38.02	52.83	2978.22	213.71	663.75	1733.35	5287.52
GST nodes	$5.2 \cdot 10^5$	$3.1 \cdot 10^6$	$5.1 \cdot 10^6$	$3.6 \cdot 10^7$	$2.5 \cdot 10^6$	$1.6 \cdot 10^7$	$2.3 \cdot 10^7$	$1.9 \cdot 10^8$

6.3   Queries

Having the GST at hand, we can now answer queries with a tree traversal followed by a single run of a shape-preserving Dijkstra. This is a dramatic improvement compared to n necessary SPD runs using the naive approach. The effect on the practical runtime is shown in Table 4. Using the combination of the GST and one SPD, all queries could be answered in less than half a decisecond. This results from the fact, that all GSTs have a very small depth, hence very few comparisons are needed to find a certain pattern and moreover the SPD run explores almost only the edges, that are part of the resulting trajectory. All in all our approach can answer map matching queries up to 8000 times faster than the naive approach and even for larger graphs this procedure might allow for real-time query answering.

Table 4. Query times (in seconds) for answering map matching queries using different approaches and comparison models. Timings are averaged over 1000 random queries.

		ST	MA	BW	SG
exact	naive	7.8665	17.1836	36.7329	245.6335
	GST+SPD	0.0011	0.0022	0.0045	0.0332
	speed-up	7151	7810	8126	7398
t=5	naive	8.0324	19.0172	42.8134	261.1443
	GST+SPD	0.0015	0.0038	0.0076	0.0458
	speed-up	5355	5004	5633	5701

6.4   Accuracy

The quality of a path p' resulting from a map matching procedure is conventionally measured by the percentage of edges of the correct path p, that are not matched by p' (called A_N), and the percentage of the length of p, that could not be covered by p' (called A_L). In our scenario there are two sources of errors for matching paths extracted from the map: Firstly, paths with a too short encoding length to be unique in the network cannot be matched at all, secondly a path with a unique encoding might still allow for a small range of different path beginnings (before the first inflection point) and path tails (after the last inflection point). But based on the density of inflection points on shortest paths, these disturbance sources have only a mild effect on the accuracy. For both quality measures we never observed an error value greater than 0.06 for $t = 5$ and 0.04 for exact queries, with the A_L value always being slightly better than A_N. So both error metric values are remarkably small for all considered graphs, even under imprecisions. To mitigate the imprecision even further when determining the current position of the vehicle, path prediction algorithms [4] can be used on the basis of the matched trajectory.

6.5   Real-World Data

To demonstrate the practicability of our approach on real-world data, we collected electronic compass measurements with our app (installed on a Nexus 4) over a period of a month on the same trajectory (so 20 measurements in total). The data was collected by bicycle, the travelled path includes streets and bicycle paths. Figure 4 provides a visualization of the trajectory in our web application. In Figure 5 we show a comparison of all introduced compass measurement techniques supported by our app. The results implied that using the average over all methods works best. (For AHRS, we tested several parameter combinations and finally considered three of them useful. There might be of course better ways to use the method.) As ground truth we used the representation of the trajectory in the underlying network. Conducting our compass measurements, we observed that the total travelled time and therefore the number of raw measurements vary significantly (by up to 20%), but the number of inflection points is very steady (11 for 18 out of 20 trajectories, 10 and 12 for the two remaining ones).

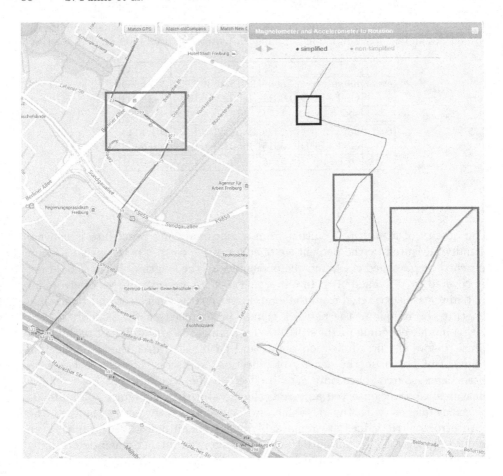

Fig. 4. GPS-based trajectory (green) visualized in the map on the left, and compass-based measurements on the same trajectory presented in a pop-up on the right side. The red box shows a zoomed-in version of part of the compass path to illustrate our line smoothing technique. The overall shape is very faithfully preserved. The pink box on the left shows a trajectory section where GPS measurements imply a curve, but the compass path truthfully reports a straight line there. The black square on the right shows a sharp turn which is not represented as single turning point in the compass path. But as we use inflection point representation, this does not affect the encoding.

In the end, we could match 13 out of 20 trajectories to the ground truth using an angle tolerance of 5°. For the remaining ones, at least one inflection point differed more from the ground truth, the maximum was at 22°. Nevertheless, considering the scenario where as soon as we found our position in the network (using e.g. the first four inflection points) and then only update our position as soon as new inflection points come in, we followed the correct trajectory in the map from beginning to end for 19 out of 20 trajectories.

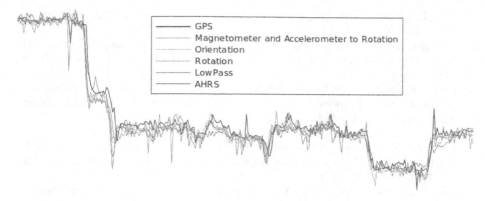

Fig. 5. Comparison of different compass measurement techniques and GPS based directions on part of our test trajectory. We observe that in general the reported values are very similar, with some outlier peaks for the Magnetometer and Accelerometer and AHRS.

So there is a clear indication that compass paths in IPR can work as standalone for precise localization (if the sensor quality is sufficient). Of course, experiments on a single trajectory are not that meaningful. In future work, a large scale study should be conducted to retrieve more information about compass-based navigation. But seeing that the scheme works for bicycles already gives hope that it might work even better for cars. As when going by bicycle one tends not to follow lanes exactly and one has a larger degree of freedom on bicycle tracks than cars have on streets.

7   Conclusions

We presented a complete pipeline to acquire compass data in a wireless manner, to process it, and to use the resulting data for localization of a vehicle moving in a street network. One important aspect to make this approach practical is our newly developed inflection point representation, which is robust against different driving styles and time-dependent data sampling. To allow for real-time localization, we designed a data structure based on generalized suffix trees, which encodes the whole street network compactly, and allows to search for a compass path in inflection point representation in fractions of a second. Future work should include more real-world experiments, better sensor value trade-offs (instead of the simple average we used), and compatibility tests with other (autonomous) information sources.

References

1. Quddus, M., Ochieng, W., Noland, R.: Current map-matching algorithms for transport applications: state-of-the art and future research directions. Transportation Research Part C: Emerging Technologies **15**, 312–328 (2007)

2. Alt, H., Efrat, A., Rote, G., Wenk, C.: Matching planar maps. J. Algorithms **49**, 262–283 (2003)
3. Yanagisawa, H.: An offline map matching via integer programming. In: Proc. 20th International Conference on Pattern Recognition (ICPR), pp. 4206–4209. IEEE (2010)
4. Eisner, J., Funke, S., Herbst, A., Spillner, A., Storandt, S.: Algorithms for matching and predicting trajectories. In: Proc. of the 13th Workshop on Algorithm Engineering and Experiments (ALENEX) (2011)
5. Funke, S., Storandt, S.: Path shapes: an alternative method for map matching and fully autonomous self-localization. In: Proceedings of the 19th ACM SIGSPATIAL International Conference on Advances in Geographic Information Systems, pp. 319–328. ACM (2011)
6. Firner, B., Sugrim, S., Yang, Y., Lindqvist, J.: Elastic pathing: Your speed is enough to track you (2014). CoRR abs/1401.0052
7. Aggarwal, P., Thomas, D., Ojeda, L., Borenstein, J.: Map matching and heuristic elimination of gyro drift for personal navigation systems in gps-denied conditions. Measurement Science and Technology **22**(2), 025205 (2011)
8. Pei, L., Chen, R., Liu, J., Liu, Z., Kuusniemi, H., Chen, Y., Zhu, L.: Sensor assisted 3d personal navigation on a smart phone in gps degraded environments. In: 2011 19th International Conference on Geoinformatics, pp. 1–6, June 2011
9. Douglas, D., Peucker, T.: Algorithms for the reduction of the number of points required to represent a digitized line or its caricature. The Canadian Cartographer **10**(2), 112–122 (1973)
10. de Berg, M., Cook IV, A.: Go with the flow: The direction-based frechet distance of polygonal curves. In: Proc. 1st Int. ICST Conf. on Theory and Practice of Algorithms in Computer Systems (TAPAS) (2011)
11. Ukkonen, E.: On-line construction of suffix trees. Algorithmica **14**, 249–260 (1995). doi:10.1007/BF01206331

A Web-Based Steam Assisted Gravity Drainage (SAGD) Data Visualization and Analytical System

Bingjie Wei[1], Rodrigo Silva[1,2], and Xin Wang[1(✉)]

[1] Department of Geomatics Engineering, University of Calgary, Calgary, Canada
{wbingjie,xcwang}@ucalgary.ca
[2] Department of Computer Engineering, University of Pernambuco, Recife, Brazil
raos@ecomp.poli.br

Abstract. To manage the voluminous and complex Steam Assisted Gravity Drainage (SAGD) data and accommodate the spatial and temporal components, a database management system working interactively with a web GIS mapping interface is designed and built. Public and proprietary SAGD data are collected from multiple sources and archived. Multiple spatial layers and flexible spatial queries can help users efficiently target SAGD wells. Furthermore, intuitive and interactive data visualization methods like attribute table, histograms and charts and time-series data viewers, as well as data mining techniques like clustering and association rule mining are implemented in the system for users to explore and comprehend SAGD data and make decisions.

Keywords: Web GIS · Oil and Gas · Steam Assisted Gravity Drainage (SAGD) · Data visualization · Data mining

1   Introduction

Western Canada is abundant in heavy oil and bitumen (oil sands), the quantity of which is the third in the world, only to the conventional oil reserves of Venezuela and Saudi Arabia [1]. In the late 1970s, steam-based in-situ process Steam Assisted Gravity Drainage (SAGD) was developed and introduced as an oil recovery technology for heavy oil and bitumen [2]. SAGD employs a horizontal well pair configuration with an upper injection well and a lower production well drilled in parallel. High-temperature steam is injected through an injector to heat up the reservoir and form a chamber, and then the heated oil bitumen at the chamber edge will drain down and flow through the producer [3]. Now SAGD is being widely used as a thermal production technology to extract oil bitumen from Alberta's subsurface oil sands deposits. Projects using SAGD technology are being more common: the number of commercial SAGD projects in Alberta has reached 16 by 2013, compared to less than 5 before year 2000 [4].

As the expansion of SAGD projects, huge and ever-growing quantities of SAGD-related data have been accumulated, involving various domains oil and gas industry could interfere with - generally like geophysics, geology, petroleum, business and

© Springer International Publishing Switzerland 2015
J. Gensel and M. Tomko (Eds.): W2GIS 2015, LNCS 9080, pp. 89–103, 2015.
DOI: 10.1007/978-3-319-18251-3_6

administration. Applications assisting in storing and managing the voluminous and complex SAGD datasets are in demand. Targeted at SAGD data, a data application should be able to accommodate the spatial characteristics of SAGD wells, provide users with access to integrative SAGD-related data and append spatial exploration and analysis functionalities.

In terms of oil and gas data applications, there are a variety of data management services and products in the market. Some commercial software, such as Accumap by IHS [5], GeoCarta by Divestco [6], geoSCOUT by geoLOGIC [7] provides access to integrated public and proprietary data in different disciplines, and integrate geographic information system (GIS) technology for the storing, displaying and analyzing spatial objects like wells, pipelines and facilities.

The commercial software products, however, not only have hardware configuration requirements for installation, but also have sequential packages to be installed as software modules or database updated. Therefore, it is desired to facilitate more convenient access to the latest software and data. Web GIS systems, GIS systems built with web technologies, give users access to the system and the mapping and analytic functionalities as long as they have access to the Internet, and are approachable by broad audience simultaneously through web browsers.

The other limitation of the existing systems is that they provide limited data visualization and analytical functions. SAGD petroleum professionals need data exploration and analysis functions to diagnose abnormal chamber development and oil recovery rate, and make decisions on corrective or improving actions. Injection, production and chamber parameters are changing continuously over time. Additional to examining those time-series data in forms of tables, information presented using data visualization methods like interactive charts and histograms can assist petroleum engineers with data comprehending and decision-making. Besides traditional data visualization methods, data mining can discover significant patterns or rules automatically or semi-automatically from large datasets [8]. Applying data mining techniques to SAGD datasets can provide engineers insightful information and lead to critical decision making faster.

In this paper, a data visualization and analysis system specialized in SAGD projects and built upon Web GIS technology is proposed. The contributions of this application are as follows.

Firstly, by integrating GIS, a GIS mapping interface and the database management system can work interactively as users explore the SAGD spatial and attributive data. Different spatial layers and flexible spatial queries can help users efficiently target spatial SAGD wells and then apply the visualization and analysis functions to the wells.

Secondly, the web GIS platform is approachable by broad audience. Users can access the GIS system and make use of the mapping and analytic functionalities through web browsers.

Thirdly, public and proprietary SAGD data are collected, and archived in a specially designed database. Intuitive and interactive data visualization methods like attribute table, histograms and time-series data viewer, as well as data mining techniques like clustering and association rule mining are implemented in the system for users to further comprehend SAGD data and make decisions.

The remainder of the paper is organized as follows. The second section introduces some related work on clustering and association rule mining techniques. The third section introduces the web-based system structure and the database design. The fourth section presents the Web GIS user interface, while the fifth section focuses on the data visualization and data mining functionalities. The last section concludes the paper.

2   Related Work

2.1   Oil and Gas Data Management Systems and Web GIS

One of the most popular commercial products for oil and gas data management in Alberta is GeoCarta by Divestco [6]. It is primarily an oil and gas data warehouse integrating locations and distributions of spatial objects, exploration and production histories and all the other relational data sources. A mapping interface and a connected data management system work interactively in order to simplify the workflows of querying and retrieving data. For this specific software, ArcMap is utilized as the GIS platform, and spatial objects can be either located in the intuitive mapping interface or searched by the industry standard location descriptions in the data management system, which is attached to ArcMap as an extension tool. Therefore, ArcGIS Desktop is required to be installed with GeoCarta; users need to manually update the oil and gas database as GeoCarta updates it regularly. All the other oil and gas data management software has a similar system design except for using the other GIS platform instead of ArcMap.

To facilitate convenient access to GIS and the appendant functionalities, web GIS has been applied to diverse applications. Different thematic applications like flood management, cultural heritage management and ecological restoration have employed Web GIS technology, proving an interactive, flexible tool [9,10,11]. There are also oil and gas information systems built by web GIS technology focusing on spatial data query [12], oil and gas industry news notification [13] and so on, which deliver valuable petroleum related information to broad users. To apply web GIS to SAGD data management and analysis is practiced and discussed in our study.

2.2   Oil and Gas Data Visualization and Analysis Methods

The current commercial oil and gas data management systems focus on data management, but have limited data analysis functionality. In terms of analyzing the large quantities of data in the oil and gas industry, visualization tools and other digital techniques have helped with exploring data, making decisions and improving production [14]. Visualization methods such as diagrams, charts, and plots are the most common and straightforward ways to summarize datasets.

By using visualized graphics, information, especially like trends, abruptions and abnormal occurrences, can be communicated to users. However, as for patterns and relationships that are implicitly contained in large datasets and can be steered towards specific goals, data mining techniques are required.

Cluster Analysis. Cluster analysis, or called clustering, aims at grouping objects with similar properties and also partition objects with dissimilarity [15]. The consistency of the clustering result of geological properties and oil and gas resources can assist in oil and gas resource exploration and evaluation [16]. K-means is one of the most popular clustering methods. K is a user-defined variable that stands for the number of clusters or groups. The algorithm initializes k random objects representing the cluster centroids and iterates the process of assigning other objects to centroids with the closest distances and calculating new centroids until there is no change in all the clusters. K-means clustering algorithm can efficiently process large datasets due to its relatively low computation complexity.

Association Rule Mining. Association rule mining (ARM) is used to find frequent associations and correlations among different attributes from large datasets. In gas and oil research field, ARM has been used in reservoir analysis and oil production [17,18]. An association rule is comprised of an antecedent part (IF) and a consequent (THEN) part. Two measures, support and confidence, are used to define rule interestingness. An example rule in the paper of Cai et al [12] can be described: IF three reservoir properties match certain levels, THEN the well oil production is high (support = 5.1%, confidence = 85.7%). Support denotes the proportion of the items in the whole dataset that satisfy the rule; confidence denotes the proportion of the objects that satisfy the consequence among the objects satisfying the antecedent condition. Frequent if/then patterns satisfying defined minimum support and minimum confidence are identified as strong association rules. Apriori is a classic ARM algorithm using particular searching approach and data structure to efficiently scan large datasets [19]. Mined rules describe the hidden relationships among multiple attributes in the datasets and can help with prediction and decision-making.

3   Design of the SAGD Data Visualization and Analysis System

Having reviewed other oil and gas data mapping and management software, a system with an integrated modular base needs to preserve a GIS environment focusing on SAGD wells and adopts new designs and implementations to perform the following functions: (a) provide a web GIS platform, making the system accessible to users through web browsers; (b) render archived SAGD data searchable by locations or attributes, and searched results exportable; (c) visualize attributive and time-series data in forms of tables, interactive charts and graphs; (d) apply clustering and ARM techniques and visualize mined spatial patterns in the interface. This section introduces the system design and presents the employed technologies and the SAGD database.

3.1   System Design

The system design is illustrated in Figure 1. The web-based application consists of four main components: the SAGD database, the data processing server, the web server and the user interface. The four components communicate, and deliver and present users information according to their requests.

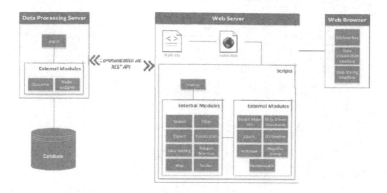

Fig. 1. System design

This system is built upon HTML5 and CSS3, which respectively structure and style webpages, and can flexibly modify and adjust webpage elements. JavaScript as an object-oriented programming language is used in developing the system, since it can be executed on the client side to avoid excessive communication with the web server and reduce the processing time. Moreover, there is a rich amount of third party JavaScript libraries, plugins and modules that can be used to accelerate the development. The other important technologies and open source libraries that have been used in this system include PostgreSQL, the Google Maps API and Node.js.

3.2   SAGD Database

Database Structure. Besides the huge quantity of data in an on-progress SAGD project, the data types can be varied, as there are static and dynamic data, numerical and categorical data, and first-hand and derived data. The dynamic injection and production processes in SAGD operations generate time-series data on the injected and produced instances and the amounts. As for the geospatial characteristics of SAGD wells, multiple SAGD well pairs (injector and producer pairs) are drilled in units of well pads; the surface locations of the horizontal wells (heels) are aggregated in the pad centers, while horizontal wells spread out underground and reach the end locations (toes) [4]. A relational database is designed and deployed with integration of basic well information, geographic coordinates, well status, and injection and production records. Figure 2 shows an overview of the database structure.

The Unique Well Identifier (UWI) is a standard well identification containing 16 characters in four components sequentially [20]. The primary purpose of UWI is to differentiate every single well. Therefore, in the database, a primary key is designed to correspond to UWI in the root table and also associate to primary keys in other tables.

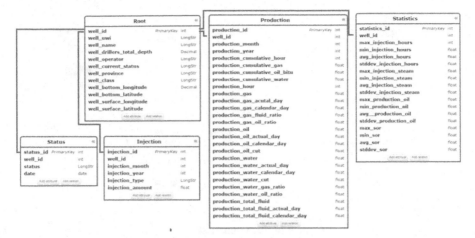

Fig. 2. SAGD database structure

The well status, injection and production histories of the SAGD wells are stored in three separate tables. The well status indicates the general phases with the corresponding periods of time that an individual well has undergone, e.g. observation, drilled and cased, abandoned. The injection or production table stores the well monthly records. For a producer, there might be some injection during the start-up for warming-up purpose; there might be small amounts of produced substances from an injector as well.

A key SAGD performance measurement, Steam Oil Ratio (SOR) calculates the amount of steam used for producing a barrel of oil [21]. Small SOR rates like around 2 represent efficient SAGD operations. Cumulative Steam Oil Ratio (CSOR) is the accumulative amount of steam divided by accumulative produced oil, which measures the efficiency since the well pair has been operated. In the database management system, SOR and CSOR are calculated for each well pair. Statistical measurements like minimum, maximum, average and standard deviation are calculated for SOR and CSOR as well as injected steam, operation hours and produced oil amount, and stored in the statistics table.

Data Collection and Preprocessing. Considering the quantity of data that SAGD projects could have been generating, public available data are limited and scattered. Some SAGD in-situ and surface facilities collect real-time data, which are compiled and only distributed within the organizations. Through Alberta Energy Regulator, annual reports on in situ performance of each SAGD projects are accessible. In the annual reports, summary information on geology and geophysics, drilling and well instrumentation, seismic, and operation performance are displayed in forms of maps and graphs. On the other hand, data can be obtained through commercial software platforms, which purchase oil and gas data through some oil and gas companies or specialized data companies. In this study, data on wells in Alberta SAGD projects are collected from Alberta Energy Regulator and Divestco GeoCarta. With the acquired UWIs and a template of data attributes, SAGD data are collected from GeoCarta data explorer and trimmed into the database structure to populate the database.

4   The Web GIS User Interface

The Web GIS user interface consists of four main components: (a) an interactive map representing the current objects; (b) a status bar indicating the selected map layers and the numbers of selected and highlighted objects on the map; (c) a table displaying the basic information of current objects; (d) manipulation tools leading to advanced functions – search, search by location, export, data visualization and data mining. Figure 3 represents the complete Web GIS user interface with panels extended for map manipulation, searching for a particular SAGD project and highlighting wells of interest, an attribute table of the searched wells (bottom right), map navigation (top left), and manipulation tool bar (top right). Pointed at one bottom well location is the auxiliary window displaying basic well information with a button, by clicking which users can access to time series data visualization on history data.

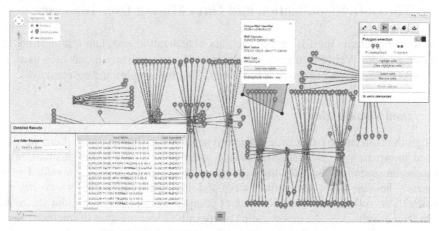

Fig. 3. The web GIS user interface of the system

One of the assets of a web-based cartographic user interface is the flexibility and interactivity provided to users. The initial setting of the system is a map filling the whole browser window with none open auxiliary windows or tabs but only clickable icons placed over the map for extending the manipulation tool bar and the attribute table. Mouse controls are for spatial navigation like zooming and panning the webbased map. Users can compile map contents based on their intentions. On the other hand, the map can be automatically zoomed in to a particular geographic area where searched wells are located.

As the organization of the three different spatial components of SAGD wells, spatial layers are used to store the heels, toes and derived lines separately. The derived line connects the heel and toe locations, standing for the well trajectory. Users can view and manipulate the spatial layers separately in the system. In terms of the map symbols, drop-shaped markers represent toes, while relatively small circle markers represent heels, as heels are more aggregated than toes. All the markers are clickable;

by clicking the marker of interest, users can explore the well history with a series of interactive graphs and charts.

To create interactive spatial queries is one of the basic but most essential applications of a geographic information system. Two kinds of search, property search and location search, are realized in the web GIS system. Based on user needs, property search, which is one extendable tab under the tool bar, can filter wells into a set of wells satisfying the search query on attributes such as UWI, operating company, and well status. Also, search queries can be composed in the attribute table. Search by location is another tab under the tool bar. Adjacently located wells can be circled by a polygon, and wells can be highlighted in blue markers. The data of searched wells is correspondingly updated in the attribute table where detailed information can be investigated.

5   The Data Visualization and Data Mining User Interface

This section presents the features of the data visualization and data mining functions additional to the Web GIS user interface. How data visualization can help users explore SAGD operation history data is illustrated with examples and case studies.

5.1   Data Visualization

Though the collected SAGD data have been archived in the database, there would be missed information if users simply retrieve and examine data in the database tables. Information graphics can help users interpret patterns and trends embedded in the datasets. The web-based data visualization and analytics system implements different visualization methods for users to conduct comprehensive analyses about the SAGD projects and wells they are investigating. Generally, users are able to interpret: (a) the history of well status, (b) the injection and production history of a well pair, and (c) the overall operation of selected wells. The additional value added to the information graphics in this system is the interactivity in the graphic components. Templates of data visualization methods are given as follows, as well as a case study on visualizing the time-series data of a specific well pair.

Data Visualization Templates. When a specific well is referred to on the interactive map, an auxiliary window of visualization on time series data (i.e. status, injection, production) is displayed. The well statuses are plotted in continuous horizontal bars with x-axis representing time, as shown in Figure 4(a). The period of each status is shown in the right side of the window when the mouse is placed on the corresponding status bar. The legend of the statuses and colors is displayed in the left side. By working with the interactive timeline, the user can not only know the chronological processes the well has been undergoing but also detailed periods of time according to each operation.

The injection and production parameters and the corresponding SOR/CSOR provide engineers the main evidences on decision-making related to operation and oil production. Interactive graphs on visualizing the time-series data are available in the system. The graph to be looked at, injection, production or SOR, is chosen on the left side in the auxiliary window. In one graph, there are four main sections where users can modify to update the graph. The layout of an example graph is shown in Figure 4(b). Firstly, users can select single or multiple attributes to be displayed by clicking them from the attribute list in the legend, and there are four types of charts- area chart, bar chart, line chart and scatterplot- that users can choose. When some data are missing on some dates, users can choose to just ignore the data or interpolate the data in line chart. Last but not least, when the users are concerned about any interesting or unusual trend in the graph, they can zoom in to the corresponding period of time in the time bar below the graph, and then the graph will be updated accordingly.

If a group of wells is selected in using search by attributes or locations, an overview of the wells can be presented in the data visualization using bar charts for numerical attributes or pie charts for categorical ones. Clicking a single bar will display additional information of the corresponding well in the right side of the visualization window. Also, clicking any of the selections in the pie chart will highlight the corresponding legend, vice versa. Figure 4(c) and Figure 4(d) show the examples for bar chart and pie chart visualization. Users can have straightforward perception about the data distribution from the histogram and pie chart.

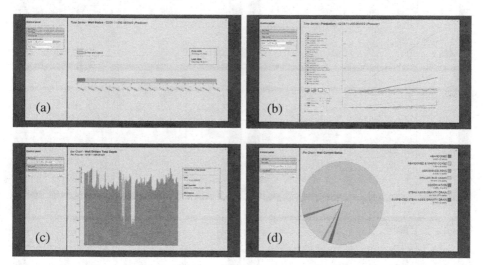

Fig. 4. Data visualization templates (a) Timeline of a producer well (UWI 02/08-11-095-06W4/0) in Suncor Firebag (b) Time-series visualization for the producer well in Suncor Firebag (c) Bar chart of well total depth for Suncor Firebag and Husky Tucker wells (d) Pie chart of status for Suncor Firebag wells

Case Study on SAGD Injection and Production History. The following are the examples of data visualization on a specific well pair (Figure 5). Based on the trends the graphs implied, it could be concluded that the performance of this well pair has been moderate and improving.

a) The injection history of the producer well was from May to November 2011;

b) The paired injector well has been injecting steam from May 2011 to August 2013 with a general increasing trend;

c) The production history of the selected producer well with production-related attributes- gas, oil and water- are plotted. Staring from October 2011 to August 2013, the oil production (represented by pink line) has been from about 2000 to 6000 m3 per month, and reached peaks in April and June 2013. The water flowing out of the producer was about 10000 to 20000 m3 per month, with almost none gas produced;

d) The oil production was in an increasing trend with three obvious busts in November 2011, June 2012 and May 2013;

e) The injected steam, produced oil, SOR and CSOR of the well pair are plotted. Both injection and production have been in increasing trends;

f) The SOR and CSOR of the well pair are zoomed in to the time period from July 2011 to July 2012, during this period of time the SOR reached a peak value of 19.94 and reduced and reached a relatively steady trend to around 3.

Fig. 5. Time-series data visualization on a specific well pair (Injector UWI 05/08-11-095-06W4/0; producer UWI 02/08-11-095-06W4/0)

5.2 Data Mining

By using data mining techniques, users can discover the hidden patterns in the SAGD wells. Classification for numerical and categorical attributes, k-means clustering and association rule mining (ARM) are implemented in the web-based GIS system. Moreover, the mapping interface displays the spatial patterns to not only communicate the mined results but also provide the exploratory capability to users. The mined patterns associated with wells are shown in the map with an interactive map legend. The map legend explains the cartographic symbols, and clicking one symbol can result in the corresponding wells appearing. Case studies are given below in respect with using data mining tools for different data analysis goals.

Users are allowed to map classified SAGD well attributes. For categorical attributes, like well current status, well type and pad, wells belonging to different categories are represented by symbols in different colors. By using categorical classification for well pads, wells in different pads are displayed in different colors, shown in Figure 6 (a). In numerical classification, wells can be classified either by equal interval or equal quantile for examining the distribution of attribute values. Figure 6 (b) presents an example of quantile classification on average oil production. Users can observe the distribution of wells in each class, like the aggregation of wells with high production or low production. Clustering is unsupervised learning from data grouping similar items and partitioning different ones. Figure 6 (c) displays the result of applying k-means clustering to SOR and oil production. Wells with similar production amount and efficiency are grouped, and different groups of wells are shown in the map in different symbols.

Figure 7 shows an ARM example for Suncor Firebag project mining the relationship between injection (hour and steam amount) and production (oil production and SOR). There are five significant rules displayed in the system. For example as shown in Figure 7 (a), the first rule states that if one well has high average injection hour with low standard deviation and low average injection steam with low standard deviation, the well might has a good SOR average with low SOR standard deviation. There are 18 out of 20 wells matching the rule. By clicking the rule in the legend, the map will be updated using three colors (dark blue, light blue and black) to represent wells matching different parts of the rules, as shown in Figure 7 (b). Dark blues wells satisfy both IF and THEN statements while light blue wells only satisfy IF part but not THEN part. When the corresponding symbol in the legend is clicked, the wells in the category will appear with other wells transparently displayed as shown in Figure 7 (c). With the interaction between users and the map, users can explore the mined rules in detail. The mined rules can be referred to when new wells are to be developed near the existing wells. Engineers can make the injection operations and expect the production efficiency from the new wells according to the rules that their adjacent wells have matched.

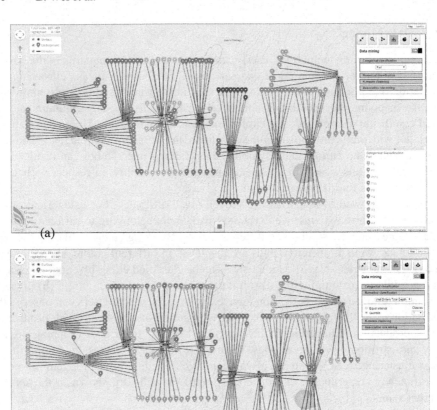

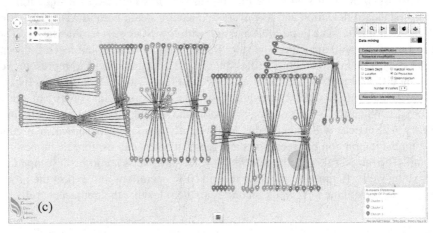

Fig. 6. Examples of categorical, numerical classification and k-means clustering of wells in Suncor Firebag project (a) Categorical classification of well pads (b) Numerical classification using quantile of well average oil production (c) K-means clustering of SOR and oil production

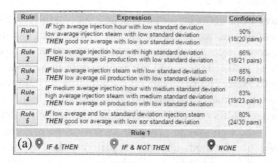

Rule	Expression	Confidence
Rule 1	IF high average injection hour with low standard deviation low average injection steam with low standard deviation THEN good sor average with low standard deviation	90% (18/20 pairs)
Rule 2	IF low average injection hour with high standard deviation THEN low average oil production with low standard deviation	86% (18/21 pairs)
Rule 3	IF low average injection steam with low standard deviation THEN low average oil production with low standard deviation	85% (47/55 pairs)
Rule 4	IF medium average injection hour with medium standard deviation high average injection steam with medium standard deviation THEN low average oil production with low standard deviation	83% (19/23 pairs)
Rule 5	IF low average and low standard deviation injection steam THEN good sor average with low sor standard deviation	80% (24/30 pairs)

Rule 1

(a) IF & THEN   IF & NOT THEN   NONE

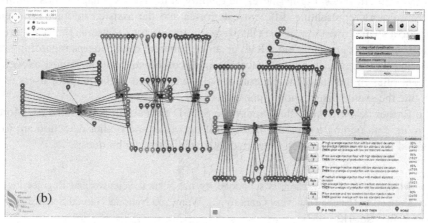

(b)

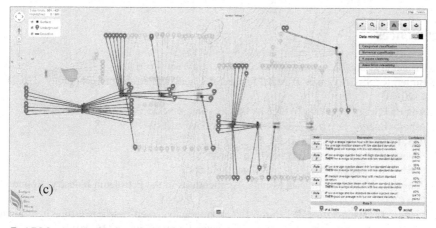

(c)

Fig. 7. ARM example for Suncor Firebag project (a) ARM result map legend (b) Map interface of association rule 1 (c) Map interface of wells fully satisfying association rule 3

6 Discussion and Conclusion

The paper has presented the development of a web-based, data visualization and analytic map system for SAGD projects and operations in Alberta. Datasets of Alberta

SAGD projects have been collected, archived and successfully exploited in the web GIS system. Meanwhile, the workflows from the selection of examined wells to the update of the interactive web-based map, from the selection of information graphic type to the display of well temporal and attributive data in an auxiliary visualization window, and from the selection of advanced data mining techniques to the update of mined patterns in the web map, have been proved feasible.

The most important additional value of this platform is the implementation of data mining algorithms in the web system. To gain a view of wells falling in different categories, the classification methods targeted at different data types can be applied to selected well attributes. Furthermore, the display in the form of maps with symbols in different colors representing different categories and the assisted interactive legends facilitate a spatial overview of the classification results for the users. Two data-driven models, k-means clustering and ARM, generate inherent data patterns regarding similarity and discrepancy in a single attribute or a combination of attributes, as well as frequent rules in the data. The patterns are also visualized in the map for users to investigate the spatial distribution of the patterns.

To further develop the system, real-time SAGD data are to be established. Moreover, more data mining techniques like neural networks and outlier detection are to be extended in the system as well as more data visualization techniques.

Acknowledgement. The research is supported by the Natural Sciences and Engineering Research Council of Canada Discovery Grant to Xin Wang and National Natural Science Foundation of China (No. 41271387).

References

1. Canadian Energy Research Institute (CERI), http://www.ceri.ca
2. Butler, R.: SAGD Comes of AGE! Journal of Canadian Petroleum Technology. **37**(07), 1–4 (2013)
3. Alberta Energy Regulator (AER), http://www.aer.ca
4. Alberta Energy, http://www.energy.alberta.ca
5. IHS, http://www.ihs.com
6. Divestco, http://www.divestco.com
7. GeoLOGIC systems ltd., http://www.geologic.com
8. Zangl, G., Hannerer, J.: Data Mining: Applications in the Petroleum Industry. Round Oak Pub (2003)
9. Lienert, C., Weingartner, R., Hurni, L.: An interactive, web-based, real-time hydrological map information system. Hydrological Sciences Journal. **56**(1), 1–16 (2011)
10. Lai, J., Luo, J., Zhang, M.: Design and Realization of the Intangible Cultural Heritage Information Management System Based on Web Map Service. Advances in Information Technology and Industry Applications. 605-612 (2012)
11. Freyman, W. A., Glennemeier, K. A.: Restoration Map: A Web-based Tool for Spatial and Participatory Adaptive Management of Ecological Restoration Projects. **32**(1), 3–6 (2014)
12. Government of Saskatchewan, http://www.infomaps.gov.sk.ca
13. PetroFeed Inc., https://www.petrofeed.com/maps

14. Evans, F., Volz, W., Dorn, G., Fröhlich, B., Roberts, D.M.: Future trends in oil and gas visualization. In: Proceedings of the conference on Visualization 2002 (VIS 2002), pp. 567-570. IEEE Computer Society, Washington, DC (2002)
15. Jiawei, H., Kamber, M., Jian, P.: Data Mining: Concepts and Techniques. Morgan Kaufman, San Francisco (2001)
16. Liu, S., Xue, L.: The Application of Fuzzy Clustering to Oil and Gas Evaluation. In: Fifth International Conference on Fuzzy Systems and Knowledge Discovery, FSKD 2008, vol. 3, pp. 644-647. IEEE Press, New York (2008)
17. Cai, Y., Wang, X., Hu, K., Dong, M.: A Data Mining Approach to Finding Relationships between Reservoir Properties and Oil Production for CHOPS. Computers & Geosciences. **73**, 37–47 (2014)
18. Aulia, A., Keat, T.B., Maulut, M.S., El-Khatib, N., Jasamai, M.: Smart Oilfield Data Mining for Reservoir Analysis. International Journal of Engineering and Technology. **10**(6), 78–88 (2010)
19. Montgomery, E.B., Clark, D.A., Gibson, B.B., Sheptycki, R.J., Batty, I.: The Canadian Unique Well Identifier (1978)
20. Agrawal, R., Srikant, R.: Fast algorithms for mining association rules in large databases. In: Proceedings of the 20th International Conference on Very Large Data Bases, VLDB, pp. 487-499 (1994)
21. Cenovus, http://www.cenovus.com

SpatioTemporal Trajectories and Navigation

Spatial Selectivity Estimation for Web Searching

Kostas Patroumpas[1,2]([⊠])

[1] School of Electrical and Computer Engineering,
National Technical University of Athens, Athens, Hellas
kpatro@dblab.ece.ntua.gr
[2] Institute for the Management of Information Systems, Athena, RC, Hellas

Abstract. Estimating how many records qualify for a spatial predicate is crucial when choosing a cost-effective query execution plan, especially in presence of extra non-spatial criteria. The challenge is far bigger with *geospatial data on the Web*, as information is inherently disparate in many sites and effective search should avoid transmission of large datasets. Our idea is that fast, succinct, yet reliable estimates of spatial selectivity could incur significant reduction in query execution costs. Towards this goal, we examine variants of well known spatial indices enhanced with data distribution statistics, essentially building *spatial histograms*. We compare these methods in terms of performance and estimation accuracy over real datasets and query workloads of varying range. Our empirical study exhibits their pros and cons and confirms the potential of spatial histograms for optimized search on the Web of Data.

Keywords: Selectivity estimation · Spatial indexing · Histograms · Query optimization · RDF · Web search

1 Introduction

Searching over the Web of Data usually implies or even requires a geographic context. For instance, a portal may provide to users not only clips and reviews for a film, but also its screening times in nearby cinemas pinpointed on a map. Tourist guides for smartphones or tablets may associate landmark places with upcoming events close by, or recommend "must see" routes. And when looking online for a hotel, aside from pricing and recent customer ratings, proximity to public transport or to city attractions could also matter for the final choice.

But it is highly improbable that all this information resides on a single server. Actually, its pieces must be retrieved from several disparate sites and then combined together to provide complete answers. In the case of distributed spatial databases, each site hosts a different spatial relation, so queries involving joins may incur high processing and data transmission costs [28]. However, the content of a single relation may be partitioned as well; e.g., disjoint subsets of points of interest for the entire planet may be retained in different machines. Besides, web documents may include explicit or implicit geographical references (like place names or postal codes), hence calling for advanced spatio-textual

© Springer International Publishing Switzerland 2015
J. Gensel and M. Tomko (Eds.): W2GIS 2015, LNCS 9080, pp. 107–123, 2015.
DOI: 10.1007/978-3-319-18251-3_7

indexing [29]. A recent trend is to represent information as web recources of
$< Subject, Predicate, Object >$, according to the *Linked Data* paradigm [7].
Such *RDF triples* [20] may be exposed from several SPARQL endpoints [26] and
can be associated together thanks to unique identifiers (IRIs). Accordingly, the
Open Geospatial Consortium (OGC) has endorsed the GeoSPARQL standard
[17] for representing and querying spatial data on the Semantic Web.

In this work, we specifically focus on selectivity estimation over geospatial
data on the Web. As in traditional relational DBMSs, query optimizers should
be able to use reliable estimates of result sizes in order to determine the most
efficient query execution plans. But things get complicated for queries with spatial predicates over large geographic datasets. First, data may consist not only of
points, but also of more complex geometries [17], like polylines, polygons, geometry collections, etc. Furthermore, geometries can be widely spread in space,
ranging from high density concentrations (e.g., points of interest in city centers)
to a few isolated places (e.g., islands in the Atlantic). Most importantly, data
may be subdivided among several remote sites, so a query has to examine each
one, collect intermediate results, and finally match them to return the qualifying answers. As in distributed spatial databases, an execution plan should avoid
naïvely shipping entire relations to the query site; instead, it should attempt to
minimize data transmissions [30]. Moreover, query optimizers must cope with
mixed queries that include both *spatial* and non-spatial (i.e., *thematic*) predicates [29]. For instance, it is not expected that a user should generally ask for
places in the city center (i.e., the search range), but distinctively for hotels or
restaurants, occasionally specifying additional thematic conditions (e.g., luxury
hotels or fish restaurants). In fact, most user requests are like this.

We deem that spatial indices and statistics on data distribution can be valuable when choosing query execution plans. A suitable plan can intertwine evaluation of spatial and thematic predicates and return answers faster. If spatial
selectivity is low (i.e., few geometries qualify), it makes sense to first evaluate the
spatial predicate guided by the index, and handle thematic criteria afterwards.
In case spatial selectivity is high (i.e., more geometries are expected to satisfy
the spatial predicate), optimizers may choose a different plan, deferring probing
of geometries. Thus, evaluation can avoid full scans, which is very costly when
millions of features are actually stored. Having even a rough estimate of how
many geometries potentially qualify for topological predicates (e.g., `contains`
or `intersects` [17]), may incur significant savings in processing costs.

The core idea of our approach is to enhance well-known *spatial access methods*
[10] in order to quickly yield approximate, yet quite reliable, spatial selectivity
estimates. In effect, we adjust variants of grid partitioning schemes, quadtrees
[23], and R-trees [4, 12] towards *spatial analogues of histograms*. Essentially, rectangular regions in space are abstracted as *"buckets"*, which can retain aggregated statistics (e.g., counts) about the geometries therein. We have extensively
tested several types of spatial histograms against query workloads of varying
range sizes and compared their performance and estimation accuracy. We stress
that our focus is mostly on the spatial part of queries. This poses the greatest

difficulty to analyze, due to skewness and non-uniform density in most geo-datasets. In perspective, our analysis could greatly assist in advanced optimization for spatial queries on distributed [28] or RDF geodata [8,15], by taking into account spatial selectivities when choosing suitable query plans, e.g., reordering joins, pushing down spatial selections, etc. Our contribution can be summarized as follows:

- We discuss the benefits of fast, reliable selectivity estimation on spatial data, chiefly in the context of distributed and RDF query processing (Section 2).
- We analyze how it is possible to extend some powerful state-of-the-art spatial access methods in order to obtain spatial selectivity estimates (Section 3).
- We conduct an empirical validation with various query workloads to assess spatial histograms in terms of performance and quality (Section 4).

2   Background and Related Work

2.1   Spatial Indexing

For fast retrieval, a spatial object is usually approximated by its *minimum bounding rectangle* (*MBR*), which fully encloses its geometry in an iso-oriented box with sides parallel to the axes. Such MBRs can be indexed with a variety of *spatial access methods* [10] as indicators of the distribution and size of exact geometries. Apart from points, these indices can also manage geometries with an extent, such as lines, polygons, or even polyhedra with $d > 2$ dimensions.

Spatial indexing is most valuable when processing numerous geometries. For example, *range queries* identify geometries intersecting with a search region q, e.g., a polygon or a circle. Spatial query processing adheres to the *"filter-and-refinement"* paradigm [21]. It first probes the index to quickly identify a superset of candidate answers; the final results are issued after exact geometric computations. Next, we outline properties of some well-known spatial indices. Without loss of generality, we concentrate on range queries over data in $d=2$ dimensions.

Uniform Grid Partitioning. A regular decomposition of a given area of interest (hereafter termed *universe* $\mathcal{U}$) is a *space-driven* access method [21]. A simple, yet effective subdivision is to overlay $\mathcal{U}$ with a uniform grid of equi-sized *cells* (a.k.a. *buckets*), as shown in Fig. 1a. Grid *granularity* c controls the number of cells per axis, leading into a total $c \times c$ cells for a $2D$ universe. Each geometry is trivially assigned to those cells it overlaps with. Thus, grids allow fast indexing and are used especially for points or frequently changing locations [25].

Grid partitioning can greatly assist in *range search*. If a cell is completely within a rectangular range q, all its geometries can be instantly returned as answers. But each object assigned to a cell partially covered by range q must be accurately probed, because it may not intersect q at all. Thus, search performance may be negatively affected if grid granularity c is too fine or too coarse.

Quadtrees [23] (known as *octrees* [24] in $3D$ spaces) are hierarchical data structures based on recursive decomposition of universe $\mathcal{U}$. The most typical variant

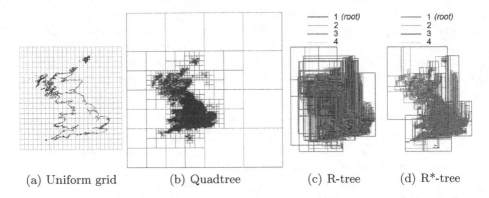

(a) Uniform grid   (b) Quadtree   (c) R-tree   (d) R*-tree

Fig. 1. Spatial indexing schemes over OpenStreetMap datasets for Great Britain

is the *region quadtree*, which subdivides $\mathcal{U}$ into equi-sized, disjoint *quadrants* by means of iso-oriented hyperplanes. The root node always represents the entire $\mathcal{U}$. In $d=2$ dimensions, every internal node has four descendants, each corresponding to a quadrant. Once a quadrant obtains more entries than its *capacity c*, it splits into four children labeled counterclockwise, as NE, NW, SW, SE quadrants of their parent node. Quadtrees are not necessarily balanced; regions densely packed with geometries are subdivided on and on, as illustrated in Fig. 1b. Leaf nodes represent data blocks for which no further subdivision is necessary.

Regarding *searching*, quadtrees resemble to binary search trees. At each node, a decision is made on which quadrant(s) require further search, by checking spatial overaps with the given query range q. This step is recursively repeated until the leaves are reached, which eventually yield the candidate answers.

Family of R-Trees. An R-tree [12] organizes a hierarchy of nested d-dimensional rectangles, with all leaves at the same level. Each node corresponds to a disk page and represents the MBR of its descendant nodes. For a leaf, its MBR is the tightest d-dimensional box covering all its geometries. As shown in Fig. 1c with the multi-coloured boxes per level, MBRs at the same level may overlap. To prevent tree degeneration and ensure efficient storage utilization, the number of entries per node (excluding the root) is between a lower bound m and maximum capacity M. Updates may affect nodes across many levels upto the root.

Searching in R-trees always starts from the root. MBRs in any visited node are tested for intersection against search region q. Qualifying entries are recursively visited until the leaf level or until no further overlaps are found. Several paths may be probed, because multiple sibling entries could overlap with q.

The data insertion phase is most critical for good search performance. Hence, the R*-tree [4] introduces *"forced reinsertion"*: upon overflow, a node is not split right away, but 30% of its entries are removed and reinserted. This is coupled with an improved splitting policy aiming to minimize overlaps between MBRs at the same level, as well as MBR perimeters (Fig. 1d). Thanks to such optimizations, R*-trees can offer up to 50% performance gain [4] compared to original R-trees.

2.2   Spatial Selectivity Estimates in Query Optimization

Prior to data processing with the possible assistance of a spatial index, choosing a suitable execution plan may be a tough task for the query optimizer. This choice is usually made according to selectivity estimates from accumulated statistics. *Histograms* are the prominent such technique in databases [13], thanks to computational efficiency and little space cost. By partitioning the data into a few *"buckets"*, they approximate well the distribution of subsets in each bucket.

Query processors usually separate evaluation of spatial predicates from thematic conditions. They (i) either evaluate the spatial part first and then match its results to the thematic condition; or (ii) execute the thematic criteria first, and check qualifying features against the spatial predicate afterwards. The decision is based on which path most likely incurs less processing. This surely applies to the case of geographical web searching, as the evaluation of spatio-textual indexing methods in [29] indicates, but it may also involve the amount of data transmitted across sites [30]. In the particular case of distributed spatial join processing, a semijoin-based operator was proposed in [28] so as to get approximate descriptors from data in remote sites and save useless comparisons. Devised specifically for geospatial RDF data and based on Hilbert encoding, the hierarchical scheme in [15] offers significant cost savings when evaluating range and spatial join queries with thematic criteria. Strabon [11], a spatiotemporal RDF prototype, profits from its underlying database optimizer and can choose good execution plans for mixed queries. Note that a suitable plan against RDF data should additionally incur the fewest result bindings among triples [3]. So, the query planner must be deeply modified to recognize a spatial index and optimize joins between spatial features and other intermediate results from graph-pattern evaluation [8].

Yet, estimating *spatial selectivity* has more challenges. Geometries may differ in shape and size, e.g., islands in the Aegean Sea. Spatial entities may not overlap, but their placement can be highly skewed (e.g., islands clustered in Cyclades, but dispersed in the Northern Aegean). Hence, spatial approximation must capture the value domain of data distribution. Estimates from sampling, equi-area or equi-count heuristics are rather poor, as the resulting buckets cannot easily adapt to fluctuations in spatial density. *Min-Skew* [1] was the first to offer selectivity estimates by constructing skew-resistant binary space partitionings using a given amount of memory. There since have been several approaches to spatial selectivity estimation, e.g., [2,9,16,22,27], most of them based on variants of spatial indices with heuristics to overcome skewness. In this work, we specifically focus on object counts per bucket, as a simple, yet powerful hint of the data distribution. With minimal modifications in standard spatial indices, we intend to offer affordable means of estimating selectivity for spatial range queries against millions of geometric objects on the Web (e.g., GeoSPARQL endpoints).

3   Employing Spatial Histograms as Selectivity Estimators

Next, we propose variants of state-of-the-art spatial access methods: *grid partitioning*, *quadtrees*, and *R-trees*. Universe $\mathcal{U}$ is approximated by a $2D$ histogram

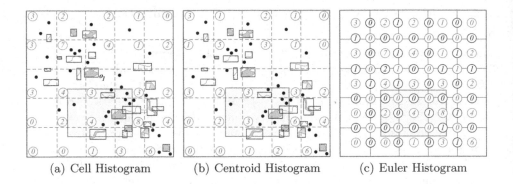

(a) Cell Histogram   (b) Centroid Histogram   (c) Euler Histogram

Fig. 2. Examples of grid-based histograms

with buckets associated to the spatial density in the subdivision, i.e., the number of geometry MBRs overlapping each bucket. Index functionality remains intact, but our main concern is to obtain selectivities directly from bucket counts after traversing the histogram, and without accessing the detailed geometries.

3.1   Grid-Based Histograms

Cell Histograms. Given a grid overlay of granularity c per axis, we propose that each square cell also retains a counter, which sums up geometries assigned to that cell. We call this structure *Cell Histogram*. Once a query range q is applied at runtime, the counts of its overlapping cells can be summed up to provide a fair estimation of the geometries involved in the search. Encircled values at cell corners in Fig. 2a indicate such counts for a setting that includes MBRs (boxes in black outline) of points, curves, and polygon geometries.

This approach is fine for points, as each location is counted only once. Unlike points that either fall inside a cell or not, a line or polygon may span several cells. If the MBR of such a geometry g overlaps with many cells, g must be referred to by each one; thus a single geometry may increment counters at multiple cells. In the example setting of Fig. 2a, the MBR of object o_1 affects counters in four cells. In case of a spatial query that covers all those four cells, o_1 will be counted four times, incurring a 300% overestimation. Obviously, when estimating selectivity from cell histograms, there is no way to avoid this *multiple-count problem* [27], other than by detailed examination, which of course has a prohibitive cost during query plan selection. Indeed, when a range query q (shown with a green rectangle) is examined against the cell histogram in Fig. 2a, estimated selectivity from the six overlapping cells is 26. Obviously, this deviates too much from the exact number of 15 geometries that query q actually intersects.

Centroid Histograms. An alternative policy is to count each MBR only once, no matter if it covers multiple cells in the underlying grid. Incrementing the counter of the cell that contains the centroid of a geometry is a plausible option;

hence, we call this scheme a *Centroid Histogram*. In this case, the grand total of the count values per cell is equal to the number of geometries indexed by the grid. Figure 2b illustrates the values of cell counters according to this approach, which provides an estimated selectivity of 22 for the range query q shown in green colour. However, this histogram has an inherent drawback: it does not account for partial cell overlaps, so estimation accuracy can be significantly biased.

Euler Histograms were introduced in [5] to specifically address the multiple-count problem, owing their concept to Euler's formula for planar, embedded, connected graphs [6]. They allocate counters not only to grid cells, but also to cell edges and vertices. Figure 2c depicts an Euler histogram for the same setting as in Fig. 2a; note that original geometries are omitted for clarity. Having additional counters for cell edges (shown in black colour) and vertices (in red) overlapping a geometry, it can distinguish between a large object spanning many cells and small objects fully contained in a single cell. Given a d-dimensional range query q, its selectivity can be calculated from an Euler histogram [5,27] as:

$$Selectivity(q) = \sum_{0 \leq k \leq d} (-1)^k F_k(q)$$

where $F_k(q)$ is a k-dimensional facet intersecting query q. In particular, a 0-d facet is a vertex, a 1-d facet is an edge and a 2-d facet is a cell box. If query range q aligns with the grid (i.e., no partial overlaps with any cells), then this estimate is accurate and incurs no error at all. The example query shown as a green rectangle in Fig. 2c intersects 4 vertices (0-d facets), 12 edges (1-d facets), and 9 cells (2-d facets) of the Euler histogram. Summing up the partial counts per facet according to the formula, provides a selectivity estimate of $(-1)^0 \times (0+0+0+0) + (-1)^1 \times (1+0+0+0+1+0+0+0+0+0+0+1) + (-1)^2 \times (4+3+3+2+4+8+0+1+3) = 25$, well above the number of 15 geometries that intersect this query range.

Multiscale Euler histograms [16] take advantage of object "scales" and offer results at multiple resolutions. But their concept is different, as they can effectively summarize specific topological relations (`contains`, `contained`, `overlap`, and `disjoint`) against a given range.

Overall, grid-based histograms are fast in estimating selectivities (especially at coarser granularities), but these values may largely deviate from actual results.

3.2   Quad-Histograms

In case that spatial indexing involves point data only, a standard region quadtree can be very efficient. But for composite geometries (e.g., curves, polygons), assigning MBRs into quadrants entails significant discrepancies in selectivity estimates due to the multiple count effect. So, we introduce *Quad-histograms*, specifically for indexing MBRs and offering reliable selectivity estimates on geometries. This data structure is loosely inspired by *MX-CIF quadtrees* devised in [14] for representing a large set of tiny rectangles in VLSI design rule checking. It is also reminiscent of *irregular octrees* [24], where each object is held only once, but objects crossing a partitioning plane (regardless of size) are retained at a higher

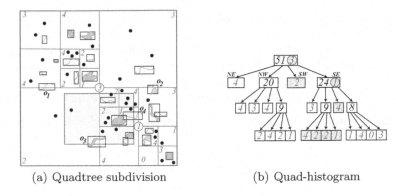

(a) Quadtree subdivision   (b) Quad-histogram

Fig. 3. Quadtree subdivision and the resulting histogram with quadrant capacity $c = 4$

level. In the context of large geodatasets on the Web, our goal is to guess how many geometries (from several quadrants) intersect a given query range.

A quad-histogram is organized similarly to a region quadtree, except that it stores entries not only in leaves, but *in internal nodes as well*. Our policy is to store each MBR in the node whose associated quadrant provides the tightest fit without intersecting this MBR. Once a leaf node A exceeds its capacity c, its region is subdivided into four equal-sized quadrants. Then, each MBR in node A is checked for inclusion in the newly formed children nodes (and subsequently deallocated from A). In case that an MBR cannot fit within a child quadrant, it remains assigned to A and is not delegated to its descendants. Our partitioning policy differs from the one in MX-CIF quadtree [14]; there, a region is repeatedly subdivided until no rectangle is fully contained in a quadrant. It also differs from *Q-histograms* [22], where, for a fixed number of buckets B, quadtree leaves are partitioned into B groups such that geometries per group are as uniformly distributed as possible. In our structure, quadrant splitting occurs once a leaf overflows, whereas internal nodes may contain more than c entries, if necessary. Figure 3 illustrates a subdivision of $2D$ universe $\mathcal{U}$ and the counts per quadrant (same setting as in Fig. 2), assuming node capacity $c=4$. The NE, NW, SW, SE quadrants are listed from left to right at each histogram level in Fig. 3b.

Aside from MBRs, each node in a quad-histogram also holds two counters:

- *The number n of local entries* pertaining to this node, because they cannot fit in any of its children. In Fig. 3, such counts are the encircled red values at the center of two quadrants. The root node holds $n=3$ MBRs itself: o_1 and o_2 are crossing the partitioning line along the x-axis, whereas MBR for o_3 is found along the y-splitting. The MBR of o_4 goes to the SE quadrant below the root, as it cannot fit into any other descendant node.
- The *total number m* of MBRs contained *in its subtree*. This value can be updated in a top-down fashion once a new MBR is inserted from the root. At every quadrant overlapping this new MBR, its associated counter m is incremented; this is repeatedly applied until either the new MBR reaches a

leaf that fully contains it or it gets assigned to an internal node. In Fig. 3a, these m values are shown at a corner of each quadrant. For example, the top NE quadrant fully contains $m=4$ geometries (three points and a curve); hence, it is filled up to capacity ($c=4$) and requires no further partitioning. Instead, its sibling top NW quadrant includes $m=20$ geometries, hence it is recursively split into finer subdivisions. Total counts m of such further split quadrants at internal nodes are shown in black colour in Fig. 3b.

To estimate selectivity for a range query q, a quad-histogram is traversed from the root like a quadtree. At each level, if the quadrant of a node A is totally within q, then visiting its subtree can be safely avoided; all relevant selectivity is readily available from counters n and m at node A. In case that q intersects (but not fully covers) a given quadrant, searching proceeds to the next level by examining each subquadrant overlapping with q. Count n of geometries locally held in node A is added to the estimate, but value m is ignored because the subtree will be further explored and a more accurate estimate can be obtained. Of course, quadrants not overlapping with range q can be safely pruned. When estimating selectivities, MBRs in leaves are never examined in detail. For query q shown in green colour in Fig. 3, the quad-histogram estimates that 19 geometries may be intersecting q. This value is obtained from green-shaded nodes in Fig. 3b and includes *local counters* from the root and its SE quadrant (values in red). This estimate is closer to the exact number (15) of qualifying geometries compared to selectivities from grid-based histograms in Fig. 2. As our experiments in Section 4 verify for various range sizes, this quadtree-based strategy has low overhead, and probing a few quadrants may suffice for a fair selectivity estimate.

3.3   Aggregate R-trees as Spatial Histograms

R-trees and R*-trees can greatly facilitate processing of various types of spatial queries, but cannot natively guide selection of an apt execution plan. To remedy this deficiency, we suggest enhancing every tree node with a counter, which simply retains the number of geometries held underneath by its subtree.

It is no surprise that such a variant R-tree has been already utilized for OLAP operations over spatial features. The *aggregate R-tree* (aR-tree) [19] inherits from R-tree the principle of clustering over input geometries, and improves it towards aggregate processing. Each entry of aR-tree holds summarized statistics about geometries residing in the underlying subtree. In the particular case of count aggregates, each MBR also retains the cardinality of objects therein. No double counting ever occurs, since each geometry only belongs to a single MBR. Updating counters is combined with insertions, as a single path is always traversed. In Fig. 4, geometries are enclosed in blue MBRs at the bottom level, and red boxes are their parents in root; numbers denote geometry counts per node. *aR*-trees* can be derived similarly from R*-trees, without altering core operations.

As soon as a spatial predicate q (e.g., the green box in Fig. 4a) is applied against this histogram, an approximate estimation of the geometries involved can be given. Like a typical range query q over an R-tree [12], it performs a check

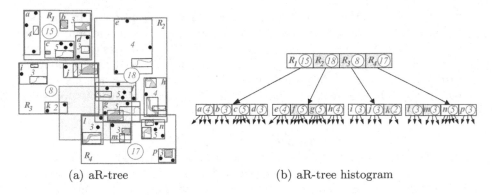

(a) aR-tree   (b) aR-tree histogram

Fig. 4. An aR-tree histogram having between $m = 2$ and $M = 5$ entries per node

against MBRs that fully or partially overlap with q. The algorithm descends the tree (perhaps at multiple paths) to detect such MBRs and simply sums up their counts. In the example of Fig. 4, searching starts from root entries R_2, R_3, and R_4, i.e., those overlapping with range q. From their respective subtrees, it is found that entries f, g, k, l, and m actually intersect q. The counters maintained in these five nodes finally provide an estimated selectivity of 18, which is much closer to the exact selectivity (15) than other spatial histograms.

However, such accuracy comes at a cost; building R-trees or R*-trees takes more time and their reorganization suffers in case of frequent updates [25]. Sometimes the number of nodes that need inspection may be high, as we discuss in the experiments. In another approach, *Rk-histograms* [9] are based on Hilbert packed R-trees and repeatedly split buckets with high skew until a given threshold, but they incur high construction time and may introduce unnecessary buckets.

4   Experimental Validation

4.1   Experimental Setup

In our use case scenario, OpenStreetMap data for Great Britain [18] were converted into RDF triples with millions of GeoSPARQL-compliant geometries. As detailed in Table 1, we have chosen indicative layers for each geometry type: points of interest, road centerlines, and polygons of natural resources.

We also generated query workloads for testing each histogram. In order for queries to be representative and conform to the actual data distribution, we randomly picked up 10 000 points from the OSM dataset and used them as centers for the respective query ranges. As the size of a query range has a strong influence on selectivity, we generated several workloads with those fixed centers but differing extents. Range size was expressed as percentage $a\%$ of the entire universe $\mathcal{U}$ (i.e., the iso-oriented MBR that encloses Great Britain). Ranges were not necessarily squares with the given centers, because we randomly modified their width and height to get arbitrarily elongated rectangles of equal area a. To

Table 1. Contents of the utilized OSM layers for Great Britain

Layer	Geometry	Cardinality
Points of interest	Point	590390
Road network	LineString	2601040
Forests, parks, waterbodies	Polygon	264570

Table 2. Experiment parameters

Parameter	Values
Number of input features	**3456000**
Number $|Q|$ of queries	**10000**
Range size ($a\%$ of $\mathcal{U}$)	0.1, 0.5, **1**, 2, 5, 10
Grid granularity c per axis	100, **200**, 300, 400, 500, 1000
Quadrant capacity c	25, **50**, 100, 200, 400
R-tree page size (in KB)	1, **2**, 4, 8

assess the impact of selectivities, we evaluated query plans involving a thematic condition as well as a spatial range. In this case, queries must also filter entities by a specific `rdf:type` (e.g., 'theatre', 'residential road', or 'waterbody').

Since we chiefly focus on selectivity of spatial predicates, all methods were implemented as standalone classes in C++ without any interaction with DBMSs or RDF stores. All data structures reside in main memory and are used to index MBRs for $2D$ points, lines, and polygons. Geometries in WKT serializations [17] are parsed from input RDF triples, and their MBRs get calculated. Afterwards, only MBRs are used in estimation and query evaluation. Estimates are based on spatial filtering, which selects any MBRs intersecting the query rectangle.

In comparing the various techniques, we used the following metrics:

- *Preprocessing cost* is the total time (in seconds) required to calculate MBRs from WKT serializations, build data structures, and populate all buckets.
- *Average number of buckets inspected per query* in order to estimate its spatial selectivity. This overhead depends on how many cells (for grid-based histograms) or nodes (for quadtrees and R-trees) overlap with query ranges.
- *Average evaluation cost per query* (in seconds) to issue final results.
- *Average Relative Error*. If SE_i is the estimated spatial selectivity according to a histogram, and AS_i is the number of geometries actually qualifying for a range query q_i, then average relative error RE [1] for query workload Q is expressed as:

$$RE = \frac{\sum_{q_i \in Q} |AS_i - SE_i|}{\sum_{q_i \in Q} AS_i}$$

We set up a XEN hypervisor running Linux on a Intel Core i7-3820 CPU at 3.60GHz with 10240KB cache, 16GB RAM, 2GB swap space, 4 CPU cores and 40GB disk space. We ran simulations using different settings for each method. Due to space limitations, we only discuss indicative results. Table 2 summarizes experiment parameters and their respective ranges; default values are in bold.

4.2   Experimental Results

First, we examine preprocessing costs required by each histogram scheme. Then, we study their behaviour for the same query workload under diverse spatial subdivisions. After choosing suitable settings per histogram, we compare their performance and quality in selectivity estimation for various query workloads.

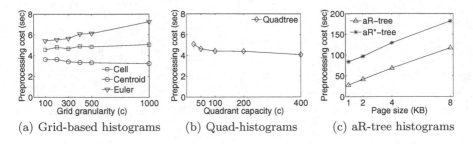

(a) Grid-based histograms   (b) Quad-histograms   (c) aR-tree histograms

Fig. 5. Preprocessing cost for various types of spatial histograms

Preprocessing cost. As depicted in Fig. 5a, the times taken to construct each grid-based histogram do not vary dramatically (8 seconds max). Centroid histograms incur less preprocessing, as they trivially need to assign a single point per geometry. Cell histograms need slightly more time, as each MBR may get assigned to multiple cells. The cost for Euler histograms is higher and rises linearly with granularity c, as more cell edges and vertices are allocated per MBR.

Regarding Quad-histograms, Fig. 5b indicates that the cost gets slightly reduced for increasing capacity c per quadrant. The more geometries accommodated in a quadrant, the less the nodes that will be created, so the resulting quadtree will have less depth. Notably, building a quad-histogram for the entire input did not take more than 5 seconds in the worst case.

But building aR-tree histograms is much more expensive, as plotted in Fig. 5c. The cost escalates with increasing page sizes per node, primarily due to the splitting overhead, and for the aR*-tree variant also due to forced reinsertions. If a node holds many entries and has to split, more comparisons must be made to share its contents. Compared to their space-driven counterparts, such data-driven spatial histograms require more time to be built (by an order of magnitude). In any case, preprocessing cost is paid only once, as long as no major geometry updates can cause readjustment of MBRs into cells or nodes.

Effect of varying spatial subdivisions. Next, we assess spatial histograms subdivided into a varying amount of buckets against a query workload of 10 000 rectangles ranging over a=1% of universe $\mathcal{U}$. Figure 6 illustrates the overhead expressed as average number of inspected buckets per query. Clearly, more cells must be checked for finer grid-based histograms (the same number in all three variants). Thus, it takes more time to compute estimates, although never more than 7 msec per query. With quad-histograms, fewer than 800 buckets per query need be probed, incurring less than 0.1 msec in estimation cost. As reflected in Fig. 6b, cost drops remarkably with increasing quadrant capacities as less buckets are created. In contrast, aR-tree histograms (Fig. 6c) must check thousands of buckets (within 3 msec max), although the number diminishes with larger page sizes (i.e., more entries per node). aR*-trees perform better, as they inherently incur less overlaps among sibling nodes and thus excel in pruning power.

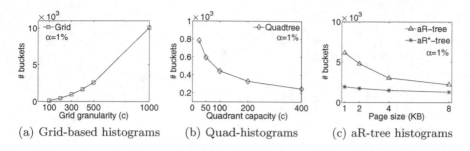

Fig. 6. Estimation overhead per query at various spatial subdivisions

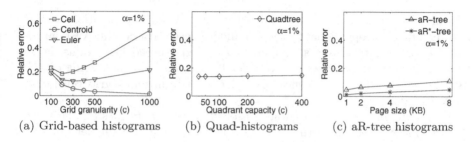

Fig. 7. Estimation quality for various spatial subdivisions

Yet, aR-trees seem unrivaled when it comes to quality of selectivity estimates. Figure 7c reveals that error is always less than 10% for standard aR-trees, reaching maximal discrepancy for larger page size (8 KB). But with aR*-trees, error never exceeds 5%, beating all other histograms. Figure 7a shows that Centroid histograms consistently surpass other grid-based variants and get more reliable for smaller cell sizes. Euler histograms are 20% off for most subdivisions, but always yield better estimates than Cell histograms. The latter are vulnerable to multiple counts, so they should not be trusted at finer granularities. For quad-histograms (Fig. 7b), error is stable around 15% no matter the quadrant capacity, as multi-counting never occurs. With the extra benefit of fast estimation, quad-histograms look robust enough to adjust even to skewed spatial distributions.

Comparison against varying range sizes. In Fig. 8 we plot how each histogram copes with varying range areas $a\%$ of $\mathcal{U}$. We report representative results for specific parameterizations per histogram (in bold in Table 2), which have shown good behaviour in previous tests. Note that these settings generate buckets of similar, *but not identical* capacity per histogram type. This happens because buckets in quadtrees are determined on-the-fly according to data distribution, whereas in aR-trees they depend on the insertion order as well.

Regarding estimation overhead (Fig. 8a), the number of inspected buckets per query naturally increases with greater ranges. Quadtrees consistently require the fewest node inspections, while standard aR-tree histograms must probe

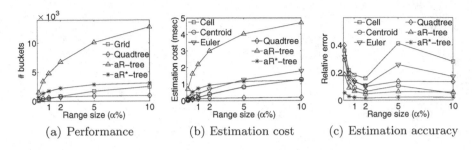

(a) Performance   (b) Estimation cost   (c) Estimation accuracy

Fig. 8. Comparison of spatial selectivity estimates for diverse range areas

thousands of nodes. This is also reflected in Fig. 8b, since estimation cost per query is directly proportional to the amount of accessed buckets. Average cost in aR*-trees for larger ranges competes that of grid-based histograms, and is always kept below 1 msec per query. Euler histograms incur increasing cost for larger ranges, as they must collect partial counts from many grid cells, edges and vertices.

But the major concern is accuracy of selectivity estimates. As Fig. 8c shows, aR*-trees are superior, incurring the less error. Especially for smaller ranges, it should be expected that the number of qualifying geometries may be significantly lower; hence, occasional false positives would lead to increasing errors. Yet, aR*-trees never exceed a 5% error, whereas aR-tree estimates may be biased even by 20% for areas as small as $a = 0.1\%$ of $\mathcal{U}$. Euler and Cell histograms fail for either too small or too large range sizes, with error up to 40%. This originates from the choice of grid granularity, which is not flexible to cope with widely diverse query extents. Unfortunately, one cell size cannot fit every variation in query ranges. This inherent weakness of flat, rigid decompositions is more pronounced due to multi-counting in the associated buckets, hence these wide discrepancies between estimated and actually qualifying geometries. Centroid histograms may avoid this trap, and yield moderately good estimates especially for larger ranges. In between, quad-histograms offer fair accuracy, about 15% off in most estimates. Thanks to their negligible cost for probing (Fig. 8b), quad-histograms may be considered as a good trade-off between overhead and quality.

Evaluation of mixed queries. Next, we use high-quality spatial selectivities estimated from aR*-trees and compare plans for mixed queries with a spatial predicate (of varying range $a\%$) and a thematic predicate θ (of diverse selectivity σ_θ too). We distinguish three alternative plans: (i) Plan *BIND* evaluates spatial and thematic predicates separately, and binds partial results with matching IRIs; (ii) Plan *Spatial FIRST* uses the spatial histogram to evaluate the range condition, and then checks if any returned features qualify for the specified θ; and (iii) Plan *Thematic FIRST* probes a hash index to identify features matching the thematic condition, and then filters out those not intersecting the given range.

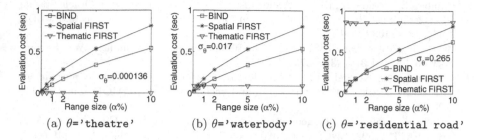

(a) θ='theatre'   (b) θ='waterbody'   (c) θ='residential road'

Fig. 9. Evaluating diverse execution plans for mixed queries at varying selectivities

Figure 9 plots average execution times per query. When thematic selectivity σ_θ is extremely low (Fig. 9a), it makes sense to evaluate thematic condition first, then filtering its few results through the spatial range, and issuing final answers almost instantly. But when more features potentially qualify for the thematic predicate, other plans may be preferred. As shown in Fig. 9c, evaluating spatial predicates first is essential for range sizes roughly smaller than 1% of $\mathcal{U}$ (i.e., low spatial selectivity), while binding partial results from separate evaluation would be preferable when both selectivities are large. Thus, availability of reliable spatial and thematic selectivities can guide choosing of cost-effective plans.

5   Concluding Remarks

In this paper, we examined techniques for selectivity estimation in queries over large geospatial datasets. We enhanced well-known indexing methods towards spatial analogues of histograms, which can quickly yield approximate, yet quite reliable selectivity estimates for topological predicates. Our empirical study provided strong evidence that histograms adjusting to spatial density and skewness can meet the performance and accuracy demands of query optimization.

It goes without saying that such selectivity estimators are also applicable in standard spatial processing (i.e., all data on a single site). But, we deem that concise histograms pay off in distributed processing, particularly when searching on the Semantic Web. As a pointer to future research, handling locality-optimized query plans in distributed RDF graphs is very challenging, since scalable evaluation of spatial predicates must incur little inter-node communication.

Acknowledgements. This work was partially supported by the European Commission grant #318159 *"GeoKnow – Making the Web an Exploratory Place for Geospatial Knowledge"*. Spiros Athanasiou and Giorgos Giannopoulos provided valuable feedback.

References

1. Acharya, S., Poosala, V., Ramaswamy, S.: Selectivity Estimation in Spatial Databases. In: ACM SIGMOD, pp. 13–24, June 1999

2. Bamba, B., Ravada, S., Hu, Y., Anderson, R.: Statistics Collection in Oracle Spatial and Graph: Fast Histogram Construction for Complex Geometry Objects. PVLDB **6**(11), 1021–1032 (2013)
3. Battle, R., Kolas, D.: GeoSPARQL: Enabling a Geospatial Semantic Web. Semantic Web Journal **3**(4), 355–370 (2012)
4. Beckmann, N., Kriegel, H.P., Schneider, R., Seeger, B.: The R*-tree: an efficient and robust access method for points and rectangles. In: SIGMOD, pp. 322–331 (1990)
5. Beigel, R., Tanin, E.: The geometry of browsing. In: Lucchesi, C.L., Moura, A.V. (eds.) LATIN 1998. LNCS, vol. 1380, pp. 331–340. Springer, Heidelberg (1998)
6. de Berg, M., van Kreveld, M., Overmars, M., Schwarzkopf, O.: Computational geometry - algorithms and applications, 2nd edn. Springer-Verlag (2000)
7. Bizer, C., Heath, T., Berners-Lee, T.: Linked Data - The Story So Far. IJSWIS **5**(3), 1–22 (2009)
8. Brodt, A., Nicklas, D., Mitschang, B.: Deep integration of spatial query processing into native RDF triple stores. In: ACM GIS, pp. 33–42, November 2010
9. Eavis, T., Lopez, A.: rK-Hist: an R-tree based histogram for multi-dimensional selectivity estimation. In: CIKM, pp. 475–484 (2007)
10. Gaede, V., Günther, O.: Multidimensional Access Methods. ACM Computing Surveys **30**(2), 170–231 (1998)
11. Garbis, G., Kyzirakos, K., Koubarakis, M.: Geographica: a benchmark for geospatial RDF stores. In: ISWC, pp. 343–359, October 2013
12. Guttman, A.: R-trees: a dynamic index structure for spatial searching. In: ACM SIGMOD, pp. 47–57, June 1984
13. Ioannidis, Y.: The history of histograms (abridged). In: VLDB, pp. 19–30 (2003)
14. Kedem, G.: The quad-CIF tree: a data structure for hierarchical on-line algorithms. In: DAC, pp. 352–357 (1982)
15. Liagouris, J., Mamoulis, N., Bouros, P., Terrovitis, M.: An Effective Encoding Scheme for Spatial RDF Data. PVLDB **7**(12), 1271–1282 (2014)
16. Lin, X., Liu, Q., Yuan, Y., Zhou, X.: Multiscale Histograms: summarizing topological relations in large spatial datasets. In: VLDB, pp. 814–825 (2003)
17. OGC Inc., GeoSPARQL Standard - A Geographic Query Language for RDF Data. URL: https://portal.opengeospatial.org/files/?artifact_id=47664
18. OpenStreetMap project. URL: http://www.openstreetmap.org/
19. Papadias, D., Kalnis, P., Zhang, J., Tao, Y.: Efficient OLAP operations in spatial data warehouses. In: Jensen, C.S., Schneider, M., Seeger, B., Tsotras, V.J. (eds.) SSTD 2001. LNCS, vol. 2121, pp. 443–459. Springer, Heidelberg (2001)
20. Resource Description Framework. URL: http://www.w3.org/TR/rdf-primer/
21. Rigaux, P., Scholl, M., Voisard, A.: Spatial Databases: with Application to GIS. Morgan-Kaufmann, San Fransisco (2002)
22. Roh, Y.J., Kim, J.H., Son, J.H., Kim, M.H.: Efficient Construction of Histograms for Multidimensional Data using Quad-trees. Elsevier DSS **52**(1), 82–94 (2011)
23. Samet, H.: The Quadtree and Related Hierarchical Data Structures. ACM Computing Surveys **16**(2), 187–260 (1984)
24. Shagam, J., Pfeiffer, J.: Dynamic Irregular Octrees. Technical Report, New Mexico State University (2003)
25. Šidlauskas, D., Šaltenis, S., Christiansen, C., Johansen, J., Šaulys, D.: Trees or grids? indexing moving objects in main memory. In: ACM GIS, pp. 236–245 (2009)
26. SPARQL 1.1 Query Language. URL: http://www.w3.org/TR/sparql11-query/

27. Sun, C., Agrawal, D.P., El Abbadi, A.: Selectivity estimation for spatial joins with geometric selections. In: Jensen, C.S., Jeffery, K., Pokorný, J., Šaltenis, S., Bertino, E., Böhm, K., Jarke, M. (eds.) EDBT 2002. LNCS, vol. 2287, pp. 609–626. Springer, Heidelberg (2002)
28. Tan, K.-L., Ooi, B.C., Abel, D.J.: Exploiting Spatial Indexes for Semijoin-based Join Processing in Distributed Spatial Databases. TKDE **12**(6), 920–937 (2000)
29. Vaid, S., Jones, C.B., Joho, H., Sanderson, M.: Spatio-textual indexing for geographical search on the web. In: Medeiros, C.B., Egenhofer, M., Bertino, E. (eds.) SSTD 2005. LNCS, vol. 3633, pp. 218–235. Springer, Heidelberg (2005)
30. Zaamout, S., Osborn, W.: A strategy for optimizing a multi-site query in a distributed spatial database. In: Liang, S.H.L., Wang, X., Claramunt, C. (eds.) W2GIS 2013. LNCS, vol. 7820, pp. 16–24. Springer, Heidelberg (2013)

A Semantic-Based Data Model
for the Manipulation of Trajectories: Application
to Urban Transportation

Donia Zheni[1]([⊠]), Ali Frihida[2], Christophe Claramunt[3],
and Henda Ben Ghezala[4]

[1] ISAMM, University of Manouba, Manouba, Tunisia
donia.zheni@gmail.com
[2] CONTOS2, ENIT, University Tunis Al-Manar, Tunis, Tunisia
alifrihida@gmail.com
[3] Naval Academy Research Institute, Brest, France
christophe.claramunt@ecole-navale.fr
[4] RIADI, ENSI, University of Manouba, Manouba, Tunisia
henda.BG@cck.rnu.tn

Abstract. Nowadays, the increasing development of positioning and wireless communication technologies favors a better real-time integration and manipulation of large spatial databases. This offers many new opportunities for the development of trajectory databases, but a number of research challenges are still open as the generated information is often unstructured, continuous, large and sometimes unpredictable. The research presented in this paper develops a modeling approach that integrates the semantic, spatial and temporal dimensions when representing spatial trajectories at the abstract and logical levels. A data manipulation language that supports the querying and analysis of large trajectory databases is also proposed. The spatial database model is based on algebraic data types, and a prototype is developed on top of the DBMS PostgreSQL/PostGIS. The whole approach and the prototype development have been experimented and applied to benchmark transportation data derived from an origin-destination survey in the region of Quebec in Canada.

Keywords: Trajectory modeling · Moving object databases · Abstract data type · Temporal GIS

1 Introduction

Over the past few years many papers have been published on spatio-temporal database modeling issues. These researches have focused on different needs such as the integration of space and time and the representation of continuous paths [3], relative motion [8], simulation and prediction of movements [9] and semantic trajectories modeling [7], [13] [15], [17].

At another level, Time Geography has also long studied and provided a modeling framework to represent the behavior of human beings in an urban space.

© Springer International Publishing Switzerland 2015
J. Gensel and M. Tomko (Eds.): W2GIS 2015, LNCS 9080, pp. 124–142, 2015.
DOI: 10.1007/978-3-319-18251-3_8

Time Geography provides a seminal and rich theoretical framework to comprehend and analyze transportation behaviors [1]. In particular, the concept of *space-time path* has been suggested by early principles of Time Geography to model human trajectories considered as a combination of dynamic (e.g., trips) and static properties (e.g., activities) (cf. Figure 1). When integrated with Geographical Information Systems (GIS), Time Geography gives a rich set of modeling and manipulation principles that could be applied to the representation of human behavior [2], [5], [6], [10].

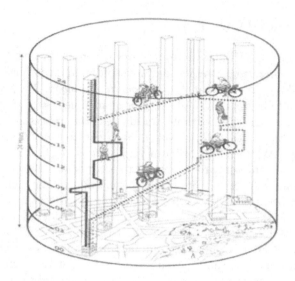

Fig. 1. The space-time path in Time Gography

However, despite its theoretical interest, Time Geography has not been fully integrated as a modeling support for the development of spatio-temporal DBMSs. So far, queries capabilities such as the ones provided by geo-relational languages do not encompass sufficient data representation and query capabilities to completely model and manipulate trajectory data. In fact, current approaches do not provide appropriate solutions to manipulate the semantics of spatio-temporal data. There is also a lack of consensus regarding the development of spatio-temporal data models.

The approach suggested in this paper introduces the principle of an Abstract Data Type (ADT) that encapsulates the spatial, temporal and semantics associated to a given trajectory. A spatial DBMS hosts the ADT as an extension plugin and is handled as a native data type as suggested elsewhere for complex data types [4], [11], [12], [14], [16], [18]. Overall, we propose a spatio-temporal (STT) abstract data type based on an algebraic modeling of disaggregated spatio-temoral trajectories. This supports the development of a set of operations that represent and cover the dynamics and the relations that depict individual moving behaviors. The STT is experimented against an origin-destination study hosted by Postgrsql/Postgis in which spatial data are handled by Quantum GIS as a map visualisation interface.

The remainder of the paper is structured as follows. Section 2 presents the main principles and definition of the STT abstract data type. Section 3 introduces a collection of spatial, temporal and spatio-temporal operations over the proposed SST abstract data type. Section 4 develops the prototype implementation and evaluation. Finally, section 5 concludes the paper and draws some perspectives.

2   STT Abstract Data Type

The specification of the STT data type requires different sorts (i.e., types). Let us assume the following usual atomic, complex, spatial and temporal data types: *Integer, Real, Boolean, String, Alist, Point, Polyline, Polygon, Time* and *Interval*. An *activity* description is formally given as a quadruple $a = (l, t_s, t_e, purpose)$ where $l \in Point$ represents its location, t_s and $t_e \in Time$ represent, respectively, its starting and ending times, and $purpose \in String$ its activity description (e.g., *shopping, working*). We formally define a trip as $d = (l_s, l_e, t_s, t_e, mode, path)$ where l_s, $l_e \in Point$ represent, respectively, its start and end locations; t_s and $t_e \in Time$ represent, respectively, its starting and ending times; $mode \in String$ denotes the mean used to make a trip. The attribute *path* represents the geometrical primitive of the trajectory, it can be directly considered as stepwise, for example using a polyline data type, or in order to approximate a continuous trip as a spatio-temporal sub-trajectory of type moving point as suggested in [4].

At the semantic level, a valid activity must start before it ends. A similar constraint applies to trips. The set of possible activity values is denoted by $D_a = \{a | a.t_s < a.t_e\}$. The set of possible trip values is denoted by $D_d = \{d | d.t_s < d.t_e\}$. Within a given STT, we assume that successive activities never temporally overlap. We denote the activity set of a STT as the temporally ordered subset A, as $A = \{a_i | \forall 1 \leq i < n : a_i \in D_a \wedge a_i.t_e < a_{i+1}.t_s\}$. Similarly, the trip set of a STT is the temporally ordered subset D, where $D = \{d_i | \forall 1 \leq i < n : d_i \in D_d \wedge d_i.t_e < d_{i+1}.t_s\}$. Consequently, a value of type STT is a pair (A, D) of temporally ordered sets. The first state of a STT is a trip d_1 succeeded by its goal, which is the activity a_1. The last state of the STT is the activity a_n. The domain of the proposed type is then specified, on the basis of temporal and spatial constraints as follows:

$$D_{STT} = \{(A, D) | (1, 2) 1 < i \leq n : d_i.l_s = a_{i-1}.l \wedge d_i.t_s = a_{i-1}.t_e + 1$$
$$(3, 4) 1 \leq i \leq n : d_i.l_e = a_i.l \wedge d_i.t_e = a_i.t_s - 1\} \tag{1}$$

Constraints (1) and (3) model the spatial relations between a trip and its previous and next activities, respectively. Constraints (2) and (4) model the temporal relations between successive states. The combination of these constraints represents the chaining of a STT. Time is indexed by the set of integers from 1 to n, the temporal granularity being application dependent.

3   STT Manipulation Operations

We introduce different kinds of operations to manipulate and verify the coherence of a STT, i.e., constructors (to create and modify a STT [11]), semantic, spatial, temporal and spatio-temporal operations. Regarding the categories proposed in our previous work [11], we added a sixth category encompassing the whole set of operations serving the validation of the database coherence. In the following paragraphs, we present short descriptions of these operations with their signatures and the semantics of the most representative ones. Overall, these operations constitute a set of core operations that can be also combined to build up more complex operations, as well as additional operations can be specified under similar principles.

3.1   Database Coherence

We introduce a set of operations that check the integrity of the STT data type. These operations may be used by a developper at the initialisation step of the STT data type. These operations permit to avoid errors related to the internal data structure. These operations can also be used to validate the whole database coherence.

The **check_activity** : $Activity \rightarrow Boolean$ and the **check_trip** : $Trip \rightarrow Boolean$ operations ensure the spatial and temporal coherence of an activity or trip. The operation **check_stt** : $STT \rightarrow Boolean$ verifies the value of a STT type. The type is valid if the set of component trips and activities respects the spatio-temporal chaining constraint previously defined. The operation **exists_stt**: $STT \times Instant \rightarrow Boolean$ checks the existence of a STT at a given time. Next, we present an example of operation semantics formally defined:

$$f_{check\_stt}(stt) := (\forall 1 \leq i \leq n : check\_activity(a_i) \wedge check\_trip(d_i) \wedge d_i.l_e =$$
$$a_i.l \wedge d_i.t_e = a_i.t_s - 1) \wedge (\forall 1 < i \leq n : d_i.l_s = a_{i-1}.l \wedge d_i.t_s = a_{i-1}.t_e + 1)(2)$$

3.2   Semantic Operations

Let us introduce a series of semantic operations that illustrate the potential of the manipulation language. Basic manipulation operations such as counting the number of components of a given trajectory or getting semantic attributes of some trips or activities in a a given trajectory have been introduced in previous works [11], [12].

Location operations: These operations retrieve the position of some specific events into a STT trip/activity chain. Let us consider a trip or an activity as an event, the values returned by this operation give an event at a determined position (e.g **Nth_Activity** : $STT \times Integer \rightarrow Activity$), an event list on a determined position (e.g **Activities_Before_Trip** : $STT \times Trip \rightarrow Alist$) or an integer denoting its position on the chain (e.g **Position_Trip** : $STT \times Trip \rightarrow Integer$).

Given an object of type STT and a trip d, a semantic example of these operations is illustrated as follows:

$$f_{Activities\_Before\_Trip}(stt, d) := \{a_i \in A | 1 \leq i \leq max\} \text{ if } (d \neq d_1) \wedge$$
$$(\exists 1 \leq max < n : d = d_{max+1}) \quad (3)$$

Semantic restriction operations: A semantic restriction operation **At_Activity_Activity** : $STT \times Activity \times Activity \rightarrow STT$ generates a new trajectory from a subset drawn from an initial trajectory. This generation fulfills several semantic parameters related to trips or activities. The parameters define which parts to be selected from the initial trajectory. Given an object of type STT and two activities a and aa such operation is defined as follows:

$$f_{At\_Activity\_Activity}(stt, a, aa) := (\{a, ..., aa\} \subset A, \{Trip\_Before\_Activity(stt, a)$$
$$, ..., Trip\_Before\_Activity(stt, aa)\} \subset D) \text{ if } \exists 1 \leq i \leq n, 1 \leq j \leq n : i < j \wedge$$
$$a_i = a \wedge a_j = aa \quad (4)$$

Semantic search operations: These operations retrieve some STT events on the basis of their semantic properties such as the transportation mode or trip motivation (e.g **Activities_With_Mode** : $STT \times String \rightarrow Alist$). Some of these operations allow to browse into the STT chain using a semantic criterion such as (**Next_Activity_With_Purpose** : $STT \times Activity \times String \rightarrow Activity$) or (**Previous_Trip_With_Mode** : $STT \times Trip \times String \rightarrow Trip$). Given an object STT and an object $m \in String$ the semantics of an example of operation is as follows:

$$f_{Activities\_With\_Mode}(stt, m) := \{a \in A | \exists d \in D : m \in d.mode \wedge a =$$
$$Activity\_After\_Trip(stt, d)\} \quad (5)$$

Projection operations: The goal of these operations is to realize a tri-dimentional projection of the trajectory as suggested by the Time Geography framework. Such operations are useful to retrieve events independently of the STT operations (e.g., **Activity_List that returns the list of activities of a given STT** : $STT \rightarrow Alist$). Below, a semantic example of these operations is given.

$$f_{Activity\_List}(stt) := stt.A \quad (6)$$

Semantic similarity operations: These operations can verify for example if two given trajectories are of the same order, $n \in \mathbb{N}$, and have a similar semantics behavior (e.g **Semantic _Similarity** : $STT \times STT \rightarrow Boolean$). Such similar semantics behavior means that each pair of activities having the same indexes into their respective STTs must also have the same purpose and each pair of trips must have the same mode. Given two objects $stt1$ and $stt2 \in STT$ then the semantics of such operation is expressed as follows:

$$f_{Semantic\_Similarity}(stt1, stt2) := (card(stt1.A) = card(stt2.A)) \wedge (\forall 1 \leq i \leq n,$$
$$stt1.A.a_i.purpose = stt2.A.a_i.purpose \wedge stt1.D.d_i.mode = stt2.D.d_i.mode) \quad (7)$$

Semantic predicates: These operations are used to verify if a trajectory is empty or if a given event belongs to the trajectory (e.g **Include_Activity**: $STT \times Activity \rightarrow Boolean$). Therefore, a semantic example illustrates the case. Given an object STT and an activity a then:

$$f_{Include\_Activity}(stt, a) := (a \in A) \tag{8}$$

3.3   Spatial Operations

Let us introduce a series of projection, manipulation and similarity operations that manipulate the spatial properties of the STT.

Projection operations into the spatial domain: These operations restrict totally or partially the trajectory to the spatial domain (cf. Figure 2). Totally, if the objective is to create "a spatial representation" of the trajectory. This case models for example the spatial path or the itinerary taken by a moving object (e.g **Itinerary** : $STT \rightarrow Polyline$). Partially, if the focus is on the activity locations of the moving object. Let us illustrate such projection operation with the following example. Given an object *stt* with a STT of cardinality $n \in \mathbb{N}$, and *concat* as a spatial operation that denotes a polyline creation resulting from the union of some adjacent polylines, we have:

$$f_{Itinerary}(stt) := \begin{cases} d_1.path & if\ length(stt) = 1 \\ l \in Polyline, \\ l = concat(< d_1.path, ..., d_n.path >) & else \end{cases} \tag{9}$$

Spatial relations: Spatial operations model topological relations between either a trajectory and a geometrical primitive or between different entities (e.g., **STT_Cross_Polyline**: $STT \times Polyline \rightarrow Boolean$) such as points (e.g., locations), polylines (e.g., itineraries) and polygons (e.g., parks). A signature and semantic example of such operation are given below. Given the object *stt*, $l \in polyline$ and assuming a topological relation *Cross*, we have:

$$f_{STT\_Cross\_Polyline}(stt, l) := Itinerary(stt)\ Cross\ l \tag{10}$$

Spatial neighborhood relations: These operations model neighborhood relations between different trajectories (e.g., **STT_SpatialNeighbour_STT**: $STT \times STT \times Real \rightarrow Boolean$) and between trajectories and spatial entities such as points, polylines and polygones. These operations can be specified using proximity calculus functions. Let us introduce the example of two objects *stt1* and *stt2*, and a real s number that materializes a proximity distance, the semantic of a neighbor operation is as follows:

$$f_{STT\_SpatialNeighbour\_STT}(stt1, stt2, s) := Neighbor(Itinerary(stt1),$$
$$Itinerary(stt2), s) \tag{11}$$

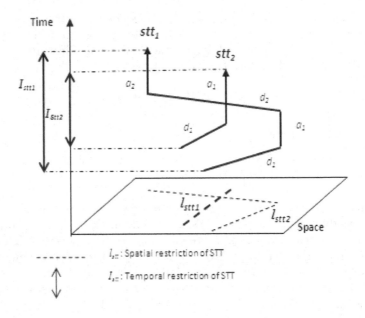

Fig. 2. Example of spatial and temporal projections

Spatial calculus operations: Spatial calculus operations can material-ize a large set of derivations such as the length of a trajectory, distance between two trajectories or between a trajectory and some spatial entities (e.g **STT_Distance_Point:** $STT \times Point \rightarrow Real$). An example of the semantic of such operations is shown below. Given an object stt, and a point entity p, we have:

$$f_{STT\_Distance\_Point}(stt, p) := distance(Itinerary(stt), p) \qquad (12)$$

Spatial search operations: These spatial search operations can retrieve some elements according to some specific spatial properties such as some trajectory activities performed at a specified location (e.g **FirstActivity_At_Point:** $STT \times Point \rightarrow Activity$), road or zone. A semantic example of these oper-ations is presented below. Given an object stt, and a point entity p, we have:

$$f_{FirstActivity\_At\_Point}(stt, p) := a_i \in A : (a_i.l = p) \wedge (if \ \exists j \neq i, 1 \leq j \leq n$$
$$such \ that \ a_j.l = p \Rightarrow i < j) \, (13)$$

Spatial similarity operations: Such operations can for example verify if two STTs follow the same spatial itinerary (e.g **Spatial_Similarity** : $STT \times STT \rightarrow Boolean$). Given two STT objects $stt1$ and $stt2$ then the semantics of this oper-ation is given as follows:

$$f_{Spatial\_Similarity}(stt1, stt2) := Itinerary(stt1) \ Equal \ Itinerary(stt2) \quad (14)$$

3.4   Temporal Operations

Let us introduce a series of projection, manipulation and similarity operations that manipulate the temporal properties of the STT.

Temporal relations operations: These operations are used to temporally compare different trajectories according to some temporal constraints (e.g **STT_After_Time** : $STT \times Time \rightarrow Boolean$). Let us introduce the signature and the semantic of an example to illustrate a temporal operation. Given an object *stt*, a time instant *t*, we have:

$$f_{STT\_After\_Time}(stt, t) := t < d_1.t_s \qquad (15)$$

Duration calculus operations: Mobile objects exhibit some specific properties that can be temporally analysed. These operations can support the analysis of the temporal properties of some trajectory activities (e.g **Activities_Duration**: $STT \rightarrow Real$) and trips' durations as illustrated in the following example. Given an object STT, we have:

$$f_{Activities\_Duration}(stt) := \sum_{i=1}^{n}(a_i.t_e - a_i.t_s) \qquad (16)$$

Temporal restriction operations: These operations restrict a given trajectory *stt* to a "sub-trajectory" fragment of *stt* given some temporal constraints. For example, the operation **At_Time** : $STT \times Time \rightarrow STT$ returns the minimal part of a STT (i.e., pair of activity/trip) which occurred at a given time. The semantics of this operation is formally obtained as follows. Given an object STT and a time instant *t* then:

$$f_{At\_Time}(stt, t) := (a_i \in A, d_i \in D) \text{if } \exists 1 \leq i \leq n : t \geq d_i.t_s \wedge t \leq a_i.t_e \quad (17)$$

Projection into the temporal domain operations: Such operations project a given trajectory to the temporal dimension. They can retrieve some specific time instants (e.g **First_Time** : $STT \rightarrow Time$) or intervals such as the the time interval during which the trajectory is defined (cf. Figure 2). For example and given a STT instance the semantics of *First_Time* is given as:

$$f_{First\_Time}(stt) := d_1.t_s \in Time \qquad (18)$$

Temporal search operation: These operations search for some specific properties of a given trajectory using a temporal criterion. For example, searching for actions performed at a particular time instant (e.g **Activity_At_Time** : $STT \times Time \rightarrow Activity$) or during a given time interval. Given a value *stt* belonging to STT and a time instant empht belonging to *Time* then:

$$f_{Activity\_At\_Time}(stt, t) := a_i \in A \text{ if } \exists 1 \leq i \leq n : t \geq a_i.t_s \wedge t \leq a_i.t_e \quad (19)$$

Temporal similarity operations: These operations can for example compare two trajectories to find out whether both trajectories have the same duration and their events the same time indexes, or not (e.g **Temporal_Similarity** : $STT \times STT \rightarrow Boolean$). Given two STT objects *stt1* and *stt2*, we have:

$$f_{Temporal\_Similarity}(stt1, stt2) := (card(stt1.A) = card(stt2.A) \wedge (stt1.D.d_1.t_s$$
$$= stt2.D.d_2.t_s) \wedge (\forall 1 \le i \le n, stt1.A.a_i.t_s = stt2.A.a_i.t_s \wedge stt1.A.a_i.t_e$$
$$= stt2.A.a_i.t_e) \quad (20)$$

3.5   Spatio-Temporal Operations

Spatio-temporal operations combine spatial and temporal operations to construct specific queries. Meanwhile, a series of native spatio-temporal operations are also considered: set (equality, difference, union, intersection), location-based and neighborhood operations. Let us introduce an example of these operations, specifically the operation **Intersection** :$STT \times STT \rightarrow STT$. Given *stt1* and *stt2* two objects of STT type, we have $f_{Intersection}(stt1, stt2)$ that returns:

– a STT object named here as *inter* which is the first fragment chain that is included in both *stt1* and *stt2*. *inter* is returned if the following conditions are satisfied:
  1. $inter = (\{a_i, a_{i+1}...., a_j\}, \{d_i, d_{i+1}...., d_j\}) : 1 \le i \le min(n_1, n_2) \wedge 1 \le j \le min(n_1, n_2))$; n1 and n2 are length of *stt1* and *stt2*;
  2. $inter \subset D_{STT} \wedge Includes(inter, stt1) \wedge Includes(inter, stt2)$;
  3. $\exists! H : (H \subset D_{STT} \wedge Includes(H, stt1) \wedge$
     $; Includes(H, stt2) \wedge STT\_Before\_STT(H, inter)$
– $\emptyset$ otherwise

A worthwhile property of the algebraic model is its ability to take into account the integration and manipulation needs of moving object applications as inspired by the Time Geography framework. It also insures a unified and flexible representation thanks to the ADT approach and the STT that encapsulates the temporal, spatial and semantics properties of a generic trajectory.

4   Implementation and Evaluation

The STT ADT has been implemented into the Postgresql/Postgis that has the advantage of being an open source spatial DBMS also compliant with Open GIS Consortium standards. It also offers several flexible tools to integrate new data types such as basic types, composite types or user defined functions. The STT has been specified as a composite type. As a new type, it is fully recognized by Postgresql. The STT is materialized as a record represented by its attributes and operations. Practically, the STT is a new "native type" and is handled as such.

STT associated operations are implemented as pl/pgSQL procedures (Post-gresql pl/sql edition). This means that the STT source code uses Postgresql native types and operations. Spatial types such as *Linestring, Point* and tem-poral types such as *Timestamp* are also taken into account. For cartographic visualization purpose, we use an open source GIS namely Quantum GIS to dis-play STT spatial trip itineraries (polylines), activities locations (points) and transportation zones (polygons).

4.1 Data Integration

The STT is composed of trips and activities. These components constitute the trajectory events chain as inspired by Time Geography concepts. Activity and trip objects are considered as composite types. This allows to represent these concepts as records made of a fields list, each being an instance of a Postgresql native type. *Geometry* type is used to represent spatial attributes and *Timestamp* served to represent temporal attributes. The implementation is realized through the Postgresql script such as:

```
CREATE TYPE Activity AS          CREATE TYPE Trip AS
(  ts timestamp,                 (  ts timestamp,
   te timestamp,                    te timestamp,
   l geometry,                      ls geometry,
   "purpose" character varying );   "mode" character varying[],
                                    path geometry );
```

A STT instance is composed of two ordered sets with the same cardinality. One handles activities whereas the other refers to trips. Two arrays are used to represent each of the *activity* objects and *trip* objects (Figure 3). These arrays can be only manipulated by the associated and implemented operations.

The STT type and its operations are implemented by the instruction "CRE-ATE TYPE AS":

```
CREATE TYPE STT AS
(   a Activity[],
    d Trip[]
); ALTER TYPE stt OWNER TO postgres;
```

The array structure permits the manipulation of the STT ordered sets. Com-parison between STTs is seamlessly performed. Semantic relations between STT events are supported because activities and trips are semantically connected (i.e., each activity is specified by a trip objective and is labeled by a specific index).

4.2 Operations Integration

Each manipulation operation presented in the previous sections is mapped to an algorithm for implementation purposes. As already mentioned, a pl/PgSQL function, i.e., CREATE FUNCTION is used to code them as procedures. An

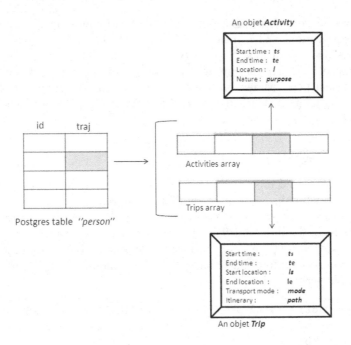

An objet *Activity*

Start time : *ts*
End time : *te*
Location : *l*
Nature : *purpose*

id   traj

Activities array

Trips array

Postgres table *"person"*

Start time :   *ts*
End time :   *te*
Start location :   *ls*
End location :   le
Transport mode : *mode*
Itinerary :   *path*

An objet *Trip*

Fig. 3. A STT object data structure

example of coded operation ADD, where check functions are called, is shown as follows:

```
CREATE OR REPLACE FUNCTION Add(t STT,a Activity, d Trip)
RETURNS STT AS $BODY$
BEGIN
  % Checking the validity of a, d and t using check operations
  %Checking chaining conditions
  IF((d.le = a.l and d.te + '00:00:01'= a.ts) AND
    (length(t)=0 OR (d.ts = t.a[length(t)].te +
    '00:00:01' AND d.ls = t.a[length(t)].l) ) ) THEN
    t.a:=t.a|| a::activity; t.d:=t.d|| d::trip;
    RETURN t;
  ELSE
    IF(not Equals(d.le, a.l)) THEN
      RAISE EXCEPTION 'error conditions couple d/a';
    ELSE
      IF(d.te + '00:00:01' <> a.ts) THEN
        RAISE EXCEPTION 'error conditions d/a';
      ELSE
        IF((d.ts <> t.a[length(t)].te + '00:00:01')) THEN
          RAISE EXCEPTION 'error conditions d/a';
```

```
   ELSE
     IF(not equals(d.ls,t.a[length(t)].l)) THEN
       RAISE EXCEPTION 'error conditions d/a';
     END IF;
   END IF.
  END IF;
 END IF;
END IF;
RETURN t;
END; $BODY$ LANGUAGE 'plpgsql' VOLATILE STRICT;
```

4.3 Experimental Data

Case study rational: In an urban context, downtown mobility is a crucial problem that might have significant impacts on human quality of life. Transportation management and planning are a difficult issue which is hampered by the continuous extension of urban areas and development of activities in the city. Studying urban mobility at different levels of abstraction is surely a valid direction to explore to provide better transportation facilities, to decrease environmental impacts and overall to improve human life quality. Studying transportation trajectories, patterns and behaviors in the city can for instance bring novel insights on:

- transportation users profiles and spatial patterns of transportation activities,
- transportation patterns per road category,
- origin, destination, duration and length of user's itineraries categorised per activity and sumamrization,
- vehicles flows from and to downtown at rush hours,
- trips motivation and kind of activities performed,
- parking practices for private vehicle or carpooling opportunities etc.

Such examples of transportation analysis may help when planning effective transportation schemes. The next section introduces an application example of our modeling approach applied to the city of Quebec and that models mobility behavior based on journey records.

Database model for the study of urban transportation in the city of Quebec: In order to test the implemented STT, let us first introduce a conceptual data model for an application that targets the analysis of mobility behaviors. A series of preliminar models to that study has been proposed in early work [12], [11]. The database schema developed is hereafter illustrated.

```
Road(id:integer, line:geometry, description:character variying)
Location(id:integer, loc:geometry, description:character variying)
City(id:integer, zone:geometry,...)
Aim(id:integer, name:character varying)
Mode(id :integer, name:charachter varying,...)
```

```
Houshould(id:integr, NbrPerson:integer,...)
Person(id:ineger, idhous:integer, sex:character)
Pattern(id :integer, idpers :integer, day :date, traj :stt)
```

Three kinds of relation are distinguished: the first category models the transportation environment: *Route*, *Location* and *City*. *City* describes a set of urban zones. *Route* model the urban road network. Each *Route* is classified, that is, Highway, Road or Tunnel. The relation *Location* describes some spatial locations of interest. The second category includes *Aim* and *Mode*. *Aim* models the motivation of the trip while *Mode* the transportation means (private vehicle, cycle, walk, public transportation, carpooling) used to reach the activity location. The last category is composed of *Houshould*, *Person* and *Pattern*. *Houshould* describes the household (e.g., members list, number of vehicles). *Person* relation describes individuals (e.g. age, sex, profession, drive license) as members of *Houshould* which aggregates them. Each individual is associated to one or more *Pattern*. The last relation describes the transportation behavior (e.g., trips, date, start time, end time, activities, mode, motivation, duration). This gives the description of the different itineraries taken by the individuals during their journey.

Origin-destination data set: The proof-of-concept STT is applied to several data sets:

- Origin-destination (O-D) survey data realized in 2001 in the Quebec region.
- Cartographic data of the Quebec region municipalities including the road network.

Origin-destination surveys have been widely used to sketch a region transportation behavior. Origin-destination surveys represent a sample of the activities and displacements performed by a region household and their members. Collected data on journeys are coded, processed and used as a reference database for different transportation analysis. The survey database stores the trips of the individuals who answered to the origin-destination conducted in 2001 by "la Société de Transport de la Communauté Urbaine de Quebec (STCUQ)". Each row of the database records the journey of a given individual. Practically, the relation *Pattern* is merged to the attribute *traj* of the *Person* relation, we obtain:

```
Person(id:integer, idhous:integer, traj:stt, day:date,...)
```

In order to fully exploit the benchmark data, a re-engineering and refinement process was undertaken. At the end of the re-engineering and refinement process, we obtained an experimental database composed of several tables. For instance the table *Houshould* holds 4144 households, the table *Person* holds 9095 samples.

4.4   Experimentation

This section illustrates the potential of the STT approach by a set of queries addressed to the experimental database and formulated according to the mobility behavior context. These queries are formulated in pseudo-code and then mapped into the Pl/pgSQL language.

Query 1: *What are the trajectories that, during the day, cross the downtown from and to different locations out of it?*

This spatial query explores the role of the downtown as a crossing area. Mapped into Pl/pgSQL, this query is shown below:

```
SELECT Itinerary(pr.traj)
FROM person pr, city AS cv
WHERE cv.nom_mun = 'Charlesbourg'
AND STT_Cross_Region(pr.traj,cv.zone)
AND not Equals(First_Point(pr.traj), Last_Point(pr.traj))
AND not contains(cv.zone, First_Point(pr.traj))
AND not contains(cv.zone, Last_Point(pr.traj));
```

Called operations are typical spatial operations. *STT_Cross_Region* evaluates the intersection between a STT and a polygon (i.e., downtown). *First_Point* and *Last_Point* retrieve the origin and destination locations. Figure 4 shows a cartographic representation of the query result.

Query 2: *Which persons leave downton by car at the end of their journey from their job location after 5 pm?*

This query retrieves the individuals working in the downtown while using their vehicle to leave their working place at a given time. To answer this query, several conditions should be verified by several constraints and retrieval conditions:

1. The last trip done by an individual should leave from its working place in the downtown.
2. At this place, the individual performed an activity "Work". This should be the last minus one in the activity list.
3. The last trip should end outside the downtown.
4. The last trip should start at 5 pm.
5. The last trip should have a vehicle as transportation mode.

This query specification is made of a set of nested queries that browse the individual records according to some constraints, e.g., mode, motivation, location, time and trip position on the itinerary chaining. Semantic restriction operations are called to limit the individual trajectory span to the trip/activity pair (i.e., last and the last minus one). The code used to run the query is shown below.

```
SELECT pr.id
FROM (SELECT pr2.id AS pr2,At_Activity_Activity(pr2.traj,
     Nth_Actvity(pr2.traj,length(pr2.traj)-1),
     Nth_Activity(pr2.traj, length(pr2.traj)-1))  AS AtAA
FROM person AS pr2) AS sub_query,
person AS pr, city AS cv
```

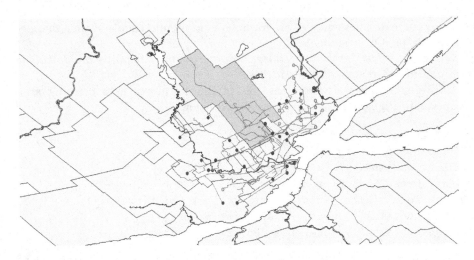

Fig. 4. Query 1 results

```
WHERE pr2 = pr.id AND length(pr.traj) >=2
AND cv.nom_mun = 'Charlesbourg'
-- Conditions 1 and 2
AND contains(cv.zone,Last_Point(AtAA))
AND Activities_With_Pupose_Count(AtAA ,'1') = 1
--Conditions 3 et 4
AND not contains(cv.zone, Last_Point(pr.traj))
AND Last_Time(AtAA)::time >= '17:00:00'::time
--Condition 5
AND Trips_With_Mode_Count(At_Activity_Activity( pr.traj,
    Last_Activity(pr.traj), Last_Activity(pr.traj)),'1') = 1
ORDER BY pr.id;
```

The figure 5 displays the location of the results.

Query 3: *For each individual making a trip to the downtown, calculate the duration and length of his/her trip. Also what is the location of each of these trips compared to the length of the other trips?*

This operation derives the first trip of each individual. Such a trip must start out of the downtown and end inside it. A semantic restriction operation is called for each trajectory in order to select a sub-trajectory that refers to the first trip/activity pair. The *First_Point* and *Last_Point* operations retrieve the trip start and end locations. The *Trips_Duration* operation returns the time duration. The *Spatial_Lentgh* returns the distance travelled. This query is defined as follows:

```
SELECT Spatial_Length(sub_traj), Trips_Duration(sub_traj),
    (Spatial_Length(sub_traj)*100)/Spatial_Length(traj))
FROM (SELECT At_Trip_Trip(pr.traj, First_Trip(pr.traj),
```

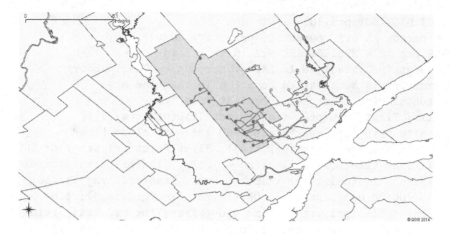

Fig. 5. Query 2 results

```
First_Trip(pr.traj)) AS sub_traj, pr.traj as traj
FROM person AS pr, city AS cv
WHERE cv.nom_mun = 'Charlesbourg'
AND not contains(cv.zone,First_Point(At_Trip_Trip(
    pr.traj,First_Trip(pr.traj),First_Trip(pr.traj))))
AND contains(cv.zone,Last_Point(At_Trip_Trip(
pr.traj,First_Trip(pr.traj),First_Trip(pr.traj))))
) as sub_query;
```

Query 4: *Which individuals can carpool towards the downtown at the start of the day with a given individual (having an ID equal to 3261401)?*

The individual ID is drawn from the survey coding procedures. Individual candidates to respond to this query should verify the following constraints:

1. They should move to the downtown at the start of the day.
2. Their location should be close to the one of the individual selected.
3. These individuals and the one selected must leave at close times.

In order to formulate this query, spatial, temporal and semantic operations should be called. Only the first trip is considered. The Postgresql spatial function *contains* checks if a spatial object contains another one. The Boolean result selects a set of records. The selected ones are browsed by the *First_Point* and *Last_Point* operations to retrieve the first and the last locations of the sub-trajectories. The distance traveled is quantified and compared to the value equal to 2500 meters. Finally, to test the temporal neighborhood, the time difference between the two trajectories and t is compared to a threshold, e.g., 30 minutes.

Figure 6 illustrates the results by displaying the itinerary of the unique individual retrieved by the query. The query as coded in Pl/pgSQL is illustrated as follows.

```
SELECT DISTINCT pr2.ID
FROM person AS pr1, person AS pr2, city as cv
WHERE pr1.id = 3261401 AND pr1.id <> pr2.id
AND length(pr2.traj) >= 1  AND cv.nom_mun = 'Charlesbourg'
--first trip's destination location in the zone area
AND contains(cv.zone, Last_Point(At_Trip_Trip(
pr2.traj,First_Trip(pr2. traj),First_Trip(pr2.traj))))
-- starts trip from near places AND leave at close times
AND distance(First_Point(pr2.traj), First_Point(pr1.traj))<= 2500
AND ((First_Time(pr2.traj)::time <= First_Time(pr1.traj)::time
And (First_Time(pr1.traj)::time -  First_Time(pr2.traj)::time)
      < '00:30:00'::interval) OR ((First_Time(pr2.traj)::time >=
      First_Time(pr1.traj)::time And (First_Time(pr2.traj)::time
      - First_Time(pr1.traj)::time)< '00:30:00'::interval)));
```

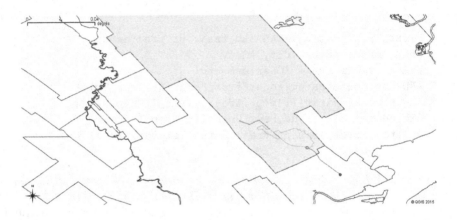

Fig. 6. Query 4 results

Query 5: *Find the trajectories that have some common activity and trip behaviors*

This query searches for individuals that made similar trips. It identifies individuals with common interests activities and displacement patterns. It calls the spatio-temporal operation *Intersects* that checks if two trajectories have some common events.

```
SELECT DISTINCT pr1.id, pr2.id
FROM person as pr1, person as pr2
WHERE Intersects(pr1.traj,pr2.traj) AND pr1.id <> pr2.id;
```

5   Conclusion

This paper introduces an ADT modeling approach oriented to the representation of a spatio-temporal trajectory. The ADT favors the description of a STT on top of a formal algebraic model. The Time Geography theoretical framework provides a support to the formal definition of the STT trips and activities that represent the trajectory semantics in time and space. These modeling abstractions facilitate the representation of mobility behaviors, trips and activities manipulation over the spatial and temporal dimensions. The modeling approach is complemented by a set of spatial, temporal and semantic operations. The potential of the STT approach is illustrated in the context of an origin-destination survey in the city of Quebec. Future work will be oriented towards an extension of the manipulation of the functions developed using Pl/pgSQL and to additional experimental and application developments.

References

1. Hägerstrand, T.: What about people in regional science ? Papers of the Regional Science Association **24**, 6–21 (1970)
2. Miller, H.J.: Modeling accessibility using space-time prism concepts within geographical information systems. International journal of geographical information systems **5**, 287–301 (1991)
3. Wolfson, O., Xu, B., Chamberlain, S., Jiang, L.: Moving objects databases: issues and solutions. In: 10th Int. Conference on Scientific and Statistical Database Management, pp. 111–122 (1998)
4. Güting, R.H., Bhlen, H., Erwig, M., Jensen, C.S., Lorentzos, N.A., Schneider, M., Vazirgiannis, M.: A foundation for representing and quering moving objects. ACM Transactions on Database Systems **25**, 1–42 (2000)
5. Wang, D., Cheng, T.: A spatio-temporal data model for activity-based transport demand modelling. International Journal of Geographic Information Science **15**, 561–585 (2001)
6. Frihida, A., Marceau, D.J., Theriault, M.: Spatio-Temporal Object-Oriented Data Model for Disaggregate Travel Behavior. Transactions in GIS **6**, 277–294 (2002)
7. Li, X., Claramunt, C., Ray, C., Lin, H.: A semantic-based approach to the representation of network-constrained trajectory data. In: Riedl, A., Kainz, W., Elmes, G.A. (eds.) 12th International Symposium on Spatial Data Handling, pp. 451–464. Springer (2006)
8. Noyon, V., Claramunt, C., Devogele, T.: A relative representation of trajectories in geographical spaces. Geoinformatica **4**, 479–496 (2007)
9. Praing, R., Schneider, M.: A universal abstract model for future movements of moving objects. In: 10th AGILE Int. Conf. on Geographic Information Science, pp. 11–120 (2007)
10. Spaccapietra, S., Parent, C., Damiani, M.L., De Macedo, J.A., Porto, F., Vangenot, C.: A conceptual view on trajectories. Data & Knowledge Engineering **65**, 126–146 (2008)
11. Frihida, A., Zheni, D., Ben Ghezala, H., Claramunt, C.: Modeling trajectories: a spatio-temporal data type approach. In: 20th International Workshop on Database and Expert Systems Application, pp. 447–451. IEE Press, Linz (2009)
12. Triki, D., Frihida, A., Ben Ghezala, H. and Claramunt, C.: Revue Internationale Internationale de Géomatique, **20**, 37–64 (2010)
13. Follin, J.M., Moreau, G., Bouju, A., Polidori, L., Soussi, M.: Enrichissement d'une base de donnes routire partir de trajectoires GPS de vhicules d'urgence. Application l'aide au choix d'itinraires. Ingnieurie des Systmes d'Information **17**, 35–54 (2012)

14. Xu, J.: Güting, R.H: A Generic Data Model for Moving Objects. Geoinformatica **17**, 125–172 (2013)
15. Parent, C., Spaccapietra, S., Renso, C., Andrienko, G.L., Andrienko, N.V., Bogorny, V., Damiani, M.L., Gkoulalas-Divanis, A., Fernandes de Macdo, J. A., Pelekis, N., Theodoridis, Y., Yan, Z.: Semantic trajectories modeling and analysis. ACM Comput. Surv., vol. 45, article number 42, 42:1–42:32, New York (2013)
16. Damiani, M.L., Güting, R.H., Valds, F., Issa, H.: Moving objects beyond raw and semantic trajectories. In: 3rd International Workshop on Information Management for Mobile Applications (IMMoA 2013), p. 4. Riva del Garda, Italy (2013)
17. Bogorny, V., Renso, C., Ribeiro, A., Siqueira, F.L., Alvares, L.O.: CONSTAnT: A Conceptual Data Model for Semantic Trajectories of Moving Objects. Transactions in GIS **18**, 66–88 (2014)
18. Pelekis, N., Frentzos, E., Giatrakos, N., Theodoridis, Y.: HERMES: A Trajectory DB Engine for Mobility-Centric Applications. International Journal of Knowledge-based Organizations, **1** (2014)

Spatiotemporal Behavior Profiling:
A Treasure Hunt Case Study

Victor de Graaff[1]([⊠]), Dieter Pfoser[2], Maurice van Keulen[1], and Rolf A. De By[3]

[1] Department of Computer Science,
University of Twente, Enschede, The Netherlands
{v.degraaff,m.vankeulen}@utwente.nl
[2] George Mason University, Fairfax, VA, USA
dpfoser@gmu.edu
[3] Faculty of Geo-Information Science and Earth Observation (ITC),
University of Twente, Enschede, The Netherlands
r.a.deby@utwente.nl

Abstract. Trajectories have been providing us with a wealth of derived information such as traffic conditions and road network updates. This work focuses on deriving user profiles through spatiotemporal analysis of trajectory data to provide insight into the quality of information provided by users. The presented behavior profiling method assesses user participation characteristics in a treasure-hunt type event. Consisting of an analysis and a profiling phase, analysis involves a timeline and a stay-point analysis, as well as a semantic trajectory inspection relating actual and expected paths. The analysis results are then grouped around profiles that can be used to estimate the user performance in the activity. The proposed profiling method is evaluated by means of a student orientation treasure-hunt activity at the University of Twente, The Netherlands. The profiling method is used to predict the students' gaming behavior by means of a simple team type classification, and a feature-based answer type classification.

Keywords: Behavior analysis · Behavior prediction · GPS data · User generated content

1 Introduction

Trajectories are more than a simple collection of geographical coordinates with timestamps added to the mix. They represent user actions and can, when interpreted properly, lead to an in-depth analysis of behavior and, consequently, user profiling. As a matter of fact, *you are what you "where"!*

Research involving trajectories has so far focussed on data management and data mining aspects at the geometrical levels. Results have led, for example, to improved telematics services using live traffic assessment by means of vehicle tracking and, more recently, map construction algorithms resulting into automatic road network generation and updates (e.g. [1]).

© Springer International Publishing Switzerland 2015
J. Gensel and M. Tomko (Eds.): W2GIS 2015, LNCS 9080, pp. 143–158, 2015.
DOI: 10.1007/978-3-319-18251-3_9

Focusing on the qualitative aspects, semantic trajectory compression methods have been introduced to reduce the size of the actual trajectory data. Essentially these methods rely on decision points, or, landmarks, in combination with movement vectors to reduce the number of position samples recorded for each trajectory. Based on such landmarks, one would be able to characterize movement at a high level based on traversed landmarks.

The scope of this work is now to identify an even higher level of abstraction and to abstract trajectories into user profiles based on their behavior as derived from movement. Specifically, we derive user profiles through spatiotemporal analysis of trajectory data to provide insight into the quality of information provided by users. The context of this work is the creation of a trajectory analysis component inside a bigger architecture where user profiles and location profiles play an important role, such as the one discussed in [2]. The presented behavior profiling method assesses user participation characteristics in a treasure hunt type event. We propose a method that allows us to map trajectories collected during a treasure hunt to a certain user typology. Our overall method consists of an analysis, and a profiling/prediction phase. The trajectory data is analyzed using a timeline and a stay point analysis, as well as a semantic trajectory inspection relating actual and expected paths. Timeline analysis detects the differences between the users and their changing behavior over time. Stay point analysis determines where teams spent a significant amount of time and helps us in assessing the impact of the environment on user behavior. Trajectory inspection is then used to distinguish between engaged teams and indifferent teams. The specific dataset used captures the answers and spatiotemporal characteristics of 100+ students using the dedicated smartphone application developed for making students acquainted with the city of Enschede. The outcome of the analysis phase is used as input to the profiling and prediction phase. This work proposes two methods, team type and answer type classification, to predict the students' gaming behavior. Team type classification uses two distinguishing features, correctness and distance, to create a total of four profile types. Answer type classification is based on a total of 10 features overall describing the teams and their answers. The generated profiles and their features are used as input to the automated generation of a decision tree to predict answer types. This is especially useful in scenarios where answer correctness is not as sharply defined, such as user generated reviews of products or places. To validate our method, we use a treasure hunt contest as a case study. The data relating to this event was collected using a mobile application. The application was used by several hundred students. This treasure hunt was one of the program elements of the welcome week for new students at the University of Twente, The Netherlands. The students used 132 devices to participate in the *Kick-In Quest* using a specific app on Android and iOS platforms. During the game, GPS data and answers were collected in real real-time. Using this data and applying our profiling methods, we can clearly distinguish characteristic user types and reason about the performance of specific profiles in the game. This final aspect demonstrates that trajectory data can be used to successfully reason about the behavior of users and that *we really are what we where*!

The outline of this work is as follows. related work is discussed in Section 2. Section 3 describes the data collection and treasure hunt game in the process. How this data is then analyzed and how profiles are derived is described in Section 4. Section 5 discusses the team type classification and the answer type prediction mechanism. Finally, Section 6 gives conclusions and directions for future work.

2 Related Work

Work on behavior profiling based on GPS data often describes the analysis and prediction of travel patterns as for example described in [3–5]. In this paper however, we focus on the *behavioral patterns* that follow from this movement, but not the actual movement patterns themselves. This was also the focus of Giannotti et al. [6] who use visited regions of interest (such as a railway station, bridge, or a museum) and sequential patterns thereof to describe peoples' movements. Zheng et al. [7] used a similar, but more formalized approach. Spaccapietra et al. [8] introduced a conceptual model using movement types and visits to specific points of interest to describe the behavior of people in sequential patterns including the movement. Yan et al. [9] introduce a framework for semantic annotation of trajectories using several abstraction layers, and discuss typical challenges when dealing with trajectory data from mobile devices.

Our timeline analysis resembles the approach taken by Guc et al. [10], but contrary to their manual annotation approach, the annotation in our work is done automatically. Our stay point analysis is based on the work by Zheng et al. discussed in [7].

Several other interesting approaches for computing with spatial trajectories are discussed in [11]. Recently, two in-depth overviews of the state of the art in the field of modeling and semantic enhancement of trajectory data were presented by Parent et al. [12] and Jiang et al. [13]. Behavior, as we discuss it in this paper, is defined as *semantic behavior* in [12]: "trajectory behavior whose predicate bears on some contextual data and possibly on some spatial and/or temporal data."

3 Case Study and Data Collection

The trajectory data used in this work was collected as part of a case study that involved 54 teams comprised of first-year university students, using a total of 132 mobile devices participating in a treasure hunt as part of the new student orientation. In the following, we describe the event during which the data was collected, the technology that was used, we provide a description of the collected data, and describe the pre-processing of the data.

3.1   Event

Every year, new students are welcomed to the University of Enschede with a voluntary, but popular welcome week called the *Kick-In*. As part of the welcome week for new Bachelor students in 2013, the *Kick-In Quest*, as seen in Figure 1, took place on a Saturday morning, from 10:00*am* until noon. The *Kick-In Quest* manifested itself as a treasure hunt, in which students had to answer questions at certain locations using a mobile app. Points were awarded for (i) answering questions correctly, and for (ii) collected GPS location data. This was explained to the students using information screens in the app. The students worked together in teams, and were motivated to use multiple devices per team to obtain more location points (resulting in more collected tracking data). The awarded amount of points for correct questions was also based on the proximity to the question location, which forced students to move around the town center of Enschede, even if the answer was already known, or could be found online. Each of the 54 teams that participated had its own designated question sequence, guiding them to 20 locations. These sequences were put together from a total of 24 questions and respective locations. It was not possible to look ahead or change a previously entered answer in the app. In case the app was closed, the app continued where it had previously stopped.

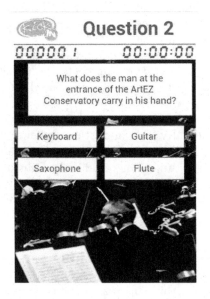

Fig. 1. Screenshot of the mobile application *Kick-In Quest*

3.2   Technology

The mobile application was developed using the PhoneGap platform [14]. This platform allows app developers to build an application as if it were a web page using HTML5, CSS, and JavaScript. The features of the mobile device, such as the GPS sensor, can be accessed through asynchronous JavaScript calls. Phone-Gap supports many different platforms, but for this app only Android and iOS were used.

3.3   Collected Data

During the game, trajectory data was uploaded from the mobile devices to a server as tuples containing the *trajectory id* and all fields of PhoneGap's *Position object*: latitude, longitude, altitude, accuracy, altitude accuracy, heading, speed, and timestamp. Furthermore, *answer data* was uploaded containing the following information: question ID, trajectory ID, answer, latitude, longitude, accuracy, and operating system (i.e., Android, or iOS).

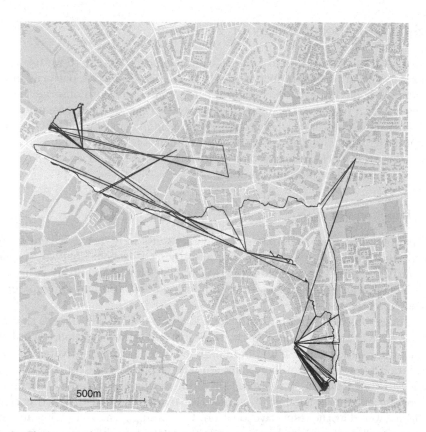

Fig. 2. Trajectory before removal of location references based on cell phone tower locations. The signal keeps jumping back and forth between relatively accurate GPS positioning and less accurate cell phone tower locations.

3.4   Data Pre-Processing

Besides several minor data cleaning tasks, such as resolving differences between the date formats of the different platforms, data pre-processing involved the removal of location references based on cell phone tower locations and trajectory point outliers.

Android offers two types of locations: *fine-grained locations* and *coarse-grained locations*. PhoneGap uses the coarse location data when the fine-grained location is unavailable. This results in trajectories as illustrated in 2. Coarse-grained locations can be detected by setting a threshold on the *accuracy value*. Removing all data points for which the accuracy value exceeds $50m$ has proven to filter out all such course points. In addition, by using a realistic threshold for the speed of the participants, extreme outliers were removed from the GPS trajectories as well.

4   Spatiotemporal Behavior Analysis

Our first goal in this work is to analyze the trajectory data. Here we use three methods to get an understanding of the data and the respective patterns in the participants' behavior. First, we perform a *timeline analysis* to observe the differences between users, and changing behavior over time. Secondly, we use a *stay point analysis* to determine where teams spent a significant amount of time, and to inspect the impact of the respective environment on the participants' behavior. Lastly, we inspect the respective trajectories with respect to the expected trajectories using the question locations.

4.1   Timeline Analysis

The spatiotemporal question-answer behavior results in a specific signature for each group. Our hypothesis is that by quantifying this behavior, we can easily identify more or less successful participants. A timeline analysis is used to relate the behavior of users by means of analyzing the spatiotemporal answering behavior.

The questions in the treasure hunt were location-bound. This means that the students were instructed to answer the question at a stated location, even if the answer would be known or found online. The students were motivated to visit the location by awarding an increasing amount of points based on the inverted distance to that location at the moment of answering the question. Therefore, to score the maximum number of points, the answers needed to be (i) correct, and (ii) answered at the respective location. Combining right and wrong answers with close or distance answer locations resulted in the four different answer types shown in Table 1.

In Figure 3, we provide the timeline analysis graph for our case study. The x-axis represents the time, the y-axis represents the team number. The teams are ordered on the time of their first answer, starting at the bottom. The bar of

Table 1. Spatial Question/Answer categories

	Close	Distant
Correct	Correct Close (CC)	Correct Distant (CD)
Incorrect	Incorrect Close (IC)	Incorrect Distant (ID)

each team consists of a sequence of answers and the time it took to answer each. The longer each bar, the longer it took to answer. The four colors represent the four answer types. CC answers are illustrated in green, CD in blue, IC in yellow, and ID in red. For each answer, the start of the bar represents the moment at which the question is presented on the screen, and the end of the bar the moment the answer is entered in the application (with a small degree of freedom for visualization purposes). For teams that used multiple devices, only the first given answer is considered, because the mobile application often hints at the correct answer after an answer is provided. This influenced the answering behavior on the other devices.

The green (CC) answers, which are correct in both actual answer and location, are more prominent towards the beginning of the game. CC answers take a substantial amount of time to obtain, since the students have to move to the right

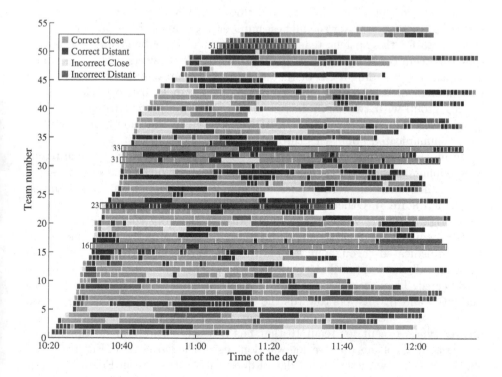

Fig. 3. Timelines of teams. Colors indicate answer types. Highlighted teams are discussed in detail below.

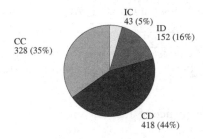

Fig. 4. Answer type frequencies. Only the first answer for each team has been taken into account, in case a team participated with multiple devices, since the explanation in the next screen often revealed the correct answer.

location. Therefore, a large part of the graph is green. Therefore, this visualization type is very suitable to get insight into the amount of time spent on certain behavior. If additionally it is of interest to see the ratio of behavior occurences, other techniques can be used, such as the pie chart of answer types in Figure 4. A closer look at Team 33, for example, shows a very green timeline, while only 9 out of the 20 answers are actually CC answers. The team with the highest percentage of CC answers was Team 16, with 12 out of the 13 answers correct and at the right location. Not only did this team have the highest percentage, the score of 12 was a tie for the highest number of CC answers. A deeper analysis of the data for this specific team gave us insight in their behavior. The reason that this team could achieve this high number of CC answers without skipping questions, by providing a CD or ID answer in between, was that it participated with four devices, and split up into a walking group with two devices, and a cycling group with two more devices. Judging by the perfect timing of which devices were used to answer the question first, we can conclude that they must have communicated about this throughout the game.

From this timeline, we can detect several *team behavior types*. Some teams were indifferent about the outcome of the entire game, which is reflected by a late starting time, short answering times, and many incorrect answers (e.g., Teams 51 and 52 in Figure 3). Other teams were indifferent about answering the questions at the right location, while still trying to answer questions correctly (e.g., Team 2). Teams like Team 1 just wanted to finish the game. Finally, teams like Team 16 were dedicated throughout the entire game. From those teams that played the game all the way until the end, there is another behavior pattern that can be detected. They rushed towards the end of the game. This can be seen by the many CD and ID answers towards the end (e.g., Team 33). Another important observation is that there were barely any teams that were consistent in their answer types, except for team 16 that has a nearly entirely green timeline. A deeper analysis of this observation was done using the bar chart in Figure 5. This chart, combined with the knowledge of question locations from Figure 6, shows that remotely located questions were fare less popular to be answered near the stated location.

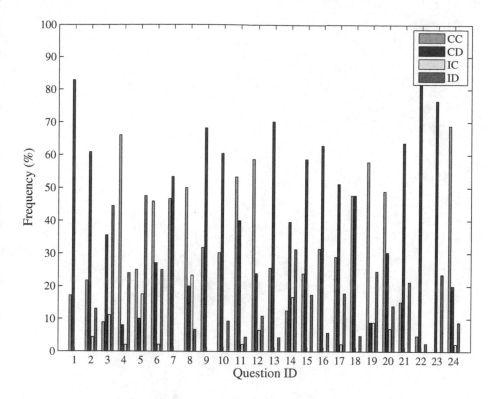

Fig. 5. Answer type frequencies by question ID. Questions 21 and 22 were located remotely, and therefore had a large amount of CD (blue) and ID (red) answers.

In addition to the timeline analysis, different visualizations are useful to compensate for the coloring bias that is induced by the fact that some behavior requires more time than other behavior. In the treasure hunt case for example, CC answers require more traveling time than CD answers. This results in an overall "greener" graph, while the pie chart in Figure 4 shows that CD answers (blue) are actually more common.

4.2   Stay Point Analysis

Stay point analysis is another form of a spatiotemporal analysis that provides insight into the most significant locations of the people's stop-and-go behavior. Stay points are defined as points where the speed was below a certain threshold for a respective time period. This analysis is uncoupled from that what the students were asked to do (answering questions), and gives us more insight into what they actually did besides playing the game.

In our case study, we use a speed threshold of $1m/s$ and a stay threshold of $30s$. To overcome the problem of GPS signals bouncing around when no, or

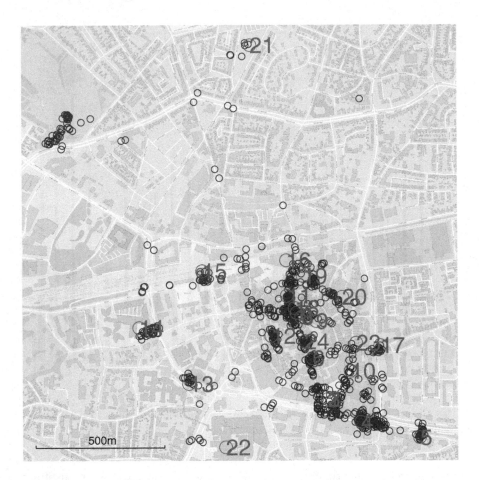

Fig. 6. Stay points derived purely from GPS data. Blue circles indicate detected stay points, the red circles and numbers indicate the question locations. The park in the northwest corner is the location of the event that took place afterwards. Question 4 (in the southeast) was in a supermarket.

little movement is observed, we did not use the typical sampling rate of $1Hz$, but compared the position with to a GPS signal sample of $5s$ ago (under-sampling).

The results of this analysis are shown in Figure 6. The red circles are the actual question locations. Blue circles are used to visualize the stay points after clustering them on a trajectory basis. Multiple blue circles located close to each other therefore represent multiple trajectories slowing down significantly in that area. For visualization purposes, the radius size of the question location circles has been reduced to $25m$, as opposed to the $100m$ used to distinguish between "close" vs. "distant" answers in the timeline analysis.

Several groups of stay points can be detected. The cluster of points in the *upper left corner* of the map reveals the location of the next program element for the students. Several teams went to this location early, or left the app running while the game was already over. The game was initiated near the center of the map. This is where the students were supposed to gather, and obtained a team code to start the app. Question no. 4 was to be answered inside a supermarket. The cluster of stay points in the lower right corner of the map surrounds that location. Judging by the time spent near this supermarket, several students went into the supermarket for more than just the answer of the question. The slow movement afterwards is probably caused by the consumption of snacks and drinks afterwards.

4.3 Trajectory Inspection

To gain further insight into the behavior of individual teams, we carried out a visual inspection of trajectories. This revealed some challenges as several teams had turned off their GPS tracking between answering questions. Also, we could cluster the trajectories into four types, (i) barely moving, (ii) not leaving the center of the town, (iii) leaving center of town once, and (iv) moving around.

Figure 7 shows examples of different trajectory types. However, no clear correlation could be found between the correctness of answers and the movement patterns of the teams. For example, Team 25 for example answered 10 questions, all correctly, without moving substantially.

5 Behavior Prediction

In many scenarios of behavior analysis, the correct behavior is unknown. An example scenario is the analysis of reviews and ratings of geo-referenced objects, such as restaurants. The ability to distinguish serious users from the less serious ones, allows us to predict the quality of their content. In the case study, we have this information on answer correctness, and used this as a ground truth to validate two prediction mechanisms built using our approach. The first one, a simple team type classification, is mainly based on the outcome of the timeline analysis. For the second one, a machine-learning approach to predict the answer types, we have used the outcome of all three analyses.

5.1 Team Type Classification

A simple team type classification categorizes teams into four groups using (i) start time and (ii) average speed of each team. Table 2 shows the resulting four types. Teams that started within $2000s$ of the first starting team were classified as early starters. The cut-off speed between the *slow and fast teams* was set at $1.2859m/s$, the median speed of all teams. For teams that participated with multiple devices, the entire travelled distance was divided by the total amount

(a) Type 1 - Team 51 barely participated and answered the questions from a cafe near the start of the event.

(b) Type 2 - Team 1 participated, but did not leave the center.

(c) Type 3 - Team 14 actively participated and moved somewhat around to answer questions.

(d) Type 4 - Team 16 actively participated, and visited even remote question locations.

Fig. 7. Raw trajectories of several teams. Each device (per team) has an own color for the trajectory. The red numbers indicate the question locations for that specific team. Teams were unable to look ahead to the next questions.

of time the devices submitted a GPS signal. Teams that answered less than 10 out of the 20 questions were not taken into account for this classification.

The radar charts in Figure 8 show the distribution of answer types for each team type. Each of the four axes represents the corresponding answer type.

Table 2. Team characteristics

	High average speed	Low average speed
Early start time	Serious	Get-It-Over-With
Late start time	Rushed	Indifferent

Again, it can be seen that IC (incorrect + close) answers are very uncommon (none of the teams had more than 20% IC answers), which also makes them hard to predict. CC answers (correct + close) are much easier to predict and are especially common among the teams classified as Serious. CD (correct + distant) answers are especially common among Get-It-Over-With teams. ID (incorrect + distant) answers can be found primarily among Indifferent teams, and to a lesser degree among Rushing teams.

5.2   Feature-Based Answer Type Classification

Rather than classifying team behavior, we, in the following, examine answer type behavior. We created nine features to describe the team's behavior in general, and one feature to compare the answer to the answer of other teams:

On a team basis we record the following features.

1. start time,
2. average speed of all the team's trajectories (total distance divided by the total time),
3. maximum covered distance,
4. time spent using the application,
5. number of devices,
6. median distances travelled between answers,
7. median time elapsed between answers, and
8. number of stay points

To relate the response to other teams, we also record

9. whether or not the answer is prevalent answer of all teams.

We use a brute force approach to find the combination of features that leads to the best F-measure (the harmonic mean of precision and recall as commonly used in Information Retrieval) for answer correctness prediction. The *best combination* of features to predict CC answers turned out to be a combination of the (i) start time, (ii) the duration, (iii) the median distance between answers, and (iv) whether or not the answer is the prevalent answer of all the teams.

To validate the results of this method, we carried out a 10-fold cross validation. Compared to the baseline method, which assumes all answers are CC answers, this prediction mechanism performs well in precision (0.5369), decent in recall (0.5321) and also performs slightly better in F-measure (0.5274) than the baseline method. Since the majority vote is a very strong feature for answer

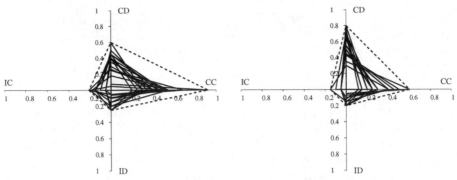

(a) Serious teams have a strong tendency towards CC answers.

(b) Get-it-over-with teams have a strong tendency towards CD answers.

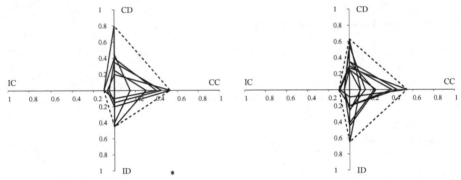

(c) Rushed teams typically have a high ratio of CD and ID answers, and very little CC answers.

(d) Indifferent teams have a strong tendency towards of ID answers.

Fig. 8. Radar charts of answer types for each team type. Each of the four axes represents the corresponding answer type.

correctness prediction, results are even better when we predict ID answers, with an F-measure of 0.8686.

This section has shown two methods of how to use aspects (features) of "rich" trajectory data to predict user behavior. While the results are encouraging, we will in subsequent work experiment with larger datasets to verify these findings and improve on our methods.

6 Conclusions and Future Work

Trajectory data is so more than a temporal sequence of position samples. Combined with the right metadata, as in this case question/answer behavior in a treasure hunt, it represents rich spatiotemporal data that can be used to analyze user behavior, which is a first step towards the creation of user profiles.

This work has shown how behavior patterns can be detected from trajectory data using several types of analyses. Although these methods have been derived in the context of a treasure hunt scenario, they are generally applicable for the analysis of "rich" trajectory data. The stay point analysis can be used to detect station locations in commuter data, taxi stops, traffic lights, and traffic bottle necks. The timeline analysis is useful for contrasting the behavior of people. In the specific visualization, the colors of the bars can represent other classification technique, such as for example sentiment analysis. Using the various analysis methods, this work demonstrates user behavior prediction based on various feature sets of the semantic treasure hunt trajectory data. Experimental evaluation has shown that indeed user behavior is codified in this trajectory data.

We can give the following directions for future work. Recently, we collected a new trajectory set using a similar setup, but with less potential for game-breaking behavior. This new data set will be used to detect Point-of-Interest visits from trajectory data, which can be used for building user profiles at another abstraction level. Similar to the virtual disc around the question locations in this paper, induced by the 100 meter vicinity criterium, *Polygons-of-Interest*, as discussed in [15], can then be used to detect the presence in a pre-defined area. Our goal will be to derive automatic methods for the profiling of users based on their rich trajectory data. Such profiling approaches will be especially helpful when trying to assess movements of large groups of people, e.g., urban commuting behavior, tourism, and large scale events.

Acknowledgments. This publication was supported by the Dutch national program COMMIT.

References

1. Ahmad, M., Karagiorgou, S., Pfoser, D., Wenk, C.: A comparison and evaluation of map construction algorithms using vehicle tracking data. GeoInformatica Journal (2015) (in press)
2. de Graaff, V., van Keulen, M., de By, R.A.: Towards geosocial recommender systems. In: 4th Intern. Workshop on Web Intelligence & Communities (WI&C 2012), Lyon, France. ACM, April 2012
3. Liao, L., Patterson, D.J., Fox, D., Kautz, H.: Learning and inferring transportation routines. Artificial Intelligence **171**(5), 311–331 (2007)
4. Zheng, Y., Li, Q., Chen, Y., Xie, X., Ma, W.-Y.: Understanding mobility based on gps data. In: Proceedings of the 10th International Conference on Ubiquitous Computing, pp. 312–321. ACM (2008)
5. Monreale, A., Pinelli, F., Trasarti, R., Giannotti, F.: Wherenext: a location predictor on trajectory pattern mining. In: Proceedings of the 15th ACM SIGKDD International Conference on Knowledge Discovery and Data Mining, pp. 637–646. ACM (2009)
6. Giannotti, F., Nanni, M., Pinelli, F., Pedreschi, D.: Trajectory pattern mining. In: Proceedings of the 13th ACM SIGKDD International Conference on Knowledge Discovery and Data Mining, San Jose, California, USA, August 12–15, 2007, pp. 330–339 (2007)

7. Zheng, Y., Zhang, L., Xie, X., Ma, W.-Y.: Mining interesting locations and travel sequences from GPS trajectories. In: Proceedings of the 18th International Conference on World Wide Web, pp. 791–800. ACM (2009)
8. Spaccapietra, S., Parent, C., Damiani, M.L., de Macedo, J.A., Porto, F., Vangenot, C.: A conceptual view on trajectories. Data & Knowledge Engineering 65(1), 126–146 (2008)
9. Yan, Z., Chakraborty, D., Parent, C., Spaccapietra, S., Aberer, K.: SeMiTri: a framework for semantic annotation of heterogeneous trajectories. In: Proceedings of the 14th International Conference on Extending Database Technology, pp. 259–270. ACM (2011)
10. Guc, B., May, M., Saygin, Y., Körner, C.: Semantic annotation of gps trajectories. In: 11th AGILE International Conference on Geographic Information Science (2008)
11. Zheng, Y., Zhou, X.: Computing with spatial trajectories. Springer (2011)
12. Parent, C., Spaccapietra, S., Renso, C., Andrienko, G., Andrienko, N., Bogorny, V., Damiani, M.L., Gkoulalas-Divanis, A., Macedo, J., Pelekis, N., et al.: Semantic trajectories modeling and analysis. ACM Computing Surveys (CSUR) 45(4), 42 (2013)
13. Jiang, S., Fiore, G.A., Yang, Y., Ferreira Jr., J., Frazzoli, E., González, M.C.: A review of urban computing for mobile phone traces: current methods, challenges and opportunities. In: Proceedings of the 2nd ACM SIGKDD International Workshop on Urban Computing, p. 2. ACM (2013)
14. Allen, S., Graupera, V., Lundrigan, L.: PhoneGap. In: Pro Smartphone Cross-Platform Development, pp. 131–152. Springer (2010)
15. de Graaff, V., de By, R.A., van Keulen, M., Flokstra, J.: Point of interest to region of interest conversion. In: Proceedings of the 21st ACM SIGSPATIAL International Conference on Advances in Geographic Information Systems (SIGSPATIAL GIS 2013), Orlando, FL, USA, (New York), pp. 378–381. ACM, November 2013

Computational Approaches,
Algorithms and Architectures

Spatial Interpolation of Streaming Geosensor Network Data in the RISER System

Xu Zhong[1]([✉]), Allison Kealy[1], Guy Sharon[2], and Matt Duckham[1]

[1] Department of Infrastructure Engineering, The University of Melbourne,
Melbourne, VIC 3010, Australia
mduckham@unimelb.edu.au
[2] IBM Research Australia, Carlton, VIC 3053, Australia

Abstract. Managing the data generated by emerging spatiotemporal data sources, such as geosensor networks, presents a growing challenge to traditional, offline GIS architectures. This paper explores the development of an end-to-end system for near real-time monitoring of environmental variables related to wildfire hazard, called RISER. The system is built upon a geosensor network and web-GIS technologies, connected by a stream-processing system. Aside from exploring the system architecture, this paper focuses specifically on the important role of stream processing as a bridge between data capture and web GIS, and as a spatial analysis engine. The paper highlights the compromise between efficiency and accuracy in spatiotemporal stream processing that must often be struck in the stream operator design. Using the specific example of spatial interpolation operators, the impact of changes to the configurations of spatial and temporal windows on the accuracy and efficiency of different spatial interpolation methods is evaluated.

1 Introduction

Geosensor networks present a range of challenges to traditional GIS architectures, including dealing with large volumes of highly dynamic data and the inherent unreliability of such geosensor networks. Nevertheless, connecting geosensor networks and web-GIS holds the potential for fine-grained monitoring in near real-time of important environmental changes.

In the paper we explore the architecture of a research prototype, called RISER, that uses geosensor networks and web GIS technologies to monitor environmental variables relevant to wildfire hazard. A key component of the architecture is the stream processing system, which provides a bridge between streaming geosensor data and a traditional spatial database, generates real-time notifications, as well as performing real-time spatial analysis. The paper demonstrates the potential of stream processing in this architecture through the example of spatial interpolation.

The key contributions of this paper are: 1. the presentation of the architecture of our system, integrating stream-processing with a geosensor network and

© Springer International Publishing Switzerland 2015
J. Gensel and M. Tomko (Eds.): W2GIS 2015, LNCS 9080, pp. 161–177, 2015.
DOI: 10.1007/978-3-319-18251-3_10

web GIS technologies; 2. a detailed investigation of the design of stream processing operators for spatial interpolation; and 3. an empirical exploration of the characteristics of spatial interpolation operators that provide a suitable balance between accuracy and efficiency.

Following a review of related literature connected with scalable and online spatial algorithms (Section 2), Section 3 describes the architecture of the RISER system, in particular highlighting the central role of the stream processing platform. Section 4 outlines the implementation of stream operators for online spatial interpolation. Section 5 tests these operators with a large simulated spatial data set, while Section 6 concludes the paper with a look at future work.

2   Background

The development of portable, low-cost, and power-efficient wireless sensor nodes and sensors is enabling the widespread use of wireless geosensor networks [19]. Sensor networks typically consist of tens or hundreds of nodes continuously sensing their environment. In the future, these networks are expected to scale to thousands or even millions of nodes.

Traditional GIS architectures are well-adapted for *offline* algorithms. In an offline environment, an algorithm is expected to have complete information about the input data to be processed. However, emerging data sources, such as wireless sensor networks, are much more suited to *online* processing. In an online algorithm, the algorithm cannot know in advance what data it will receive, and must instead deal with new data sequentially as it arrives [1]. Clearly, realtime geosensor networks require an online information processing environment, accepting new data as it is generated. Conventional offline spatial algorithms cannot always be easily adapted to an online environment, because of the computationally intensive nature of many spatiotemporal algorithms combined with the need for generating results in real time [11].

Fundamental spatial algorithms are frequently computationally intensive. For example, spatial interpolation methods such as thin plate spline [8] and Kriging [18] require the solution a large set of linear equations. Similarly, although efficient database joins have been developed in the specific instances of object tracking and spatial event detection [2,3,13], in general the problem of spatiotemporal joins remains computationally challenging in an online environment. Thus, a key challenge for online spatial algorithms is scalability.

One approach to increasing efficiency that has a long history in GIS is parallelization [10,14]. The challenge of parallelization is to identify a decomposition of the computation that can be efficiently solved using a divide-and-conquer approach. This decomposition is frequently spatial, an instance of data parallelism. For example, Nittel et al. [15] solved the online k-mean clustering problem for spatial data by first dividing data into spatial subregions small enough to be stored in the in-operator memory. Serial k-mean clustering is then conducted over each subregion to obtain a set of weighted centroids. These are then recombined using a single, efficient pass of a weighted k-mean clustering. Data parallelization is also used in [11], where source and target data points are divided using a uniform grid decomposition to efficiently compute an IDW (inverse distance weighting) interpolation. Our approach in this paper similarly uses a uniform grid decomposition of source data points as a part of one of our interpolation operations.

An alternative to spatial decomposition is decomposition by task. For example, task decomposition schemes have been developed for IDW [5,6,17,24] and Kriging [9] spatial interpolation. These interpolation algorithms runs in parallel for each target point in the surface. Thus, every target point in the surface is interpolated with access to the whole source data, leading to an exact solution, but no reduction in overall computational load. Combinations of task and spatial decomposition are also possible (e.g., [7]).

Instead of parallelization, another possibility is to subsample the data streams, reducing the computational overheads by computing with a smaller data set. Uniform (blind) sampling is simple and fast, but it does not take into account the spatial and temporal characteristics of the data stream. Instead, Jin et al. proposed a spatial subsampling approximation to the k-mean clustering problem in [12]. The algorithm first applies serial k-mean clustering to a small random (blind) subsample from the original data set. Next, the algorithm iteratively adds further data points from the complete data set to this initial subsample based on proximity to the boundary of clusters. Dependent on the number of iterations, the approach reduces both the time complexity and the accuracy of the clusters produced, although the requirement to store the entire data set does not change the space complexity. In a similar way, Ali et al. used stored sensor data about past changes to estimate the likelihood that new data will provide important information about monitored events [4]. The approach then subsamples and prioritizes processing based on this estimate. Another important area for subsampling strategies has been streaming trajectory data. Subsamples may be based, for example, on whether new data strongly indicates a change in the direction of movement of an object [21] or deviation from its expected trajectory [23].

In this work, we apply ideas from both parallelization and subsampling in the development of a stream operator for spatial interpolation in the context of an online algorithm.

3   Architecture

The RISER project (resilient information systems for emergency response) aims to develop new technologies and information systems capable of capturing, collating, and communicating timely and relevant information, even in the extreme and unexpected circumstances surrounding an emergency. As part of this project, a prototype system for real-time environmental monitoring of changes relevant to wildfire hazard has been developed and deployed. The RISER system has three main components:

- **RISERnet**: RISERnet is a redeployable research wireless sensor network for monitoring environmental changes. The network currently consists of 70

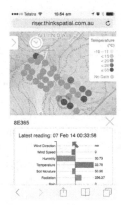

a. RISERnet geosensor mote   b. RISERview iPhone interface

Fig. 1. RISERnet wireless sensor mote in Olinda, Victoria (a) and RISERview web-interface to real-time sensor data (b)

wireless sensor motes (Libelium Waspmotes), with on-board sensors monitoring environmental parameters including temperature, humidity, soil moisture, solar radiation, wind speed and direction. The network has been deployed in wildfire-prone environments in Olinda, in Powelltown, and in Anglesea, in Victoria, Australia (Figure 1a). The motes are on average about 80m from their nearest neighbor. Different network topologies have been adopted across the three sites. The Olinda network consists of 40 sensor motes which were deployed on a 4 × 10 grid. In Anglesea, a star topology was adopted. The Powelltown site has heterogeneous vegetation so an irregular deployment was used, in order to form a robust multi-hop mesh network. The motes were distributed more densely in dense-vegetation regions, where RF attenuation is higher. In sparse-vegetation regions, the motes are farther from each other.

– **RISERview**: RISERview is a web-based interface to data from RISERnet. The Leaflet-based map interface includes a timeslider to allow access to both real-time and historical sensor data, as well access to detailed current and historical data from individual nodes (Figure 1b).

– **Middle-tier**: The architecture middle tier is constructed from a PostGIS spatial database for historical data storage and a stream processing system for notifications, spatial analysis, and bridging the PostGIS spatial database and the streaming sensor data.

The overall RISER system architecture is shown in Figure 2. Each geosensor node in the RISERnet network captures data from its on-board sensors a regular intervals (configurable, but by default every 15 minutes). Nodes communicate real-time sensed data to on of four special gateway nodes (called Meshliums) via a wireless (WiFi) multihop mesh network. Gateway nodes forward aggregated data via a 3G WAN connection to the stream processing platform, implemented in IBM InfoSphere Streams. The stream processing platform is discussed further in the following section. Amongst its functions the stream processing platform updates the PostGIS spatial database with new data tuples. In turn the RISERview user interface presents current and historical data from stored in the spatial database based on a Node.js server, a Leaflet map interface, and a D3.js interface to the graphs of historical data at each node.

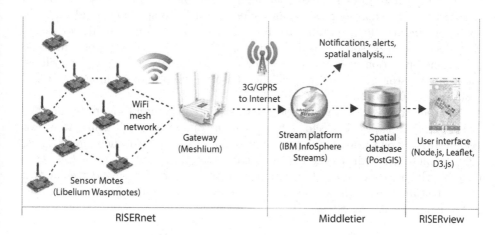

Fig. 2. RISER system architecture

3.1 Stream Processing

Stream processing systems are amongst the most familiar class of information systems that adopt an online approach to information processing. In a stream processing system, online algorithms are implemented as operators that can be applied to dynamic, sequential input data sources (termed "streams"). Just like a GIS, one can approach the architecture of a stream processing platform from the perspective of the key functions of a spatial database: data capture, storage and management, retrieval, and analysis.

Data Capture. Traditional databases are not well-adapted for frequent updates and highly dynamic data (a challenge that some other areas, such as moving object databases, have also faced [25]). In most spatial databases, the capture of new data is a relatively infrequent operation, with data occasionally input, for example, from stored spatial data files. By contrast, in stream processing systems, data capture is continually occurring. Typically, such data consists of a sequence of timestamped *tuples*, each containing a spatial reference (e.g., a point or polygonal region), some measured observations (such as temperature or soil moisture), and potentially an object identifier (e.g., the identity of the person or vehicle to which that tuple refers). In stream processing, data steams are not allowed to be blocked in any situation: the stream processing system must be ready to accept new data items at any time, even at uncertain and time-varying rates.

Data Storage and Management. In traditional databases, data once captured can be restructured and managed at any time, for example through generation of indexes. In stream processing systems, however, data once captured must be managed "in motion" and input tuples may only be seen once at a stream's input port [16]. Thus, stream processing systems involve the design and definition of a *workflow*, where data is passed through a sequence of stream operations as it is received. Stream operations can include "split" (to split and send multiple copies of the stream in parallel to different process); "filter" (to discard data that does not meet some criteria); "aggregate" or "functor" (to perform some processing operation upon the data, such as spatial analysis, below); as well as, for example, storage in a traditional database for subsequent offline query and analysis (cf. Figure 2).

Another key restriction of stream data storage and management is that the order of input tuples is decided by upstream operators [16]. Thus, it is not possible to rely on tuples arriving at an operator in the order of their timestamps. The distinction is akin to the conventional distinction between *valid time* (the time at which a change or observation occurred in the world) and *transaction time* (the time when transaction involving a data item occurred in the database) in temporal database systems [26]

Data Retrieval. Efficient retrieval of data is a key function of databases. A wide range of ingenious spatial indexes, for example, ensure that complex and voluminous spatial data can still be retrieved efficiently from a spatial database. However, because of the continuous and high rate of update of data streams, an important challenge of stream processing systems is to make efficient use of volatile (rather than persistent) memory. Thus a key restriction of stream processing systems is that only a limited number of tuples can be saved in the in-operator (volatile) memory [16]. Tuples that are not needed frequently can still be stored and indexed in persistent database storage, and retrieved as required. However, efficient and low-latency stream operations also typically require a significant amount of data in volatile working memory.

Data Analysis. Finally, at the core of any stream processing system is its stream operations: the online algorithms that enable efficient and accurate processing of dynamic data. Just like a spatial database system, a spatiotemporal stream processing platform is expected to implement spatial data analysis functions, such as computing geometric or topological spatial relations, performing network analysis, or spatial interpolation. The challenge of designing spatiotemporal stream operators is to scale to large data volumes and high data rates, at the same time as achieving low latency, near real-time execution [17]. Further, the results of a stream operator should still be of comparable accuracy as the conventional offline alternative [16]. Balancing the needs for both high scalability and high accuracy is at the core of spatiotemporal stream operator design.

3.2   Stream Processing Platform

RISER uses IBM InfoSphere Streams, a commercial stream computing platform with a modular, component-based programming model. Developers are able to build user-defined functions and operators with C++ and Java APIs, integrated using InfoSphere Streams own Stream Programming Language (SPL). The platform offers specific functionality within a number of toolkits:

- *SPL Standard toolkit*: includes data source and sink operators, utility operators, and relational operators.
- *Geospatial toolkit*: offers a limited number of functions for spatial analysis and supports different earth models (e.g., WGS84). Developers can define point, line, and polygon objects; calculate the distance between two points under different earth models (`distance` function); convert distance between different unit systems; and determine whether an objected is contained in a polygon object (`isContained` function).
- *Database toolkit*: provides a set of SPL operators that can integrate a stream programs with most external database systems.
- *Complex Event Processing toolkit*: developers can define their own "patterns" for events to detect and track.
- *Mining toolkit*: provides operators for data classification, clustering, regression, and associations.
- *R-project toolkit*: provides access to the R statistical computing environment.
- *TimeSeries toolkit*: facilitates time series data analysis on the InfoSphere Streams.

In RISER, the stream processing platform forms the bridge between the data streams emanating from the geosensor network and all the other uses of these streams. For example, a notification service can easily be implemented as a stream operator to immediately alert engineers when nodes or sensors appear to have developed a fault (e.g., become non-responsive or generate spurious data), or when sensor values go beyond predefined thresholds. The stream processing platform also updates a conventional spatial database (PostGIS) as new data from the sensor network is received, which in turn is used for the basic user interface (RISERview, Figure 2). However, in the following section, we examine the development of a suite of stream operators to perform online spatial analysis on the sensor data streams.

4   Stream-Based Spatial Interpolation Operator

While the positions of sensor nodes in the field may be irregular (as described in section 3), bushfire spread simulation tools, such as PHOENIX RapidFire [22], require regular, gridded inputs. Hence in order to connect the RISERnet streams to such tools, the measurements need to be interpolated spatially. Moving beyond using streams for simple notification and database update, a stream-based interpolation operator was required for monitoring spatial change no only over the point locations of sensors, but interpolated over the whole monitored space. The operator needed to be efficient, scaling to not only tens or hundreds of nodes, but the thousands of nodes or more envisaged in future larger deployments.

Before exploring the performance of the interpolation operator, in the following section, In this section, we briefly outline the key design concepts used in constructing the stream interpolation operator, with reference to two fundamental stream constructs: ports and windows.

4.1   Ports

A fundamental part of the anatomy of any stream operator are its input and output *ports*. Input ports accept data from streams, as well as potentially other sources (such as configuration parameters); the results of processing the input streams itself produces one or more data streams, generated at the output ports. Operators in InfoSphere Streams are composable, where the outputs of stream operators can be connected to the inputs of other operators in a workflow (see Figure 3).

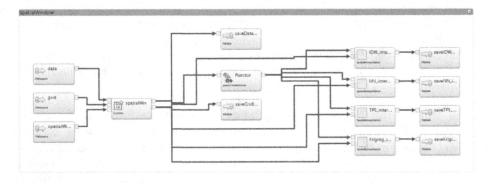

Fig. 3. Polymorphic spatial interpolation operators embedded in RISER stream workflow

Our stream interpolation operator is designed to support four common spatial interpolation algorithms: inverse distance weighting (IDW), natural neighborhood (NN), thin plate spline (TPS), and ordinary Kriging (OK). While these spatial interpolation techniques differ widely in their specific algorithmic details, from the perspective of a stream processing system they are structurally similar, requiring two input ports and one output port (see Figure 3).

The first input port is configured to accept the source points for the interpolation (in our case, those data items from the geosensor network). The attributes of these source tuples must include the coordinates and values at the source points. The second input point accepts tuples describing the set of target (output) points for which data will be interpolated. These tuples contain simply the coordinates of the target points. The single output port outputs the interpolation results: the values interpolated at the target points based on the data from the source points.

InfoSphere Streams allows stream operators to be *polymorphic*. Given the commonality in underlying structure, all four spatial interpolation algorithms were implemented within a single stream operator. The underlying code implementing each specific algorithm was written using a combination of Perl and C++. A configurable parameter allows the underlying structure to be reused, and the user to specify which of the four interpolation algorithms are required at a particular time.

4.2   Windows

Another fundamental concept in stream operator design is *windowing*. For many operations, including spatial interpolation, it does not make sense to process each input data tuple individually, immediately it is received. Rather, incoming data from a stream may need to be held in a buffer for a short while in order for a stream operator to process a batch of recent data together. A port's windowing type and policy defines the characteristics of that buffer.

Temporal Windows. Temporal windows decompose data streams into discrete units for processing. Two of the most common types of temporal window are *tumbling* windows and *sliding* windows. A tumbling window has a *flush* policy, which specifies when the entire contents of the window is expunged. Thus, streaming data is continually input into the window, until the flush policy is triggered and the process begins again. A sliding window is akin to a FIFO list, and is configured through a *trigger* policy and an *eviction* policy. When the trigger policy is satisfied, the window generates an event to execute a function on the tuples currently in the window. When the eviction policy is satisfied, the window expunges old tuples from the window.

These policies can be *count-based* (e.g., dependent on the number of tuples in the window); *time-based* (e.g., dependent on the maximum difference in timestamps between valid tuples in the window); *delta-based* (dependent on the maximum difference in value between valid tuples in the window); or in the case of tumbling windows *punctuation-based* (based on an "signal" from an upstream operator that the window should be flushed). Although not all stream processing platforms implement all policy types, count-based and time-based policies at least are common to any stream processing system (cf. [20]).

In the case of our spatial interpolators, the windowing type and policy has a critical role in controlling the stream operator. The second input port (target points) of the operator supports only punctuation-based tumbling windows. This ensures as many target points as needed can be provided, and only explicit punctuation by an upstream operator can cause the target points to be reset.

The first input port (source points) of our operator is configured as a tumbling window, rather than a sliding window, since source points need to be processed once, as a set, once sufficient source data has been received from the stream. This port supports any of count-based, delta-based, time-based, and punctuation based tumbling temporal window configurations. When this port's window is flushed, an event is generated that causes the expunged set of tuples from the window to be treated as source points for the chosen spatial interpolation. The values at the target points are interpolated and submitted to the output port, followed by a window marker punctuation to inform the downstream operators that the most recent interpolation is finished.

Spatial Windows. Unlike temporal windows, InfoSphere Streams does not offer native support for spatial windows. However, it was straightforward to develop code for implementing four types of spatial windows—extent-based, distance-based, k-proximity, and tessellated spatial windows, after [20]—based on existing functionality.

Distance- and Extent-based Spatial Windows. Distance-based windows filter out data in the stream that is greater than some specified distance from a known point. Extent-based spatial windows generalize distance-based windows by filtering out data in the stream that falls outside the extents of a defined region, potentially of arbitrary shape. In practice, however, the region covered by an extent-based spatial window must be able to be defined by an expression with finite number of variables (such as a polygon).

In implementing distance- and extent-based spatial windows, a custom stream operator was constructed using the `distance` and `isContained` functions native to the Geospatial Toolkit (distance-based and extent-based spatial windows, respectively).

k-proximity Spatial Windows. k-proximity windows are applied over the locations in the stream, finding the k-nearest neighbors (kNN) for each of a set of input seed points [20]. A k-proximity spatial window operator was implemented in a similar way to the distance-based spatial window, with the addition of an efficient k-nearest neighbors search algorithm (based on the nn-c library).

Tessellated Spatial Windows. A tessellated spatial window operator is a generalization of an extent-based spatial window to a partition of space (such as a grid). Thus the tessellated spatial window operator works in a similar fashion to the extent-based spatial window. The key difference is instead of filtering out tuples outside the defined extent, the tessellated spatial window operator adds a new attribute to every tuple based on the ID if the region in which the tuple is contained.

As we shall see, spatial windowing, and in particular tessellated spatial windows, play an important role in making spatial interpolation scalable in the cases of OK (ordinary Kriging) and TPS (thin-plate spline) interpolation.

5   Results

The spatial interpolation stream operators were successfully implemented, and operate smoothly and in real-time upon the geosensor network data generated by RISERnet. However, in order to provide a more rigorous test, the operators were also tested on simulated data for two reasons: 1. simulated data allows us to know the "true" surface and compare evaluate accuracy of different operator and windowing options; 2. simulated data allows arbitrarily large sets of source data points to be generated, where today's real geosensor networks are still limited in size to only tens or hundreds of nodes.

5.1   Experimental Design

Simulated Surface. A dynamic temperature field was simulated using a mixture of 2,000 Gaussian functions. The signs of these functions obey a first-order binomial distribution $B(1, 0.5)$. The centers of the Gaussian functions are distributed uniformly across the test area. The ranges of the Gaussian functions is a uniform random number between 0.2 and 0.3. A snapshot of the temperature field is shown in 4.

Fig. 4. A snapshot of the "true" simulated surface to be interpolated

Simulated Network. Further, up to 32,000 randomly distributed wireless sensor nodes connected via a total of 16 gateways were assumed to be deployed across the simulated testing area. Like a real sensor network, the simulated sensor nodes formed a multi-hop mesh network and forwarded sensed data to their nearest gateway (see Figure 5a, with gateways marked and subnetworks differentiated using different colors). The input tuples to the stream interpolation operator was generated by sampling this surface with data captured at these points by simulated sensor nodes. As for RISERnet, the nodes and the subnetworks are synchronized, with nodes reporting sensor readings to the associated gateway periodically. The gateways then relay the readings to the stream system.

However, geosensor networks are inherently unreliable. Nodes may occasionally fail to correctly generate or communicate data for a variety of reasons, and

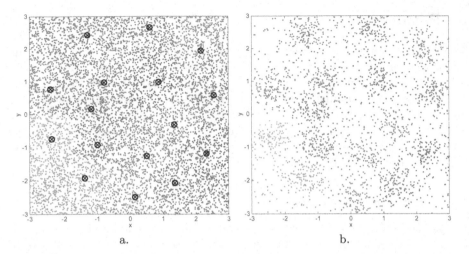

a.   b.

Fig. 5. Simulated temperature field and wireless sensor network (a), along with subset of dots of which the colours illustrate the subnetworks. Gateways are represented by the circles with a cross.

data is frequently lost either in communication or at the source. Nodes further from the associated gateway require more hops to relay a message, increasingly the likelihood of data loss. To improve the realism of our simulation, the possibility of successful communication is also modeled as:

$$P(r) = (1 - g) \exp\left(-\frac{r^2}{2\sigma_r^2}\right) + g \tag{1}$$

where r is the distance from the node to the associated gateway, $g = 0.1$ is the nugget, and $\sigma_r = 0.25$. Figure 5b shows an example realization of the subset of successfully communicating nodes at one particular epoch. In practice, this means approximately 30% of the data from the network is successfully received by the stream processing operator at any one epoch. Thus for a network of 8,000 nodes, on average 2,500 data points may actually be received and processed at any one epoch. This high level of attrition reflects the extremes of our practical experience with real networks wireless geosensor networks like RISERnet, where at any one epoch substantial proportions of data may be lost, even though over time very large volumes of data are received.

Spatial Windowing. The computationally intensive nature of spatial interpolation necessitated the use of tessellated spatial windows to partition the networks into tractable subregions. Three different spatial partitions were tested, shown in Figure 6: a regular grid; the Voronoi diagram, based on the locations of gateways as seeds; and a customized scheme based on the Delaunay triangulation of the gateway locations.

To aid comparison, the three partitions were designed with the same number of elements in the partition (16). The grid-based decomposition is straightforward

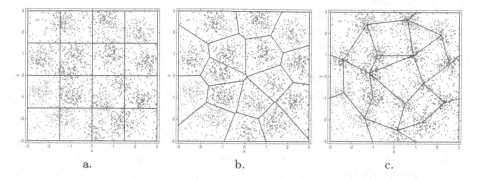

Fig. 6. Three tessellated spatial window schemes: (a) uniform grid; (b) Voronoi diagram; and (c) Delaunay triangulation-based partition

to generate. The Voronoi-based decomposition reflects the subnetworks. The Delaunay-based triangulation explicitly combines data from different subnetworks. Later experiments will investigate the effects of the different windowing schemes.

5.2   Interpolation Technique

Figure 7 depicts typical results from applying the different interpolation operators, in this case to a simulation with 8,000 sensor nodes (approximately 2,500 tuples points at each epoch). Figure 7a shows the mean processing time for our stream operator to generate the output using the different interpolation methods and Voronoi-based spatial windowing. Figure 7a shows the mean error (RMSE) of the output generated, when compared with the original simulated surface.

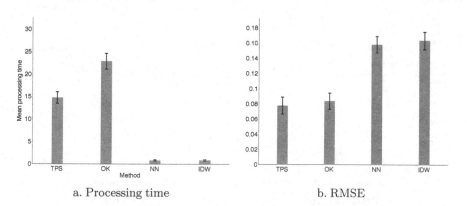

a. Processing time   b. RMSE

Fig. 7. Mean processing time (a) and error (b) for four interpolation techniques, based on 8,000 sensor nodes ($\approx$2,500 data points)

As might be expected, the results show the NN and IDW interpolation schemes are substantially faster to compute than TPS or OK, due to their lower computational complexity. However, all interpolations could be computed in a reasonable amount of time for a practical stream processing system, less than 25 seconds in the worst case, and less than one second in the case of NN or IDW. As might also be expected, the increased efficiency of NN and IDW comes at the cost of decreased accuracy. The benefit of using TPS and OK are that the provide a better characterization of the surface. In practice, the best balance between efficiency and accuracy will depend on the specific application. For example, in cases where the interpolated surface is required as an input to a bushfire simulation system, higher accuracy interpolation is highly desirable, due to the likely amplification of errors in the interpolated surface due to error propagation. On the other hand, where the surface is required purely for visualization or real-time applications, more efficient but less accurate methods are more appropriate, especially for larger geosensor networks.

5.3   Scalability of Kriging

Taking Kriging as the least efficient interpolation method, further experiments examined the balance of efficiency and accuracy of ordinary Kriging over the a range of network sizes and spatial windowing options. Figure 8 shows the processing time and output RMSE for the OK stream operator for 625, 1.25K, 2.5K, 5K, and 10K data points (i.e., 2K, 4K, 8K, 16K, and 32K sensor nodes). The Figure clearly shows that the Voronoi tessellated spatial window scheme is consistently the most efficient, outperforming either the uniform grid or the Delaunay-based spatial windows. Conversely, the Voronoi scheme is consistent the *least* accurate, outperformed by both uniform grid and Delaunay-based schemes. Statistical hypothesis tests confirm this observation in all cases at the 5% level, with the only exception of the runtimes of the very smallest data sets (625 and 1.25K data points).

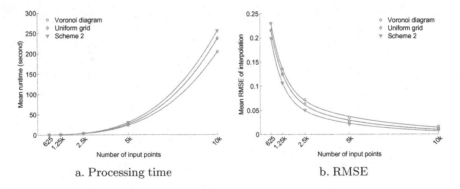

a. Processing time   b. RMSE

Fig. 8. Mean processing time (a) and error (b) for OK interpolation over 625, 1.25K, 2.5K, 5K, and 10K data points (2K, 4K, 8K, 16K, and 32K sensor nodes)

The explanation for these differences comes from the structure of source points within each cell of the tessellation. The nature of the Voronoi tessellation means that in general the set of Voronoi cells tend to have a similar number of source points. As a consequence, the performance of the stream interpolator within each spatial window is similar. However, cutting across Voronoi cells, the Delaunay-based tessellation tends to have rather more variable numbers of source points in each window. The overall time taken for interpolation is limited by the worst case of each individual spatial window, and hence the Delaunay-based tessellation tends to perform worst.

However, in terms of accuracy, the structure of the Voronoi cells means the Voronoi boundaries tends lie in locations where there is least information from the sensor nodes (because those nodes are necessarily furthest from the gateway, and so more likely to suffer data loss). As a result, edge effects reduce the accuracy of interpolation across the Voronoi cells. Conversely, the Delaunay-based triangulation cuts across Voronoi cells, averaging data from different subnetwork in the interpolation, and reducing edge effects. In both cases, the grid-based decomposition provides and intermediate case between these two extremes.

6   Conclusions

In this paper we have showcased the RISER system, which combines data from a redeployable geosensor network currently in a wildfire prone area of Victoria, Australia, with web-GIS technologies for data storage and presentation. However, the inherently dynamic, voluminous, unreliable data from geosensor networks demands the use of online processing methods, such as stream processing, rather than the offline, batch-based processing commonly used with GIS. Thus, the overall system architecture has a stream processing platform at its heart. The paper explores the characteristics of the stream processing core, as well as the detailed design of a stream processing operator for spatial interpolation, implementing four different interpolation techniques. An brief empirical exploration of the performance of this operator highlights the balance between efficiency and accuracy that must be struck in stream-based interpolation. More efficient interpolation techniques and spatial windowing structures tend to lead to less accurate results, and vice versa.

Current work is investigating further the development of substantially more efficient stream-based interpolation algorithms, for example, by taking advantage of temporal autocorrelation in sensor readings. Future work will also investigate a wider range of streaming spatial analysis operations, as well as investigating other approaches to stream interpolation that may have a larger influence upon the balance between efficiency and accuracy, such as stream subsampling.

References

1. Albers, S.: Online algorithms: A survey. Mathematical Programming **97**(1–2), 3–26 (2003)

2. Ali, M.H., Aref, W.G., Kamel, I.: Scalability management in sensor-network phenom-enabases. In: 18th International Conference on Scientific and Statistical Database Management, 2006, pp. 91–100. IEEE (2006)
3. Ali, M.H., Mokbel, M.F., Aref, W.G.: Phenomenon-aware stream query processing. In: 2007 International Conference on Mobile Data Management, pp. 8–15. IEEE (2007)
4. Ali, M.H., Mokbel, M.F., Aref, W.G., Kamel, I.: Detection and tracking of discrete phenomena in sensor-network databases. In: SSDBM, pp. 163–172 (2005)
5. Armstrong, M.P., Marciano, R.J.: Local interpolation using a distributed parallel supercomputer. International Journal of Geographical Information Systems 10(6), 713–729 (1996)
6. Cramer, B.E., Armstrong, M.P.: An evaluation of domain decomposition strategies for parallel spatial interpolation of surfaces. Geographical Analysis 31(2), 148–168 (1999)
7. Ding, Y., Densham, P.J.: Spatial strategies for parallel spatial modelling. International Journal of Geographical Information Systems 10(6), 669–698 (1996)
8. Duchon, J.: Splines minimizing rotation-invariant semi-norms in Sobolev spaces. In: Constructive theory of functions of several variables, pp. 85–100. Springer (1977)
9. Guan, Q., Kyriakidis, P.C., Goodchild, M.F.: A parallel computing approach to fast geostatistical areal interpolation. International Journal of Geographical Information Science 25(8), 1241–1267 (2011)
10. Hawick, K.A., Coddington, P.D., James, H.A.: Distributed frameworks and parallel algorithms for processing large-scale geographic data. Parallel Computing 29(10), 1297–1333 (2003)
11. Huang, Q., Yang, C.: Optimizing grid computing configuration and scheduling for geospatial analysis: An example with interpolating DEM. Computers and Geosciences 37(2), 165–176 (2011)
12. Jin, R., Goswami, A., Agrawal, G.: Fast and exact out-of-core and distributed k-means clustering. Knowledge and Information Systems 10(1), 17–40 (2006)
13. Kamel, I., Al Aghbari, Z., Awad, T.: Mg-join: Detecting phenomena and their correlation in high dimensional data streams. Distributed and Parallel Databases 28(1), 67–92 (2010)
14. Kidner, D.B., Rallings, P.J., Ware, J.A.: Parallel processing for terrain analysis in GIS: Visibility as a case study. GeoInformatica 1(2), 183–207 (1997)
15. Nittel, S., Leung, K.T.: Parallelizing clustering of geoscientific data sets using data streams. In: Proceedings of the 16th International Conference on Scientific and Statistical Database Management, 2004, pp. 73–84. IEEE (2004)
16. Nittel, S., Leung, K.T., Braverman, A.: Scaling clustering algorithms for massive data sets using data streams. In: ICDE, vol. 4, p. 830 (2004)
17. Nittel, S., Whittier, J.C., Liang, Q.: Real-time spatial interpolation of continuous phenomena using mobile sensor data streams. In: Proceedings of the 20th International Conference on Advances in Geographic Information Systems, pp. 530–533. ACM (2012)
18. Oliver, M.A., Webster, R.: Kriging: A method of interpolation for geographical information systems. International Journal of Geographical Information System 4(3), 313–332 (1990)
19. Palpanas, T.: Real-time data analytics in sensor networks. In: Managing and Mining Sensor Data, pp. 173–210. Springer (2013)
20. Patroumpas, K., Sellis, T.: Semantics of spatially-aware windows over streaming moving objects. In: 2007 International Conference on Mobile Data Management, pp. 52–59. IEEE (2007)

21. Potamias, M., Patroumpas, K., Sellis, T.: Sampling trajectory streams with spatiotemporal criteria. In: 18th International Conference on Scientific and Statistical Database Management, 2006, pp. 275–284. IEEE (2006)
22. Tolhurst, K., Shields, B., Chong, D.: Phoenix: development and application of a bushfire risk management tool. Emergency Management Australia 23(4), 47–54 (2008)
23. Trajcevski, G., Cao, H., Scheuermanny, P., Wolfsonz, O., Vaccaro, D.: On-line data reduction and the quality of history in moving objects databases. In: Proceedings of the 5th ACM International Workshop on Data Engineering for Wireless and Mobile Access, pp. 19–26. ACM (2006)
24. Wang, S., Armstrong, M.P.: A quadtree approach to domain decomposition for spatial interpolation in grid computing environments. Parallel Computing 29(10), 1481–1504 (2003)
25. Wolfson, O., Xu, B., Chamberlain, S., Jiang, L.: Moving objects databases: issues and solutions. In: Proc. Tenth International Conference on Scientific and Statistical Database Management (SSDM), pp. 111–122 (1998)
26. Worboys, M.: A unified model of spatial and temporal information. Computer Journal 8(4), 26–34 (1994)

Opportunistic Trajectory Recommendation for Task Accomplishment in Crowdsourcing Systems

André Sales Fonteles[(✉)], Sylvain Bouveret, and Jérôme Gensel

LIG, Université Grenoble Alpes, F-38000 Grenoble, France
{andre.sales-fonteles,sylvain.bouveret,jerome.gensel}@imag.fr

Abstract. Crowdsourcing market systems (CMS) are platforms that enable one to publish tasks that others are intended to accomplished. Usually, these are systems where users, called workers, perform tasks using desktop computers. Recently, some CMS have appeared with spatiotemporal tasks that requires a worker to be at a given location within a given time window to be accomplished. In this paper, we introduce the trajectory recommendation problem (or TRP) where a CMS tries to find and recommend a trajectory for a mobile worker that allows him to accomplish tasks he has some affinity with without compromising his arrival in time at destination. We show that TRP is NP-hard and then propose an exact algorithm for solving it. Our experimentation proved that using our algorithm for recommending trajectories is a feasible solution when up to a few hundred tasks must be analyzed to find an optimal solution.

Keywords: Spatial task assignment · Task recommendation · Spatial crowdsourcing

1 Introduction

Over the last years, many crowdsourcing market systems (CMS) in which a group of users, called workers, can contribute to achieve goals or solve tasks have appeared. These systems make use of the human intelligence to accomplish tasks that computers alone are not efficient in or not able to accomplish themselves [8], such as text translation, voice transcription, semantic tagging of images, content creation and others. The Amazon Mechanical Turk (MTurk) is probably the best known example of such kind of systems that also includes names as CrowdFlower[1] and oDesk[2].

More recently, a different kind of CMS has appeared, e.g. Sereale[3], TaskRabbit[4], Medusa [13], where a *requester* may publish a *spatiotemporal* task that

---

[1] http://www.crowdflower.com
[2] http://www.odesk.com
[3] https://www.sereale.fr
[4] https://www.taskrabbit.com

© Springer International Publishing Switzerland 2015
J. Gensel and M. Tomko (Eds.): W2GIS 2015, LNCS 9080, pp. 178–190, 2015.
DOI: 10.1007/978-3-319-18251-3_11

requires a worker to be in a specific location within a given time window in order to accomplish it. For example, a spatiotemporal task may request someone to go to the intersection of two streets within a specific time window and record a short video using his smartphone in order to allow a third party system or someone else to analyze the current traffic status there. In general, most spatiotemporal tasks requires the worker to use a mobile device (e.g., smartphone and tablet) and its embedded sensors (e.g., camera, GPS, microphone) to be accomplished. However, some other tasks such as "clean up my house between 8:00 am and 11:30 am" may be still considered spatiotemporal tasks, although not requiring a smartphone for accomplishing.

In this work, we focus on CMS containing spatiotemporal tasks. More specifically, we focus on the following scenario. A worker wants to travel from a location to another and the CMS opportunistically recommends a trajectory for accomplishing spatiotemporal tasks in chain without compromising his arrival in time at the destination. According to Musthag and Ganesan [11,12], providing workers with such trajectory recommendation can improve their efficiency when dealing with spatiotemporal tasks. Moreover, such "action plans" have shown to be useful to workers in online crowdsourcing [9], and could be useful for spatiotemporal tasks as well.

When recommending a trajectory, besides respecting the deadline, other aspects must be also taken into account. For example, every task is associated with a time window during which it can be accomplished. Thus, a trajectory must lead a worker to arrive at a task within its time window. Furthermore, rather than recommending a shortest path to the worker, the goal of the system is to recommend a trajectory with tasks with which the worker has the greatest possible affinity,[5] and consequently very likely to be accepted. We call the problem of finding such trajectory for a worker a Trajectory Recommendation Problem, or TRP. The main contributions of this paper are the presentation and formalization of TRP and an exact algorithm for solving it.

The remaining of this work is organized as follows. In Section 2, we define formally the Trajectory Recommendation Problem and study its complexity. In Section 3, we present a brute-force approach for solving TRP and then propose a better exact algorithm. Section 4 reports the results of our experiments. In Section 5, we review the related works. Section 6 concludes the paper and presents our future work.

2   Trajectory Recommendation Problem

2.1   Preliminary Definitions

A task s is a request for a service to be fulfilled by a worker in a given location within a given time window. We characterize a task as $s = (l^s, \tau_1^s, \tau_2^s, \delta^s)$, where l^s is the location where the task must be accomplished, $\tau_1^s \in \mathbb{N}$ and $\tau_2^s \in \mathbb{N}$

---

[5] The affinity (or interest) of the worker for a task s is represented as a utility function $u(s)$.

are respectively the earliest time and the latest time (time window) in which a worker must start doing it, and δ^s is the duration of a task.

2.2   Problem Definition

Definition 1. *An* instance of the trajectory recommendation problem TRP *is a tuple* $(\mathcal{S}, u, l_o, l_d, \tau_o, \tau_d, \mathcal{G})$, *where:*

- $\mathcal{S} = \{s_1, \ldots, s_n\}$ *is a set of tasks;*
- $u : \mathcal{S} \rightarrow \mathbb{R}^+$ *is a utility function, which maps each task* s_i *with a utility, that we write* $u(s_i)$, *specifying the interest of the worker for this task;*
- l_o *is the initial location (origin) of the worker;*
- l_d *is the final location (destination) that the worker has to reach;*
- $\tau_o \in \mathbb{N}$ *is the earliest time in which the worker can start traveling from location* l_o;
- τ_d *is the latest ending time (deadline) at which the worker must arrive at location* l_d;
- $\mathcal{G} = (V, E, d)$ *is a weighted directed graph, where* $V = (\{l^s | s \in \mathcal{S}\} \cup \{l_o, l_d\})$ *is the set of* vertices *(or locations),* $E \subset V^2$ *is the set of* edges, *with* $v \neq v'$ *for each* $(v, v') \in E$, *and* d *is a* cost *function mapping each edge* $(v, v') \in E$ *to a number in* $\mathbb{N}$ *specifying the time it takes to travel from location* v *to* v'.

Let $\mathcal{I} = (\mathcal{S}, u, l_o, l_d, \tau_o, \tau_d, \mathcal{G})$ be an instance of the TRP. A *trajectory* for $\mathcal{I}$ is a sequence $T = \langle (s_1^T, t_1), \ldots, (s_m^T, t_m) \rangle$ of tasks to be executed attached with a respective time of arrival. The time of arrival is defined as follows:

$$t_i = \begin{cases} \max(\tau_1^{s_1^T}, \tau_o + d(l_o, l^{s_1^T})) & \text{if } i = 1 \\ \max(\tau_1^{s_i^T}, t_{i-1} + \delta^{s_{i-1}^T} + d(l^{s_{i-1}^T}, l^{s_i^T})) & \text{if } i > 1 \end{cases}$$

where *max* models that a worker may wait for $\tau_1^{s_i^T}$ in order to accomplish task s_i^T if he arrives before its time window.

A trajectory T is *valid* if and only if it satisfies all the following conditions:

1. for all $(s_i^T, t_i) \in T$, $t_i \in [\tau_1^{s_i^T}, \tau_2^{s_i^T}]$ (a task should be done in the correct time window); and
2. $t_m + \delta^{s_m^T} + d(l^{s_m^T}, l_d) \leq \tau_d$ (the worker must arrive at his destination before the deadline).

For the sake of simplicity, in the remaining of the paper, sometimes we refer to a trajectory as a sequence of tasks. For example, let A, B, and C be tasks and $T = \langle (A, t_A), (C, t_C), (B, t_B) \rangle$ be a trajectory on these tasks. The trajectory T can be also represented as $\langle A \rightarrow C \rightarrow B \rangle$.

Given a valid trajectory T, the *utility* of T is simply the sum of the utilities associated with every task executed on the trajectory, namely:

$$u(T) = \sum_{(s_i^T, t_i) \in T} u(s_i^T)$$

We can now put things together and define the *trajectory recommendation problem* as follows:

Problem TRP

Input:	A tuple $(\mathcal{S}, u, l_o, l_d, \tau_o, \tau_d, \mathcal{G})$.

Question: What is the valid trajectory T, if any exists, with the highest utility?

2.3 Problem Complexity

In the following sections, we will assume that for any TRP instance considered, both u (the utility function) and d (the cost function) are polynomial-time computable. Under this assumption, we prove that the decision version of TRP is NP-complete by reduction from the *Traveling Salesman Problem* (TSP) defined as follows:

Problem TSP

Input:	A set $C = c_1, \ldots, c_m$ of m cities, a distance function $d : C \times C \to \mathbb{N}$, and an integer k

Question: Is there a permutation σ of $[1, m]$ such that $d(c_{\sigma(m)}, c_{\sigma(1)}) + \sum_{i=1}^{m-1} d(c_{\sigma(i)}, c_{\sigma(i+1)}) \leq k$?

Theorem 1. *Given a tuple $(\mathcal{S}, u, l_o, l_d, \tau_o, \tau_d, \mathcal{G})$ and a number k, deciding whether there exists a valid trajectory T, such that $u(T) \geq k$ is NP-complete. That is, the decision version of* TRP *is NP-complete.*

Proof. Membership to NP follows from the fact that the validity of a trajectory can be checked in polynomial time, as well as the computation of its utility. For hardness we can use the following reduction. From an instance $((\mathcal{C}, d), k)$ of the TSP, we can create the instance $((G, \mathcal{S}, u, l_o, l_d, \tau_o, \tau_d), k')$ of the decision version of TRP defined as follows:

- $\mathcal{G}$ is a complete graph between m vertices $(v_1, \ldots, v_m)$, and $d(v_i, v_j) = d(c_i, c_j)$;
- $\mathcal{S} = \{s_1, ..., s_m\}$, where $l^{s_i} = v_i$, $\tau_1^{s_i} = 0$, $\tau_2^{s_i} = k$ and $\delta^{s_i} = 0$;
- $u(s_i) = 1$ for all i;
- l_o can be any vertex in the graph;
- $l_d = l_o$;
- $\tau_o = 0$;
- $\tau_d = k$;
- $k' = m$.

Suppose that there is a valid trajectory T in this TRP whose utility is greater than or equal to $k' = m$. It means that all the tasks are accomplished in T. Given the definition of a valid trajectory, it means that: (i) the trajectory passes through all the nodes in the graph, and (ii), the total duration of this trajectory is less than k (the deadline). This is exactly a solution for the initial instance$((\mathcal{C}, d), k)$ of the TSP.

Conversely, suppose that there is a solution σ to the initial TSP instance. Suppose $w.l.o.g$ that $v_{\sigma(1)} = l_o$ and $s_{\sigma(i)}$ is a task whose location is $v_{\sigma(i)}$. Then one can easily see that the following trajectory:

$$\langle s_{\sigma(1)} \rightarrow s_{\sigma(2)} \rightarrow s_{\sigma(3)} \rightarrow \cdots \rightarrow s_{\sigma(m)} \rangle$$

is a valid trajectory (with a total duration of at most k).

3   Algorithms

A brute-force approach to solve TRP is to find all possible trajectories, verify which ones are valid and then which one presents the highest utility among them. Although this brute-force algorithm guarantees correctness, it is computationally very expensive. The total number of trajectories to be created and analyzed by the algorithm is the permutation of k tasks from a total of n, being $n = |S|$, where k varies from a trajectory of one task to a trajectory involving all the n tasks:

$$\sum_{k=1}^{n} \frac{n!}{(n-k)!} = \frac{n!}{0!} + \frac{n!}{1!} + \cdots + \frac{n!}{(n-1)!}$$

For example, a set $S = \{s_1, s_2\}$ would derive in a total of 4 possible trajectories, 2 with two tasks ($k = 2$): $\langle s_1 \rightarrow s_2 \rangle$ and $\langle s_2 \rightarrow s_1 \rangle$; and 2 with just one task ($k = 1$): $\langle s_1 \rangle$ and $\langle s_2 \rangle$.

3.1   Exact Algorithm

In this section, we present an approach that also gives as an output an exact answer for TRP with non negative utilities for tasks. This algorithm is based on the following lemma.

Lemma 1. *For all trajectories $T \subset T'$, $u(T') \geq u(T)$ if the utility of a task can not be negative.*

Proof. Obvious from its definition.

For example, the trajectory $T' = \langle A \rightarrow B \rightarrow C \rangle$ derived from the trajectory $T = \langle A \rightarrow B \rangle$, i.e., $T \subset T'$, has a utility $u(T')$ at least as high as $u(T)$, since $u_A + u_B + u_C \geq u_A + u_B$. Hence, if any valid trajectory T can be expanded by the addition of a new task and the result is a valid trajectory, the former can be discarded as an answer for TRP, because there is another trajectory $T' \supset T$ with a utility at least as high as $u(T)$. Thus, to define an answer for TRP, this algorithm finds the set of valid trajectories that can not be expanded any further by the addition of new tasks and compare its elements' utilities. In the following, we present the main function of the proposed algorithm.

```
Input   : An instance of TRP
Output : A trajectory with maximal utility
1  for s ∈ S do
2  |   if τ₁ˢ > τ_d OR τ₂ˢ < τ_o then
3  |   |   S = S - {s} ;
4  |   end
5  end
6  for s ∈ S do
7  |   Trajectory T = new Trajectory() ;
8  |   Set candidateTasks = S.clone() ;
9  |   expand(T, s, candidateTasks, u, l_o, τ_o, l_d, τ_d, *bestTrajectory, G);
10 end
11 return *bestTrajectory;
```

Algorithm 1. Proposed algorithm

In the main function, the first step performed is to prune the set of tasks S by removing all those that are can not be accomplished during the period between τ_o and τ_d. Then, for each task left it calls the algorithm's most important function: *expand*. The *expand* function is responsible for creating/finding valid trajectories recursively. The intuition behind *expand* is simple. First, it tries to add a new task to the end of a trajectory and then verifies if the new trajectory is valid. If it is, the function tries to expand even further recursively. If it can not expand further, it compares the trajectory with the best trajectory yet found and prunes the invalid trajectory. Following we present *expand* in details.

The expand function first verifies if it is possible for the worker to travel from the location (called *position*) of the last task of the trajectory to the new task, accomplish it and travel to the destination arriving before the deadline τ_d. If it is not the case, the task is removed from the set *candidateTasks*, i.e., from the set of tasks that may be added to the current trajectory in order to expand it further. This decision is due to the fact that if a task E can not be added to the end of a trajectory $\langle A \rightarrow C \rightarrow B \rangle$ without compromising its deadline, then it, of course, can not be added to the end of the expanded version $\langle A \rightarrow C \rightarrow B \rightarrow D \rangle$. Thus, this task is never analyzed again when expanding the original trajectory or any of its derived trajectories.

In case, for example, a new task s' can be added to the end of a trajectory T without compromising its deadline, the function checks if a worker that follows T would be able to arrive within the time window $[\tau_1^{s'}, \tau_2^{s'}]$. If so, the new task is added to the end of the trajectory, removed from *candidateTasks* and the function calls itself recursively for all tasks left in *candidateTasks*. Finally, if the trajectory is not expanded for all *candidateTasks*, the function compares its utility with the one of the best trajectory yet found. If it is higher, the new trajectory found is considered to be the best one and so on.

It is worth noting that other prune strategies can/should be also implemented in the algorithm. For example, the best possible utility for a trajectory is the one of a trajectory with all tasks $s \in S$. This could be a stop condition in

```
1  Function expand(T, s, candidateTasks, u, position, τ, l_d, τ_d,
   *bestTrajectory, G)
2  |   τ = max((τ + G.distance(position, l^s)), τ_1^s);
3  |   dTaskToDestination = G.distance(l^s, l_d);
4  |   if τ + δ^s + dTaskToDestination ≤ τ_d then
5  |   |   if τ ≤ τ_2^s then
6  |   |   |   position = l^s;
7  |   |   |   T.add(s, τ);
8  |   |   |   τ = τ + δ^s;
9  |   |   |   candidateTasks = candidateTasks.clone();
10 |   |   |   candidateTasks = candidateTasks −{s};
11 |   |   |   canExpand = false;
12 |   |   |   for s' ∈ candidateTasks do
13 |   |   |   |   canExpand = canExpand OR expand(T.clone(), s',
   |   |   |   |   candidateTasks, u, position, τ, l_d, τ_d, *bestTrajectory, G);
14 |   |   |   end
15 |   |   |   if NOT canExpand then
16 |   |   |   |   if *bestTrajectory = null OR u(T) > u(*bestTrajectory)
   |   |   |   |   then
17 |   |   |   |   |   *bestTrajectory = T;
18 |   |   |   |   end
19 |   |   |   end
20 |   |   |   return true;
21 |   |   end
22 |   else
23 |   |   candidateTasks = candidateTasks −{s};
24 |   end
25 |   return false;
26 end
```

Function expand

the algorithm if found. However, for the sake of simplicity it is not added in this paper.

Example: Consider an instance of TRP as shown in Figure 1 where $S = \{A, B, C\}$, τ_o =1:15 pm and $\tau_d = 2$:00 pm. In this example, the algorithm first tries to remove from S any task having a time window completely disjoint from the time window [1:15 pm, 2:00 pm] ($[\tau_o, \tau_d]$), though all tasks are within this periods. Then, for each task in S, the function *expand* is called passing also an empty trajectory as parameter. When executing on task A, the algorithm verifies if trajectory $\langle A \rangle$, the result of adding A to the end of an empty trajectory, is valid. Since it is, it tries to expand further by calling *expand* recursively for each task $s \in \{B, C\}$ passing now trajectory $\langle A \rangle$ as parameter. The trajectory $\langle A \to B \rangle$ is also valid therefore the algorithm tries to expand further. However, this time, $\langle A \to B \to C \rangle$ is found to be invalid because a worker could not complete it and arrive before the deadline at l_d. Since $\langle A \to B \rangle$ can not be

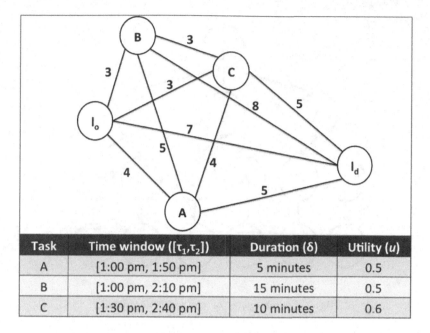

Task	Time window ($[\tau_1,\tau_2]$)	Duration (δ)	Utility (u)
A	[1:00 pm, 1:50 pm]	5 minutes	0.5
B	[1:00 pm, 2:10 pm]	15 minutes	0.5
C	[1:30 pm, 2:40 pm]	10 minutes	0.6

Fig. 1. Tasks configuration in an example of TRP instance

expanded and there is no current best trajectory yet, it is considered to be the best one found. After that, the function returns the recursion to $\langle A \rangle$ and tries to expand it to $\langle A \rightarrow C \rangle$, which is also valid and can not be expanded further. The utility of trajectory $\langle A \rightarrow C \rangle$ is then compared against the one of $\langle A \rightarrow B \rangle$, and as it is higher, $\langle A \rightarrow C \rangle$ becomes the current best trajectory. Following, the recursion returns and the algorithm searches new trajectories using $\langle B \rangle$ as a baseline. By expanding $\langle B \rangle$, a new best trajectory is found: $\langle B \rightarrow C \rightarrow A \rangle$. Finally, the algorithm searches for better trajectories using $\langle C \rangle$ as baseline, but no trajectory better than the current best one is found, and thus, $\langle B \rightarrow C \rightarrow A \rangle$ is returned as an answer for the TRP problem. Figure 2 shows the full search space of trajectories in this given example. Dark gray tasks are tasks present in invalid trajectories that were pruned, while light gray are also in invalid trajectories but were analyzed. Although in this example only one invalid trajectory is pruned, our experiments with synthetic data sets have shown that our prune strategy greatly reduces the execution time of the algorithm for bigger entries compared with the brute-force approach.

4   Experiments

In order to analyze the feasibility of using our proposed algorithm for solving TRP, we have conducted some experiments over synthetic data sets. These data sets were obtained through a small program created where it is possible to enter as input a number of tasks and receive as output a randomly generated instance

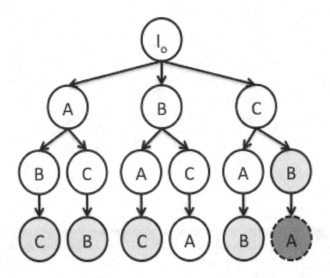

Fig. 2. Search space for the exact algorithm

of TRP. Although essentially random, all data sets shared some two common characteristics. First of all the total time length $[\tau_o, \tau_d]$ of a trajectory was fixed to 1 hour. Second, all tasks generated presented an intersection between their time window and $[\tau_o, \tau_d]$. Our experimentation were performed using a Mac Book Pro Retina with OS X Yosemite as operating system, a 3GHz Intel Core i7 processor and 8Gb 1600MHz DDR3 ram memory. The experiments were implemented using Java as programming language.

During the experimentation, we first analyzed the execution time of the brute-force approach compared with the one of the algorithm we proposed. Our first experiment has consisted in executing each algorithm 1000 times for randomly generated inputs of each size: 5, 6, 7, 8 and 9 tasks. Thus, in total we first executed 5000 times for each approach. Figure 3 shows a comparison between the average execution time in milliseconds of our proposed approach and the brute-force one. It is possible to see that with 9 tasks, the time for solving TRP using brute-force is already 250 milliseconds while our approach is still next to zero. In fact, even with 9 tasks the average execution time of our approach was 0,064 milliseconds. Although in the worst case (when all possible permutations of tasks are valid) our approach can generate as much trajectories as the brute-force one, our prune strategy is responsible for this difference between the two execution times.

In our second experiment, we have analyzed the execution time of our approach individually. We have executed our algorithm 500 times for randomly generated inputs of sizes varying from 10 to 100 task, 10 by 10. In total, it ran 5000 times. Figure 4 shows the results of the experiment in milliseconds. Even with 100 tasks as input, our algorithm proved to be capable of providing an

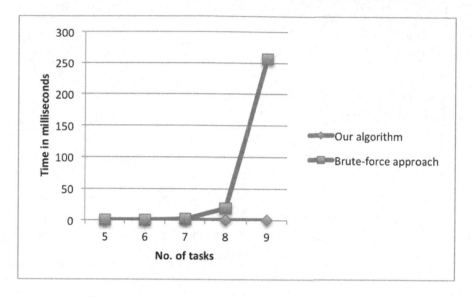

Fig. 3. Comparison of our algorithm and the brute-force one

answer for TRP in an average of 80 milliseconds. Although not presented in the graph, we have also performed some tests with data sets of 200 hundreds tasks, the average execution time was already about 2,5 seconds.

Our experiments have proven that our proposed algorithm is a feasible solution for TRP providing an optimal answer for up to 100 tasks in average less than 80 milliseconds. Moreover, if the CMS does not need a result for the trajectory recommendation immediately, even an instance of TRP with a few hundred tasks can be processed within a few seconds. As mentioned earlier in this section, although our algorithm present a worst case that generates as much trajectories as the brute-force approach, the experiments has shown that our prune strategy greatly reduces its search space and execution time.

5   Related Work

In this section, we present a review of task recommendation in CMS and discuss works related to task scheduling in crowdsourcing systems. Then, we present a related problem called Time-Constrained Traveling Salesman Problem or TCTSP.

In order to leverage the overall number of tasks accomplished in a CMS, some researchers have proposed the usage of recommendation systems to suggest tasks with high utilities for a worker without considering their sequence. Although in a first look it may appear simple to recommend a task according to this ranking of utilities, the real challenge here is to find or estimate the utility of a task to a worker. In general, the literature [1,5,10,14] propose to estimate such values based on the interests/preferences and skills of a worker that are

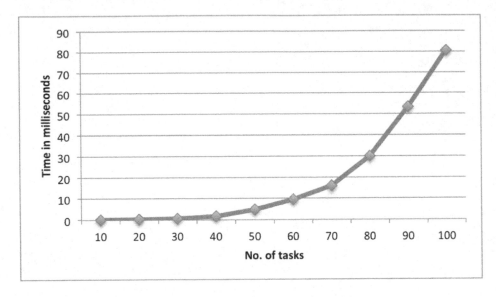

Fig. 4. Execution time of our algorithm

implicitly discovered by analyzing his usage of the CMS. Some other works may differ slightly. For example, Difalla et al. [4] use a similar approach for utility estimation according to the preferences and skills of a worker. However, such information is discovered from his profile extracted from social platforms, and not by his usage history of the CMS. The main differences between our approach and these works using task recommendation is that the sequence in which the tasks must be accomplished is not taken into account in the later. When not dealing with spatiotemporal tasks, this sequence may not be always relevant. However, for tasks with strict time window and location to be accomplished the order plays an important role. In this work, we use the concept of utility of task to estimate the overall utility of a trajectory under the assumption that the utility of all task is already estimated and given as an input of the TRP problem.

Another area related to our work is task scheduling in spatial crowdsourcing systems. Kazemi and Shahabi [6] propose an approach where a system, provided with a set of workers, their locations and a set of spatiotemporal tasks, tries to assign a schedule to workers that maximizes the overall number of tasks accomplished. Another similar work by Kazemi et al. [7] has for goal to maximize the number of spatiotemporal tasks done. In order to do so, it assigns as many tasks as possible to workers matching their locations and the reputation of a worker with the reputation required by a task. Finally, Deng et al. [3] propose a way to recommend a schedule to a single worker, given his location and a set of spatiotemporal tasks, that maximizes the number of tasks accomplished by him. The originality of our work is based on the following characteristics. First, none of these works considers the preferences of the worker when recommending or assigning. If a set of tasks that displeasure a worker is recommended or assigned to him, he may refuse to accept the suggestion or even worse, follow the schedule providing bad results for tasks. Furthermore, the spatiotemporal tasks in these works are considered to have a deadline, but not an earliest start time, i.e. a task does not present a time window. Finally, none of these works focus on the particular scenario where a worker is moving from an origin to a destination where he must arrive before a given deadline.

Finally, it is also worth noting a variation of TSP, known as TCTSP, which is very similar to the TRP. In particular, this variation also includes time window constraints for visiting a city and the possibility to wait for a time window to open [2]. The main differences between the TCTSP and our approach is that the goal of the former is to minimize the time/distance necessary for visiting all cities and the later is to maximize the utility of a trajectory. Moreover, smaller differences are also present in the problem formalization. For example, no deadline is defined for the arrival at the final destination.

6   Conclusion

In this paper, we have introduced and formalized the trajectory recommendation problem TRP that allows a worker to accomplish tasks he has affinity with, without compromising his arrival in time at destination. Moreover, we have proven that TRP is NP-hard and proposed an exact algorithm for solving it. Our experimentation has demonstrated that it is feasible to use our algorithm in a scenario with up to one hundred tasks having an average response time of a few milliseconds and a few seconds for a few hundred tasks.

As a future work, we plan to study the feasibility of adaptation of algorithms for the TSP/TCTSP to the TRP. We also plan to propose approximation algorithms to provide an answer to TRP when more tasks are to be handled. We also plan to experiment the acceptance ratio of recommended trajectories by workers. Further, we plan to investigate whether the similarity between a recommended trajectory and the one the worker usually follows may influence the acceptance or not.

Acknowledgments. This work has been supported by the French Ministry of Higher Education and Research (Ministère de l'Enseignement Supérieur et de la Recherche de la France - MESR).

References

1. Ambati, V., Vogel, S., Carbonell, J.G.: Towards task recommendation in micro-task markets. In: Human Computation (2011)
2. Baker, E.K.: Technical note - an exact algorithm for the time-constrained traveling salesman problem. Operations Research **31**(5), 938–945 (1983)

3. Deng, D., Shahabi, C., Demiryurek, U.: Maximizing the number of worker's self-selected tasks in spatial crowdsourcing. In: Proceedings of the 21st ACM SIGSPA-TIAL International Conference on Advances in Geographic Information Systems, SIGSPATIAL 2013, pp. 324–333. ACM, New York (2013). http://doi.acm.org/10.1145/2525314.2525370

4. Difallah, D.E., Demartini, G., Cudré-Mauroux, P.: Pick-a-crowd: tell me what you like, and i'll tell you what to do. In: Proceedings of the 22Nd International Conference on World Wide Web, WWW 2013, International World Wide Web Conferences Steering Committee, Republic and Canton of Geneva, Switzerland, pp. 367–374 (2013). http://dl.acm.org/citation.cfm?id=2488388.2488421

5. Fonteles, A.S., Bouveret, S., Gensel, J.: Towards matching improvement between spatio-temporal tasks and workers in mobile crowdsourcing market systems. In: Proceedings of the Third ACM SIGSPATIAL International Workshop on Mobile Geographic Information Systems, MobiGIS 2014, pp. 43–50. ACM, New York (2014). http://doi.acm.org/10.1145/2675316.2675319

6. Kazemi, L., Shahabi, C.: Geocrowd: enabling query answering with spatial crowd-sourcing. In: Proceedings of the 20th International Conference on Advances in Geographic Information Systems, SIGSPATIAL 2012, pp. 189–198. ACM, New York (2012). http://doi.acm.org/10.1145/2424321.2424346

7. Kazemi, L., Shahabi, C., Chen, L.: Geotrucrowd: trustworthy query answering with spatial crowdsourcing. In: Proceedings of the 21st ACM SIGSPATIAL International Conference on Advances in Geographic Information Systems, SIGSPATIAL 2013, pp. 314–323. ACM, New York (2013). http://doi.acm.org/10.1145/2525314.2525346

8. Kittur, A., Smus, B., Khamkar, S., Kraut, R.E.: Crowdforge: crowdsourcing complex work. In: Proceedings of the 24th Annual ACM Symposium on User Interface Software and Technology, UIST 2011, pp. 43–52. ACM, New York (2011). http://doi.acm.org/10.1145/2047196.2047202

9. Kokkalis, N., Huebner, J., Diamond, S., Becker, D., Chang, M., Lee, M., Schulze, F., Koehn, T., Klemmer, S.R.: Automatically providing action plans helps people complete tasks. In: Workshops at the Twenty-Sixth AAAI Conference on Artificial Intelligence (2012)

10. Lin, C.H., Kamar, E., Horvitz, E.: Signals in the silence: Models of implicit feedback in a recommendation system for crowdsourcing (2014)

11. Musthag, M., Ganesan, D.: The role of super agents in mobile crowdsourcing. In: Human Computation (2012)

12. Musthag, M., Ganesan, D.: Labor dynamics in a mobile micro-task market. In: Proceedings of the SIGCHI Conference on Human Factors in Computing Systems, pp. 641–650. ACM (2013)

13. Ra, M.R., Liu, B., La Porta, T.F., Govindan, R.: Medusa: a programming framework for crowd-sensing applications. In: Proceedings of the 10th International Conference on Mobile Systems, Applications, and Services, MobiSys 2012, pp. 337–350. ACM, New York (2012). http://doi.acm.org/10.1145/2307636.2307668

14. Yuen, M.C., King, I., Leung, K.S.: Task recommendation in crowdsourcing systems. In: Proceedings of the First International Workshop on Crowdsourcing and Data Mining, CrowdKDD 2012, pp. 22–26. ACM, New York (2012). http://doi.acm.org/10.1145/2442657.2442661

G2P: A Partitioning Approach for Processing DBSCAN with MapReduce

Antonio Cavalcante Araujo Neto(✉), Ticiana Linhares Coelho da Silva,
Victor Aguiar Evangelista de Farias, José Antonio F. Macêdo,
and Javam de Castro Machado

Federal University of Ceará, Fortaleza, Brazil
antonio@alu.ufc.br, {ticianalc,javam}@ufc.br,
{victorfarias,jose.macedo}@lia.ufc.br

Abstract. One of the most important aspects to consider when computing large data sets is to distribute and parallelize the analysis algorithms. A distributed system presents a good performance if the workload is properly balanced. It is expected that the computing time is directly related to the processing time on the node where the processing takes longer. This paper aims at proposing a data partitioning strategy that takes into account partition balance and that is generic for spatial data. Our proposed solution is based on a grid model data structure that is further transformed into a graph partitioning problem, where we finally compute the partitions. Our proposed approach is used on the distributed DBSCAN algorithm and it is focused on finding density areas in a large data set using MapReduce. We call our approach G2P (Grid and Graph Partitioning) and we show via massive experiments that G2P presents great quality data partitioning for the distributed DBSCAN algorithm compared to the competitors. We believe that G2P is not only suitable for DBSCAN algorithm, but also to execute spatial join operations and distance based range queries to name to a few.

Keywords: Partitioning · Graph partitioning · DBSCAN · MapReduce

1 Introduction

One of the most important aspects to consider when computing large data sets is the parallelization of the analysis algorithms. Computationally or data-intensive problems are primarily solved by distributing tasks over many computer processors [1]. However, algorithm parallelization is not sufficient to guarantee efficiency because it depends on data partitioning. Clearly, in case of high skew data distribution the processing time will be bounded by the node where the process takes longer. Moreover, a data partition technique should take into account how the data is handled by the algorithm. Thus, specific data partitioning techniques should be developed for coping with algorithms needs. With this problem in mind, we focus, in this paper, on a particular data partition technique for DBSCAN algorithm.

© Springer International Publishing Switzerland 2015
J. Gensel and M. Tomko (Eds.): W2GIS 2015, LNCS 9080, pp. 191–202, 2015.
DOI: 10.1007/978-3-319-18251-3_12

Among many types of clustering algorithms, the density-based ones are more suitable to detect clusters with varied densities and different shapes in spatial data. One of the most important density-based clustering algorithms is the DBSCAN (Density-Based Spatial Clustering of Application with Noise) [7]. Its advantages over other clustering techniques are: DBSCAN groups data into clusters of arbitrary shape, it does not require the number of clusters *a priori*, and it also deals with outliers in the dataset. However, DBSCAN is a time-consuming algorithm compared to other clustering algorithms such as k-means. Moreover, the increasing amount of data using only a single processor in the clustering process is an inefficient approach. Recently, many researchers have begun to use cloud computing infrastructure in order to solve scalability problems of traditional algorithms that run on a single machine [5]. Therefore, the strategy to parallelize the DBSCAN in shared-nothing architecture is considered an efficient solution to solve such problems [18].

In our previous work [4] we proposed a distributed and parallel version of the DBSCAN algorithm through the MapReduce paradigm. However, its partitioning strategy is developed for a particular application (traffic jam identification), and it still does not guarantee the load balance among the processing nodes. As we know, a distributed system presents a good performance if the workload is well balanced, as the total computing time is expected to be directly related to the node where the processing takes longer.

The main contribution of this paper is a partitioning strategy that takes into account partition balance and that is generic for spatial data. Our proposed solution is based on a grid model data structure that is further transformed into a graph partitioning problem, where we finally compute the partitions, as described in Section 4.1. Our approach is named G2P (Grid and Graph Partitioning). We believe that G2P is not only suitable for DBSCAN algorithm, but also to execute spatial join operations and distance based range queries to name a few.

Related works, such as [5] and [9] also use MapReduce to parallelize the DBSCAN algorithm but both take advantage of data replication. [5] requires some parameters for tuning data partitioning, although a way to estimate the value of these parameters is not presented in that paper. In our experiments we confirm that our approach presents better results than [5]. We show the quality of our partitioning approach with respect to the load balance.

The structure of this paper is organized as follows. Section 2 presents the related works and Section 3 our problem statement. The Section 4 addresses the methodology and implementation of this work, which involve the solution of the problem. The experiments are described in Section 5. Finally, the conclusion and future work are presented in Section 6.

2   Related Work

The algorithms OPTICS [2] and DBCURE [20] discover clusters based on the density of points, but with widely varying densities. PDBSCAN [12] is a parallel implementation of DBSCAN. However, PDBSCAN does not take advantage of the the MapReduce model. Another related work is GRIDBSCAN [16] that is not suitable for large amounts of data. In this work we use a distributed and parallel version of DBSCAN with MapReduce that is suitable for handling large amounts of data.

The paper [9] proposes an implementation of DBSCAN with a MapReduce of four stages using grid based partitioning. After that, the dataset is partitioned. The authors also presents a strategy for joining clusters that are in different partitions and contain the same points in their boundaries. Such points are replicated in the partitions and the discovery of clusters which can be merged in a single cluster is analysed from them. Note that the number of replicated boundary points can affect the clustering efficiency, as such points not only increase the load of each compute node, but also increase the time to merge the results of different computational nodes.

Similar to the previous work, [5] also proposes a DBSCAN implementation using MapReduce and a grid based partitioning, called DBSCAN-MR. To partition the points, [5] presents a great cost to create the grid, moreover this phase is centralized. The dataset is partitioned in order to maintain the uniform load balancing across the compute nodes and to minimize the number of points to be replicated in the several partitions. Another disadvantage is that the strategy proposed depends on two input parameters, which are not trivial to set in order to get a good partitioning. The DBSCAN algorithm runs on each compute node for each partition using a kd-tree index. The merge of clusters that are in distinct partitions occurs when there is a point that belongs to both partitions and it is a core point in any of the them. If it is detected that two clusters should merge, they are renamed to a single name. This process also occurs in [9].

Our work is similar to the papers [9] and [5], as they consider the challenge of handling large amounts of data using the MapReduce paradigm to parallelize the DBSCAN algorithm. However, our paper presents a generic partitioning strategy that offers a small overhead and does not depends on additional parameters as [5] depends. The data distribution is well balanced among the processing nodes, once we transformed our problem into a graph partitioning problem as shown in Section 4.1. Furthermore, the strategy we use to merge clusters does not require replication as presented in [5]. The paper [19] also presents a strategy for distributed DBSCAN using MapReduce, however it is not a suitable solution for commodity cluster computing as our approach.

3 Problem Statement

The distributed DBSCAN strategy used in this work focuses on finding density areas in spatial data using MapReduce. The first phase in this strategy is partitioning the data among the processing nodes. However, the partitioning should not be specific for a particular application (e.g. traffic jam identification), and we need to guarantee the load balance among the processing nodes.

There are many problems that are modeled as a graph partitioning problem. They involve a surprising variety of techniques in this context. The applications include parallel processing, road networks, image processing, VLSI design, social networks and bioinformatics. We also map our partitioning problem as a graph partitioning problem. Before defining the version of graph partitioning problem used in our work, we need to introduce some definitions.

Definition 1 (Graph definition). *Let $G = G(V, E)$ be an undirected graph, where V corresponds to the set of vertices and E corresponds to the set of edges. Both vertices and edges are weighted. Let $\psi(v_i)$ denotes the weight of a vertex $v_i \in V$. For each edge $(v_i, u_j) \in E$, $\omega(v_i, u_j)$ denotes its weight and it is defined as $\omega(v_i, u_j) = \psi(v_i) + \psi(u_j)$.*

Let $S \subseteq V$, $S = \{(v_1), ..., (v_m)\}$, the weight of S is $\Psi(S) = \sum_{i=1}^{m} \psi(v_i)$. Similarly $R \subseteq E$, $R = \{(v_1, u_1), ..., (v_n, u_n)\}$, the weight of R is $\Omega(R) = \sum_{i=1}^{n} \omega(v_i, u_i)$.

Definition 2 (k-partition definition). *A k-partition of the graph $G(V,E)$ is a mapping of V into k disjoint subsets S such that $\cup S \subseteq V$ and $V \subseteq \cup S$.*

Definition 3 (Cut Edge definition). *A cut edge $C=(S,T)$ is a partition of V of a graph $G=(V,E)$ into two subsets S and T. The cut edge set of a cut $C=(S,T)$ is the set $R = \{(v_i, u_j) \in E | v_i \in S, u_j \in T\}$ of edges that have one endpoint in S and the other endpoint in T.*

For the (k,x) balanced partition problem [22], the objective is to partition $G(V,E)$ into k components S of at most size $|S| \leq x * (\frac{|V|}{k})$, while minimizing the weight of a cut edge set R ($\Omega(R)$).

It's worth noting that this problem has many well-known tools implementing an approximative solutions for it. In this work we will use METIS [21]. So we can formulate our problem statement as follows:

Problem Statement: Given a data set of d-dimensional points $DS = \{p_1, p_2, ..., p_n\}$ and a set of virtual machines $VM = \{vm_1, vm_2, ..., vm_k\}$, the problem consists in partitioning DS in k disjoint sets according to the following criteria:

1. The partitions should be balanced. Considering that in a distributed environment, the total processing time is expected to be directly proportional to the size of the largest partition, since it takes longer to compute.

Table 1. Notation

Notation	Meaning
G	Graph G(V,E)
$\psi(v_i)$	The weight of vertex $v_i \in V$
$\Psi(S)$	The weight of a vertex set $S \subseteq V$
$\omega(v_i, u_j)$	The weight of edge $(v_i, u_j) \in E$
$\Omega(R)$	The weight of a edge set $R \subseteq E$
DS	spatial data set
GDS	grid data structure

2. As the data partitioning is the first phase in the distributed DBSCAN algorithm, each cluster should be entirely contained in a single partition in order to decrease the number of merge cases in the proposed approach.

We will use these two criteria to evaluate our approach in Section 5. Next, we propose a new partitioning approach G2P (Graph and Grid Partitioning) which is generic and takes into account the data distribution. Table 1 summarizes some concepts explained in this section and that are used in what follows.

4   Methodology and Implementation

In this section, we present our partitioning approach G2P and the distributed DBSCAN used in this work.

4.1   G2P: Graph and Grid Partitioning

One of the main advantages of G2P proposed for distributed DBSCAN is taking into account partition balance and being generic for spatial data.

The partitioning problem addressed in this work is modeled as a graph partitioning problem. Foremost, we group the data with aid of a grid data structure that distributes the data in its cells. Thus, points with near spatial positions are in the same cells or in adjacent cells. Therefore, we convert this grid to the input graph for the graph partitioner algorithm. Thus, our approach is carried out in two phases:

1. **First phase:** Transform the input of our partitioning problem into the input of the graph partitioner problem. We present it in Section 4.1.1.
2. **Second phase:** Generate the partitions by transforming the output of the graph partitioner problem into an output for our partitioning problem. This phase is presented in Section 4.1.2.

4.1.1   First Phase.
In this section, we describe how to transform an input of our partitioning problem into an input for the graph partitioner problem, i.e., how to use the data set DS and VM information to build a graph G with weight assigned to its vertices and edges. We also show that the output of the graph partitioner problem is a partitioning to G in such way that we can construct a partitioning for DS.

In order to generate G, we introduce an intermediate step. Firstly, we build a grid data structure (GDS) from DS. Then, we build G from GDS as described next.

4.1.1.1   Grid building First, we build a grid data structure GDS from DS. As we consider the spatial position of each point in the dataset, it is necessary to assume a coordinate system that will be used as a reference to position the points in the different cells. Each cell $C_{i,j}$ of GDS is composed of a subset of points that belong to DS. Note that i and j indicate the position of the cell in the space region using the coordinate system and i and j may be negative. Therefore, we choose a random point from DS to be the reference point.

Let $o = (x,y)$ be a point chosen as reference for the coordinates system to be adopted and $p = (x',y')$ be some point that we aim to find the cell that it belongs to. So that, p belongs to $C_{i,j}$ where

$$i = \left\lceil \frac{(2 * \sqrt{2} * (x - x')) - eps}{2 * eps} \right\rceil \tag{1}$$

and

$$j = \left\lceil \frac{(2 * \sqrt{2} * (y - y')) - eps}{2 * eps} \right\rceil \tag{2}$$

These equations are obtained by setting the diagonal of any two adjacent cells $C_{i,j}$ and $C_{k,l}$ (i.e., where either $|i - k| = 1$ or either $|j - l| = 1$) equal to eps.

4.1.1.2   Graph building After the grid GDS is constructed, the next step corresponds to generate an input graph G that will be given as input for the graph partitioner problem.

Let $|C_{i,j}|$ be the number of points in the cell $C_{i,j}$. From that, we construct the input graph $G(V, E)$ which is generated according to the following steps:

1. For each cell $C_{i,j}$ in GDS, add a vertex $v_{i,j}$ to V and set $\psi(v_{i,j}) = |C_{i,j}|$.
2. For each pair of adjacent cells $C_{i,j}$ and $C_{k,l}$ where either $|i - k| = 1$ or either $|j - l| = 1$, add edge $(v_{i,j}, v_{k,l})$ to E and set $\omega(v_{i,j}, v_{k,l}) = \psi(v_{i,j}) + \psi(v_{k,l})$.

In this way, the inputs for the graph partitioning problem are the graph G, the number of machines k as the number of partitions to find and x equals to 1. We set the parameter x equals to 1 because our goal is load balance the partitions.

4.1.2   Second Phase. There are many well-known tools that implement approximative solutions for the graph partitioning problem. As stated before, we chose to use METIS in this work. The output of METIS is a k-partition of G in k disjoints subsets S.

Our approach provides well-balance partitions because it is an output of METIS which ensures high quality partitions [21]. For an edge $(v_i, u_j) \in E$ of $G(V,E)$, the weight $\omega(v_i, u_j)$ represents the density of the region comprised by the corresponding cells u_j and v_i in the grid GDS. As we map our problem to the graph partitioner problem and it minimizes the weight of the cut-edges, we avoid that two cells that compose a high-density region are allocated to distinct partitions. This prevents that each density cluster be contained in more than one partition in order to decrease the number of merge cases in our proposed approach.

Considering this, note that our approach obeys to the criteria enumerated before. Next, we present the distributed DBSCAN algorithm used in this work. The DBSCAN main idea is to analyze, for each point in the dataset, whether it has a certain number of points ($MinPts$) within a radius of eps or not, using this criteria to define clusters. Both, $MinPts$ and eps are input parameters.

4.2   Distributed DBSCAN using MapReduce

In this section, we detail the phases to parallelize DBSCAN using the MapReduce programming model. These phases are illustrated in Figure 1.

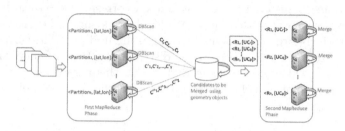

Fig. 1. All the phases of distributed and parallel DBSCAN execution

In the first Map phase, each row from the dataset is described as a pair $\langle key, value \rangle$, such that the key refers to the partition identifier and the value refers to a geographic location where the data was collected, which may be in any coordinate system. Next occurs the Reduce phase, which receives a list of values that have the same key, i.e. geographical locations of the same partition. The DBSCAN algorithm is applied in this phase using the kd-tree index [3] and the result is stored in a database. This means that the id of each cluster and the information about their points, such as latitude, longitude or if a point is a core point or noise, are saved.

As the DBSCAN algorithm is processed in a distributed manner and the dataset is partitioned, it is necessary to check and discover which clusters of different partitions intersect and might be merged into a single cluster. In other words, two clusters may have points at a distance less than or equal to eps, in such way that if the data were processed by the same reduce or even if they were in the same partition, they would be grouped into a single cluster. Thus, the clusters are also stored as geometric objects in the database and only the objects that are at a distance of at most eps will be able to go to the next phase which is the merge phase. Tuples with pairs of candidate clusters to merge are given as input with the same key to the next MapReduce process.

The next phase aims at checking the merge of clusters and it is also described by a MapReduce process. The Map function is the identity function. It simply give as input each key-value pair to the Reduce function. The Reduce function

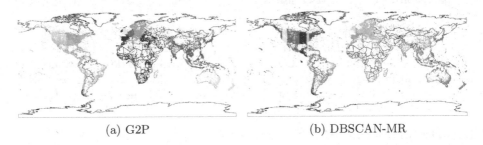

(a) G2P   (b) DBSCAN-MR

Fig. 2. Partitioning example

receives as key the lowest *id* cluster from all the clusters that are candidates to be merged into a single cluster. The value of that key corresponds to the other merge candidates clusters' *id*s. In this phase, if two clusters should be merged into a single cluster, the information about their points are updated. The correctness of this merge clustering strategy and of the distributed DBSCAN algorithm were presented on, [4]. Differently from related works, this algorithm considers the chance of a noise point in a cluster to become a border or a core point after the clusters are merged.

5   Experimental Evaluation

We analysed the quality of G2P with regard to the load balance rate across several scenarios. We compared our results to the data partitioning approach (PRBP), proposed in DBSCAN-MR [5] and the results showed that G2P produces much more balanced partitions than DBSCAN-MR.

As in both solutions the partitioning is a centralized phase, the infrastructure used in the experiments is composed of a single machine, running Ubuntu 14.10 as operating system, and 8GB of RAM available.

The dataset used in this evaluation is composed of geolocations of photos from Flickr all over the world, provided by Yahoo! Webscope [23]. It contains about 49 million geotagged photos. We performed experiments with subsets of this dataset that have different sizes in order to measure how does the strategies behave when the dataset grows. Also, for each strategy, the parameters *eps* and β that describe the partitions sizes were varied. The parameter β will be explained below.

Also, it is important to notice that G2P is capable of cutting the space in multiple directions, i.e., it does not only cuts the space horizontally or vertically, as shown in Figure 2a. The PRBP strategy, instead, only considers these two types of cutting, what might easily split a cluster into different partitions, causing an increase in the processing time of the merge phase of DBSCAN. As shown in Figure 2b, some dense areas are split into several ones.

For G2P, we varied the parameter K (number of partitions) from 1 to 24, for all the datasets. That makes, for each of k value, ideal partition sizes. We

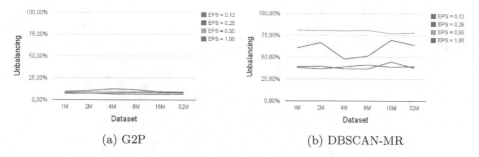

(a) G2P   (b) DBSCAN-MR

Fig. 3. Unbalancing analysis

compare the size of the larger partition to the ideal size to measure how far it is from the perfect partitioning.

For DBSCAN-MR we varied the β parameter, that specifies the maximum size for a partition. For some scenarios, the partitioning algorithm might not be able to split some datasets, what might cause the not attendance of this requirement and, consequently, load unbalance.

Effect of the Dataset Size

In these experiments, the size of the dataset varies from 1.000.000 to 32.000.000 points. We can observe in Figure 3 that for both strategies the unbalancing floats around the same values for all the dataset sizes. Furthermore, we can notice that G2P has a much lower unbalancing in comparison to DBSCAN-MR strategy in all the scenarios.

Effect of Eps

Increasing the value of *eps* means increasing the size of the cells of the grid, which implies directly on the region of the space it covers. Thus, the larger the cells, more points fit in it. One can easily see that it is easier to reach a better load balance among partitions if there is more cells with less points in each one of them, than if the grid is composed of less cells with more points in each one.

As shown in the Figure 3, the higher the *eps* value, the higher the unbalancing. Although, for the same values of *eps*, we observe that G2P has varied, in average, about 4% from the lower value of *eps* to the higher one. On the other hand, PRBP increased its unbalancing around 40% in average.

Effect of K

We also performed experiments varying the number of partitions k. When partitioning the dataset, a higher number of partitioning implies directly on the size of these partitions. As the partitions are smaller, a little variation cause a much higher unbalance. As shown in the Figure 4, the aggregated unbalance for the higher values of k is noticeable greater than for the lower ones. Although the unbalance increases, it is, for all the experimented scenarios, below 10%.

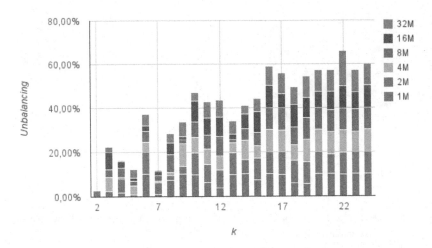

Fig. 4. The aggregate unbalancing for the datasets from 1 million points to 32 million points as K increases

6   Conclusion and Future Work

We proposed G2P (Grid and Graph Partitioning), a data partitioning strategy that takes into account partition balance and that is generic for spatial data. G2P is based on a grid model data structure that is further transformed into a graph partitioning problem entry, where we finally compute the partitions. G2P is used on the distributed DBSCAN algorithm and it is focused on finding density areas in a large data set using MapReduce. We performed massive experiments which confirmed that our approach produces very well balanced partitions in comparison to our related work DBSCAN-MR.

As future work, we would like to focus on other techniques that are able to speed up the clustering processing. When dealing with huge amounts of data, mechanisms to assist the acceleration of the clustering process may be proposed in the various stages of processing. The use of the grid data structure can be useful in computing clusters at the partitioning stage, which might certainly save time in later steps. We also intend to study the reuse of results of previous computations, adjusting just the clustering parameters, which is a problem that was not addressed by any work in the literature to the best of our knowledge.

References

1. Schadt, E.E., Linderman, M.D., Sorenson, J., Lee, L., Nolan, G.P.: Computational solutions to large-scale data management and analysis. In: Nature Reviews Genetics, pp. 647–657. Nature Publishing Group (2010)

2. Ankerst, M., Breunig, M.M., Kriegel, H.-P., Sander, J.: Optics: ordering points to identify the clustering structure. ACM SIGMOD Record **28**(2), 49–60 (1999)
3. Bentley, J.L.: Multidimensional binary search trees used for associative searching. In: Communications of the ACM, vol. 18, pp. 509–517. ACM (1975)
4. Coelho da Silva, T.L., Araujo, A.C.N., Magalhaes, R.P., Farias, V.A.E., de Macedo, J.A., Machado, J.C.: Efficient and distributed dbscan algorithm using mapreduce to detect density areas on traffic data. In: ICEIS (2014)
5. Dai, B.-R., Lin, I.-C.: Efficient map/reduce-based dbscan algorithm with optimized data partition. In: 2012 IEEE 5th International Conference on Cloud Computing (CLOUD), pp. 59–66. IEEE (2012)
6. Dean, J., Ghemawat, S.: Mapreduce: simplified data processing on large clusters. Communications of the ACM **51**(1), 107–113 (2008)
7. Ester, M., Kriegel, H.-P., Sander, J., Xu, X.: A density-based algorithm for discovering clusters in large spatial databases with noise. KDD **96**, 226–231 (1996)
8. Giannotti, F., Nanni, M., Pedreschi, D., Pinelli, F., Renso, C., Rinzivillo, S., Trasarti, R.: Unveiling the complexity of human mobility by querying and mining massive trajectory data. VLDB J. **20**(5), 695–719 (2011)
9. He, Y., Tan, H., Luo, W., Mao, H., Ma, D., Feng, S., Fan, J.: Mr-dbscan: an efficient parallel density-based clustering algorithm using mapreduce. In: 2011 IEEE 17th International Conference on Parallel and Distributed Systems (ICPADS), pp. 473–480. IEEE (2011)
10. Jensen, C.S., Lin, D., Ooi, B.-C.: Continuous clustering of moving objects. IEEE Transactions on Knowledge and Data Engineering **19**(9), 1161–1174 (2007)
11. Jeung, H., Yiu, M.L., Zhou, X., Jensen, C.S., Shen, H.T.: Discovery of convoys in trajectory databases. Proceedings of the VLDB Endowment **1**(1), 1068–1080 (2008)
12. Kisilevich, S., Mansmann, F., Keim, D.: P-dbscan: a density based clustering algorithm for exploration and analysis of attractive areas using collections of geo-tagged photos. In: Proceedings of the 1st International Conference and Exhibition on Computing for Geospatial Research & Application, p. 38. ACM (2010)
13. Li, X., Ceikute, V., Jensen, C.S., Tan, K.-L.: Effective online group discovery in trajectory databases. IEEE Transactions on Knowledge and Data Engineering **25**(12), 2752–2766 (2013)
14. Li, Y., Han, J., Yang, J.: Clustering moving objects. In: Proceedings of the Tenth ACM SIGKDD International Conference on Knowledge Discovery and Data Mining, pp. 617–622 (2004)
15. Lin, J., Dyer, C.: Data-intensive text processing with mapreduce. Synthesis Lectures on Human Language Technologies **3**(1), 1–177 (2010)
16. Uncu, O., Gruver, W.A., Kotak, D.B., Sabaz, D., Alibhai, Z., Ng, C.: Gridbscan: grid density-based spatial clustering of applications with noise. In: IEEE International Conference on Systems, Man and Cybernetics, SMC 2006, vol. 4, pp. 2976–2981. IEEE (2006)
17. Vieira, M.R., Bakalov, P., Tsotras, V.J.: On-line discovery of flock patterns in spatio-temporal data. In: Proceedings of the 17th ACM SIGSPATIAL International Conference on Advances in Geographic Information Systems, pp. 286–295. ACM (2009)
18. Pavlo, A., Paulson, E., Rasin, A., Abadi, D.J., DeWitt, D.J., Madden, S., Stonebraker, M.: A comparison of approaches to large-scale data analysis. In: Proceedings of the 2009 ACM SIGMOD International Conference on Management of data, pp. 165–178. ACM (2009)

19. Welton, B., Samanas, E., Miller, B.P.: Mr. scan: extreme scale density-based clustering using a tree-based network of gpgpu nodes. In: Proceedings of SC13: International Conference for High Performance Computing, Networking, Storage and Analysis, p. 84. ACM (2013)
20. Kim, Y., Shim, K., Kim, M.-S., Lee, J.S.: DBCURE-MR: an efficient density-based clustering algorithm for large data using MapReduce. In: Information Systems, pp. 15–35. Elsevier (2014)
21. Karypis, G., Kumar, V.,: Metis-unstructured graph partitioning and sparse matrix ordering system, version 2.0. Citeseer (1995)
22. Andreev, K., Racke, H.: Balanced graph partitioning. In: Theory of Computing Systems, pp. 15–35. Springer (2006)
23. Yahoo! Webscope. Yahoo! Webscope dataset YFCC-100M (2014)

Author Index

Printed in the United States
By Bookmasters

Printed in the United States
By Bookmasters